THE FRIENDLY SOCIETIES IN ENGLAND
1815–1875

AMICITIA AMOR ET VERITAS

Frontispiece

The emblem of the Independent Order of Oddfellows, Manchester
Unity, with Certificate of Admission.

THE
FRIENDLY SOCIETIES
IN ENGLAND
1815-1875

P. H. J. H. GOSDEN

MANCHESTER UNIVERSITY PRESS

Printed in Great Britain by Butler & Tanner Ltd., Frome and London

PREFACE

I HAVE approached the development of friendly societies in England topically rather than chronologically. The multiplicity and variety of these societies was such that a strictly chronological account could hardly form a coherent whole. Moreover my aim has been not only to show how the societies grew in size and how different forms of organisation emerged, but also to show the ways in which they met some of the needs of large sections of the population during this period. I found that I was better able to achieve this aim by examining in turn the development of the various aspects of the friendly society movement and of its work.

The preparation of this study has left me indebted to many. I am grateful to Dr. Hobsbawn of Birkbeck College for his valuable criticisms. My thanks are due to numerous officials of friendly societies and librarians for help in tracing material and especially to the staff of the Goldsmiths' Reading Room of the University of London Library who have shown great patience in meeting my frequent requests. Finally, I would like to thank the National Conference of Friendly Societies whose munificence has done much to facilitate publication.

P. H. J. H. GOSDEN.

Leeds University,
  December, 1960.

ACKNOWLEDGEMENTS

AUTHOR and publishers are greatly indebted to the National Conference of Friendly Societies for a generous contribution to the cost of this volume, and to the officers of the Independent Order of the Manchester Unity of Odd Fellows Friendly Society for their interest and ready co-operation in its production.

In addition to the purchase of copies by the Societies as a whole, the following have joined in the contribution towards the cost of publication:

Independent Order of Odd Fellows Manchester Unity Friendly Society
Ancient Order of Foresters Friendly Society
Loyal Order of Ancient Shepherds (Ashton Unity) Friendly Society
Independent Order of Rechabites.

CONTENTS

LIST OF ILLUSTRATIONS

ABBREVIATIONS

Chief Registrar's   Annual Report of the Chief Registrar of Friendly Societies
Report   from 1876.

R.C.F.S.   Report from the Royal Commission appointed to inquire
into Friendly and Benefit Building Societies, 1871–1874.

Registrar's Report   Annual Report of the Registrar of Friendly Societies in
England.

S.C.F.S.   Report of the Select Committee of the House of Commons on Laws respecting Friendly Societies, 1825.

Stanley   Report of E. L. Stanley, Assistant Commissioner to the
Royal Commission appointed to inquire into Friendly
and Benefit Building Societies, 1874.

Young   Report of Sir George Young, Assistant Commissioner to
the Royal Commission appointed to inquire into Friendly
and Benefit Building Societies, 1874.

A Note on the Spelling of 'Oddfellow'

Throughout this book 'Oddfellow' is spelt as one word; this is the form
adopted in the Shorter Oxford English Dictionary and widely used in the
period with which this book is concerned. On the other hand, the form of
spelling 'Odd Fellow' is now and was then also in general use.

CHAPTER ONE

INTRODUCTION

ONE of the most interesting aspects of the history of the development of friendly societies between 1815 and 1875 is the light which it sheds upon the social life and ideas of the classes which joined them. Many of the theories which were current among members and their sympathisers purporting to describe the origins of these societies are of little value to those concerned with their historical origins, but do serve to illustrate that desire for an ancient and hallowed pedigree which was typical of such organisations during much of the nineteenth century. A variety of myths and legends circulated among Oddfellows which placed their origin among the Romans and other ancient peoples,[1] while the Foresters, not to be outdone, traced their ancestry back to Adam who was the 'first Forester'.[2]

Some sympathisers with the friendly society movement who did not accept such legends showed interest in providing the societies with a lengthy ancestry. H. Tompkins, who was a member of the staff of the Registry of Friendly Societies a century ago, published a *Lecture on the Friendly Societies of Antiquity* in which he described the fraternities connected with the performance of religious rites in the temples of ancient Greece as friendly societies. He felt that he was justified in doing this since these fraternities not only met together to sacrifice to certain gods, but also assisted members who fell into want and provided for their funerals. Other writers claimed that the medieval gilds were the ancestors of friendly societies and even that a direct connection could be established between them. The secretary to the Royal Commission on Friendly Societies, J. M. Ludlow, wrote in 1873: 'I feel convinced that there is no historical gap between the gild of old

[1] See note below, p. 27.
[2] C. Hardwick, *A Manual for Patrons and Members of Friendly Societies*, 1859, p. 40.

times and the modern friendly society; that if we knew all, we could trace the actual passage from the one to the other.' [1]

Friendly societies which would have been recognisable as such to a nineteenth-century member can be traced from the late seventeenth century for it was in 1687 that the Friendly Benefit Society of Bethnal Green was founded. This was one of seventy-three societies founded before 1780 which were still believed to be in existence in 1883.[2] The societies seem to have begun to increase rapidly in numbers from about 1760. It is impossible to determine either the number of members or the number of societies in existence for lack of comprehensive records, but there is some evidence of a marked increase during the last forty years or so of the eighteenth century. An idea of the rapid increase from about 1760 is given by the dates of foundation of registered friendly societies printed as Appendix I to the report of the Chief Registrar of Friendly Societies in 1880. This list only shows the small number of eighteenth-century foundations which eventually found their way on to the Register, but it seems likely that the increased numbers after 1760 are a fair indication of the more rapid expansion from about that time.

TABLE I

Date of Foundation	Number of Societies Founded
1711–20	4
1721–30	1
1731–40	3
1741–50	3
1751–60	8
1761–70	24
1771–80	27
1781–90	48

The increased rate of industrial development in the second half of the eighteenth century and the needs of the growing number of industrial workers account for this much more rapid rate of growth.

Another indication of the extent to which friendly societies (or

[1] *The Contemporary Review*, April, 1873, p. 748.
[2] Chief Registrar's Report, 1883, pp. 9–13.

box clubs as they were sometimes called) were becoming an element in the social pattern of the eighteenth century is given by the publications devoted to them and their problems by a variety of writers. In 1728 a pamphlet advocating the establishment of societies was published entitled *A Method for the Regular Management of those Societies called Box Clubs*. Defoe had advocated them in his *Essay on Projects* in 1697. In 1752 Alcock published his *Observations on the Poor Laws* in which he discussed the work of friendly societies among tradesmen in the West of England. Dr. Price, who in 1789 made the first attempt to produce generally applicable tables of contributions and benefits for friendly societies, issued his first scheme for a society 'which would probably thrive' in 1771. In 1773 Baron Maseres put forward his 'Proposal for Establishing Life Annuities in Parishes for the Benefit of the Industrious Poor'. This would have made compulsory membership of societies controlled by the churchwardens and providing for old age. A typical view of those hostile to the societies was expressed in the Board of Agriculture's 'General View of the Agriculture of the County of Essex' in 1793; this concluded 'that benefit clubs, holden at public houses, increase the number of those houses, and naturally lead to idleness and intemperance; that they afford commodious opportunities to foment sedition, and form illegal combinations, which they have sometimes actually done; and that as far as I have read and observed, there is not the smallest probability in their general extensive application, that they ever have, or ever will diminish our poor rates but just the contrary . . .'

There were no affiliated orders in England before 1810 and it is worth noticing that the clubs which were called 'Oddfellows' in the eighteenth century would hardly have been recognised as friendly societies in the nineteenth century. In the second half of the eighteenth century there were societies known as Oddfellows clubs meeting for social evenings at inns. The earliest Oddfellows club of which there are records appears to be the Aristarcus meeting at the Oakley Arms, Southwark, the Globe Tavern, Hatton Garden, or the Boar's Head in Smithfield—as the Noble Master directed. Minutes of a meeting held in 1748 at the Globe Tavern were seen by James Spry and summarised by him in his *History of*

Oddfellowship. The evening opened with a prayer followed by a toast, a resolution to admit a new member, an oration in praise of the society, a second toast, a song, a report that Brother Hughes was in King's Bench Prison and in great want—for him a guinea was voted—the loving cup was passed round and alms amounting to 11s. 6d. were collected, the Master announced that he would attend St. Saviour's, Southwark, on Easter Sunday to hear the Rev. Brother Dr. Howard preach, the last toast was given and the meeting closed with the chaplain's benediction. The rules showed no provision for any insurance and the contributions from members 'in support of the Festivals, Fund of Charity and Grand Circuit Quarterage' were heavy, two guineas annually, 'one to be paid at the feast of St. Janus and the other on the feast of St. John'. It was from clubs such as this that the nineteenth-century 'unities' of Oddfellows took their name and, perhaps, their convivial nature, although the foundation of the Abercrombie lodge in Manchester about 1810 marks the beginning of the Oddfellows as a friendly society in the usual sense of the term.

The most comprehensive attempt to provide overall figures showing the extent of friendly societies in England at the end of the eighteenth century was that made by Eden. He realised that his inquiries could not give a complete picture because of the reluctance of local clubs to reveal full particulars of their activities to even the most sympathetic inquirers of the upper classes. In his *State of the Poor* he showed that societies were to be found in virtually every part of England in 1794 and 1795. He reported that there were 34 friendly societies in Wolverhampton, 51 in Nottingham, 50 in Hull, 10 in Preston, 18 in Lancaster and so forth, but in other places he could obtain no information; there was no mention of friendly societies in the entry for Manchester.[1]

In 1801 Eden published his *Observations on Friendly Societies* and in this he estimated the total membership of the societies. According to the list which he gave, 5,117 local clubs had registered under the act of 1793 by this time.[2] He added to this one-third for clubs which had not had their rules registered, giving a total of 7,200

[1] F. M. Eden, *The State of the Poor*, 1797, vols. II and III.
[2] F. M. Eden, *Observations on Friendly Societies*, 1801, p. 7.

societies. Since he found that in 400 clubs there were 38,800 members or an average of 97, he took 90 as the average membership figure. In this way he estimated that there were 648,000 members of friendly societies. A useful comparison may be made with the Poor Law return of 1803 where the question 'What friendly societies hold their usual meetings in your parish or place?' produced a total of 9,672 societies in the overseers' returns. The further question as to the number of members in these societies gave a total membership for England and Wales of 704,350.[1]

The earliest general act dealing with friendly societies was that passed on the initiative of George Rose in 1793. Rose was Secretary of the Treasury and took a keen interest in the societies; later he was to do much to encourage the formation of savings banks. This act conferred various rights on friendly societies and their members, the most important of which was the recognition of registered societies as bodies which could sue and thus protect their funds.[2] The main aim of the act was to encourage the formation of friendly societies so as to reduce the demand for poor relief. This aim was not achieved but the act certainly helped to secure a wider recognition of the value of friendly societies and to give them a standing in the eyes of the authorities which led to their exclusion from the ban on combinations in 1799.

Although the earliest general act concerning friendly societies was not passed before 1793, yet it was in 1757 that the societies first came to attract the attention of the legislator. The measure of 1757[3] compelled coalheavers working on the River Thames to contribute to a friendly society to be administered under the superintendence of an alderman of the City of London. Employers were ordered by the act to retain two shillings in each pound from the men's wages and hand this money over to the society. The expenses of administration were to be met from these contributions and benefits were to be paid at the rate of seven shillings per week during sickness and sixpence per day in old age. Provision

---

[1] Returns relative to the expense and maintenance of the Poor, 1803–4.
[2] The terms are discussed more fully below, pp. 338, 339.
[3] 31 Geo. II, c. 76.

was also made for burial expenses and for a payment to the widows and orphans of deceased coalheavers. The act was repealed in 1770, 'having been found ineffectual to answer the purposes intended'.[1]

A similar measure was enacted in 1792 to compel shippers and keelmen employed in the coal trade on the Wear to join a friendly society since most of them had to live in the place where they worked 'so that when they or their families became objects of parochial relief, either the parish or the township in which they are settled is grievously burthened, or sufficient provision is not made for their support'.[2] A compulsory deduction was to be made from the men's wages at the rate of one halfpenny for each chaldron of coal carried in their keels. Benefits were to be paid from the fund accumulated for sickness, old age, and to widows and orphans. Writing of such compulsory schemes in 1797, Eden commented that 'There are great objections to all compulsory schemes for erecting friendly societies: whatever benefit is intended the Poor, obliging them to subscribe, is, in effect, taxing them; nor can I imagine a severer tax, in the present confined state of financial resource, than a twenty-fourth, or a thirty-sixth, of a man's daily earnings, imposed as a direct tax'.[3]

There were few members of the governing classes who showed anything approaching such understanding of the point of view of the friendly society member in the years before 1875 as Eden showed in this comment. In the earlier part of the nineteenth century the societies were regarded as useful organisations for lowering the poor rate but potentially dangerous in a political sense. The efforts made directly by the governing classes to run societies were aimed principally at reducing the poor rate and such societies attracted comparatively little support. The friendly society movement, as it developed between 1815 and 1875, sprang from the efforts of those who became members and it owed comparatively little to outsiders. In this respect it might be compared with the trade unions or the co-operatives, both of which grew as a result of the energy and determination shown by

[1] 10 Geo. III, c. 53.   [2] 32 Geo. III, c. 9.
[3] Eden, *State of the Poor*, vol. I, p. 603.

the members they served. These three movements represent, in a
sense, the ways in which those without political power sought to
protect themselves in an increasingly industrialised society.

The friendly societies might even be considered as the pioneers
of this self-help movement among the working men of the time.
Large and influential friendly societies such as the Oddfellows or
Foresters emerged earlier than comparable organisations in the
trade union or co-operative spheres. They were pioneers not only
in time but also in size throughout this period; they had far more
members than either the trade unions or the co-operative societies.
The known membership of those friendly societies which made a
return in 1872 was 1,857,896; that of trade unions making a
return 217,128, and that of co-operatives 301,157.[1] The actual
number of members of friendly societies at this date was estimated
by the Royal Commission at 4,000,000 while it is unlikely that
there were more than 1,000,000 trade unionists.[2] These figures
provide some measure of the relative importance of friendly
societies in the self-help movement among working men and, indeed, in the social life of the nineteenth century.

In these circumstances it is to be expected that parallels to the
developments in friendly societies during this period can be found
in the trade unions. Among the small local societies which were
the characteristic friendly societies of 1815 the organisation was
virtually the same as in trade unions of the same period. A form
of primitive democracy was practised, government was in the
hands of the general body of members assembled at the club room
while the executive functions were carried out by officials chosen
not by election but by a system of rotation of office.[3] Later on the
growth of the orders led to more complicated constitutional
forms in affiliated friendly societies and these societies owed much
to the efficiency of their full-time bureaucracy. The central
organisation of the unions became in some cases stronger than

[1] R.C.F.S., 4th Report, Appendix I.
[2] According to S. and B. Webb, *A History of Trade Unionism*, Appendix V,
the membership of the 34 unions for which statistics could be given was 297,615
in 1875 and these were said to comprise about one-third of the whole body of
trade unionists.
[3] Infra, p. 18. See also S. and B. Webb, *Industrial Democracy*, 1902 ed., p. 8.

B

that of the affiliated orders where lodge funds did not during this period ever come directly under the control of the central government of the orders. The needs of industrial warfare made such control by the centre imperative in the case of some trade unions,[1] but whatever the actuarial advantage might have been of adopting this course, the friendly society lodges insisted on maintaining their own sickness and management funds distinct from the central funds of the Order. Local control of funds remained a principle of the organisation of the co-operative societies also, for here, again, no overwhelming need could be shown to make the local societies surrender their autonomy to some central body. Before a permanent headquarters came to be established, some trade unions changed their seat of government regularly from one district to another so that no one area or group of members should seem to dominate the rest. A similar arrangement prevailed well beyond the close of this period in the Ancient Order of Foresters whose headquarters were moved each year.

Friendly society development before 1875 played an important part in fashioning the legislative and administrative policies to be followed in future by the state towards working-class organisations in general. Legislation and administrative machinery originally devised to deal with friendly societies came to be extended to cover trade unions, co-operatives, building societies, loan societies and local savings banks.

The legislation followed friendly society development, it did not anticipate it or even guide it to any marked degree. Those who formed and maintained the societies were extremely independent in their attitude and were most unwilling to be patronised or guided by the governing classes. Baernreither in his *English Associations of Working Men* felt that stability and financial success would have attended the efforts of the societies much sooner if they had been less suspicious of the state, its magistrates and officials. But such evidence as exists does not indicate that magistrates and officials were any wiser than those who did in fact run the societies. The approval of the justices for tables of contribu-

[1] S. and B. Webb, *Industrial Democracy*, 1902 ed., pp. 90 ff.

tions and benefits required in the act of 1819 was dropped because
it really achieved no useful purpose.[1]

The friendly society legislation itself was used by trade unions
from the early days; they often called themselves friendly societies
and registered as such in order to protect their funds and—before
1824 at least—to secure a less troubled existence. In the act of 1855
provision was made for the mere deposit of rules without examination at the Registry; this was framed to facilitate the admission
of trade unions and was taken advantage of by many of them.
This is shown by the list given in the return for 1869 which
included the Amalgamated Society of Engineers, Machinists,
Millwrights, Smiths and Pattern-makers, the Friendly Society of
Ironfounders of England, Ireland and Wales, the Amalgamated
Society of Carpenters and Joiners and the Operative Bricklayers
Society. The outcome of the case of *Hornby* v. *Close* was that the
aims of a trade union were held by the courts not to be analogous
to those of a friendly society and the Trade Union Act of 1871[2]
declared that the friendly society acts should not apply to trade
unions even although it enabled them to obtain a similar status to
friendly societies through a procedure nearly the same as that of
the friendly society acts.

Co-operative societies first gained legal protection under the
Friendly Society Act of 1834[3] which authorised the registration
of societies for 'any other purpose [than those specified] which is
not illegal'. A separate Industrial and Provident Societies Act was
passed in 1852.[4] This act still kept these societies administratively
within the field of the Registrar of Friendly Societies and all

[1] A letter published in the *Gentlemen's Magazine* in 1795 (vol. LVI, p. 1082)
gives some idea of the possible consequences of magisterial supervision. This
letter, from Lichfield, complained that the magistrates had struck out a rule on
registering a society which had excluded a member if he joined the services. It
appeared that they had done this to other societies also.

The members were 'fearful that their funds will not support the probable
charges of maintaining crippled or disabled soldiers or sailors, who had been
fellow members with them in societies, as they are certainly more liable to accident
than those that stay at home'. The magistrates' understanding of actuarial matters
seems to have been considerably less than that of the members.

[2] 34 & 35 Vict., c. 31.   [3] 4 & 5 Wm. IV, c. 40.
[4] 15 & 16 Vict., c. 31.

provisions of the friendly societies acts were to apply except where this act stated otherwise. The Benefit Building Societies Act of 1836[1] applied to building societies all the provisions of the existing friendly societies acts. The result of this measure was that these acts remained in force for building societies long after they were repealed by amending legislation so far as friendly societies were concerned.

The effect of the friendly society legislation was to create not only a code of practice to be applied to similar organisations, but also to set up an administrative department to apply the code. The early administration was through the courts—registration was the business of the J.P.s—and the change to a central registry of friendly societies is a good example of that movement from administration through a court of law to administration through a government department to which parallels may be found in other fields at this time. Tidd Pratt, the first Registrar, was described in one of the appendices to the Report of the Royal Commission as 'minister of self-help to the whole of the industrious classes' since his administrative functions had grown so varied. Whether a man joined a savings bank, a friendly society or a trade union, shopped at the co-operative store or bought his house through a building society, the Registrar's certificate would follow him. The Royal Commission made the claim that the Registrar had become to the working man 'the embodiment of the goodwill and protection of the state, in all that goes beyond police, the poor law, justice and the school'.[2]

A study of the practices of friendly societies in this period throws some light on the way in which the 'industrious classes' sought to let a little entertainment and colour enter their drab lives. In the early years the convivial activity of the societies was of the utmost importance, and while it may have been less important in 1875, it was still regarded as an essential part of the life of any self-respecting society. The ritual of initiation, the good fellowship of the lodge room and the celebrations of the annual 'club day' meant much to members. The early trade unions indulged in somewhat similar practices and met a similar need. The

[1] 6 & 7 Wm. IV, c. 32.   [2] R.C.F.S., 4th Report, 1874, Appendix I.

elaborate initiation ceremonies in use among the Bradford wool-
combers and the Rochdale flannel weavers in the 1820s were said
to have been taken from the ceremonies of the Oddfellows.[1] Both
friendly societies and trade unions usually held their lodge meetings at public houses and the practice of paying the rent of the
room by buying a pre-arranged quantity of 'lodge liquor' prevailed in both. It is interesting to notice that the pressure to end
the practice and to substitute a formal cash rent came from the
central organisation in both the unions[2] and in the most highly
organised affiliated order, the Oddfellows of the Manchester
Unity. The whole question of conviviality was one on which the
Registrar frequently gave his opinion; it was quite illegal for any
registered society to spend funds on it. When the orders began to
develop their own bureaucracies, their own central officials condemned the use of lodge funds for this purpose. Yet, in spite of
such condemnation, these practices took an unconscionable time
in dying, as the Royal Commission found out. In order to preserve harmony in the lodge, the friendly societies usually excluded
all discussion of politics at lodge meetings and this practice was
also to be found among the older craft unions.

The principal internal development in the history of friendly
societies between 1815 and 1875 was the emergence of the nation-
wide affiliated order. These orders took their origin in the areas
which felt earliest the impact of the industrial revolution—Lancashire and the West Riding. As the period progressed so did the
orders spread both geographically and socially and by 1875 not
only the better-paid working men of the towns but also the agricultural labourers were able to join them. These orders became
the leaders and spokesmen of the friendly society movement and
in some respects helped to bring about developments whose
benefits extended far beyond their immediate membership.

The affiliated orders, and the Manchester Unity of Oddfellows
in particular, were responsible for gathering and assessing the data
on which much actuarial science came to be based. The study of
the probability of sickness among working men had not been
undertaken systematically until the needs and experience of the

[1] Webb, *History of Trade Unionism*, p. 113 n.   [2] Ibid., pp. 185-6.

orders made it both necessary and possible. The industrial insurance companies were able to venture with comparative safety later on into the territory opened up by the orders. Moreover, in an age when professional services were coming to be more widely available, the affiliated orders did much to make the services of a doctor available to working men. Their contract system whereby a doctor undertook to attend sick members in return for an annual capitation fee paid by the society was the only practical basis for providing medical attendance at the time and it has now been adopted by the state for its national health service.

No attempt has been made in this book to consider the friendly societies of the colonies, dominions and foreign countries. Yet it would be wrong in writing of their development in England not to mention that it was these English societies which provided the inspiration and in many cases the actual founders of societies abroad, especially in the Empire and in the United States. The Manchester Unity had a large number of members in the Empire who continued to accept the leadership of the home country. Although the Oddfellows of the United States ultimately broke their connection with Manchester yet they owed their origin to those emigrants from England who 'carried the seed of Oddfellowship with them'. The world-wide character of the English affiliated orders was one of the results of the emigration from this island in the nineteenth century.

CHAPTER TWO

THE DEVELOPMENT OF ORGANISATION
AND GEOGRAPHICAL DISTRIBUTION

THE GROWTH OF THE SOCIETIES BETWEEN 1815 AND 1875

IT is not possible to give precise figures for the total membership of friendly societies in any particular year of this period, but it is possible to make estimates, based on such figures as are available, which show the extent to which these societies grew in the sixty years following the Napoleonic Wars.

The main sources of statistics are the Reports of the Registrar of Friendly Societies along with the Reports of Parliamentary and Royal Commissions—the Reports of the Commissions were sometimes based on figures supplied by the Registrar. Owing to the voluntary nature of registration, many thousands of societies never at any time came under the surveillance of the Registrar, there was no means by which he might know of their existence. Of those societies which were registered, many failed to keep proper records or to make returns. The Registrar's Report for the year 1872 was one of the fullest to be issued and a higher proportion of returns were actually received that year than was usually the custom—probably due to the interest stimulated by the Royal Commission which was then sitting—but even in 1872 while 21,819 blank forms were sent to societies asking for returns, only 12,267 were in fact received back by the Registry.[1] Thus even in this year not many more than half of the registered societies provided particulars about their membership.

By the 1870s the most important element in the friendly society movement was the affiliated societies, and as these grew larger and more reliable, so were they anxious to make known their achievements; thus they began about the middle of the century to publish particulars concerning their membership and wealth.[2] In view

[1] Registrar's Report, 1872, Appendix, p. 192.
[2] Examples: List of Lodges of the Independent Order of Odd Fellows, Manchester Unity. Annual Directory of the Ancient Order of Foresters.

of the purpose which lay behind this collecting and publishing and because of the intense loyalty which the officers felt towards the orders they served, some of the earliest figures may be a little over-generous, yet they are a valuable source of information to anyone wishing to follow the development of friendly societies. Along with the figures provided by the great affiliated orders may be classed the official publications of the county and other large societies. But even when all these sources of information are considered, there still remains a great mass of small local societies which have left few records.

Perhaps the most accurate estimate of the membership of friendly societies at the end of this period was that made by the Secretary to the Royal Commission.[1] After studying both the Report of the Registrar for 1872 and the Report of the Assistant Commissioner who visited Lancashire and the North, the Secretary analysed in detail the position in Lancashire and then proceeded, 'If, without examination of the details, we took the figures of the summary in the Registrar's Report confining ourselves to thousands as respects funds and members, and applied the same proportions of 1,388,000 members and £1,457,000 funds, we should obtain for the whole of England (inclusive of Wales) over 32,000 societies of all sorts with over 4,073,000 members and over £11,942,000 funds.' To check his estimate, the Secretary attempted another forecast based on the Registrar's Report alone; this time he obtained a total membership of 4,078,101 and total funds of £11,912,567. From these figures it seems probable that there were over four million members of various sorts of friendly societies, including burial societies, by 1872.

The societies themselves by this date were of various types; the Royal Commission found it convenient to classify them in seventeen groups including:
  (1) Affiliated societies or orders.
  (2) Ordinary large (or general) societies.
  (3) County societies and other patronised societies not purely local.
  (4) Local town societies.

[1] R.C.F.S., 4th Report, 1874, Appendix IV.

(5) Local village and country societies.
(6) Particular trade societies.
(7) Dividing societies.
(8) Deposit friendly societies.
(9) Collecting societies and burial societies generally.
(10) Annuity societies.
(11) Societies of females.

There were also cattle insurance societies, certain benevolent societies, societies established by authority of the Secretary of State under section ix of the act of 1855 and societies only depositing their rules as well as unregistered societies. Not all of these organisations could have been defined as institutions 'whose object is to enable the industrious classes, by means of the surplus of their earnings, to provide themselves a maintenance during sickness, infirmity and old age'.[1] While in the eyes of the law they were all covered by friendly society legislation, yet the phrase 'friendly society' as commonly used in 1875 meant above all the affiliated societies and the various types of local societies. Accordingly it is largely with these types of society rather than with all organisations covered by friendly society legislation that this book is concerned.

The categories adopted by the commissioners were by no means mutually exclusive: societies of females could also be local town or local village or deposit or annuity societies; a local town society might be a dividing society or a deposit society and so on. Yet these categories are useful in showing the variety of demands which the societies had come to meet by 1875. Thus by the time the societies came under the scrutiny of the Commissioners, both in respect of their extent and their complexity of organisation, many friendly societies differed greatly from the small groups of working men whose combinations for the purpose of mutual help had met with so much suspicion in 1815.

The difficulty of obtaining any accurate estimate of the membership of friendly societies in 1815 is considerably greater. Before the establishment of the office of Registrar the only contact

[1] The definition given by Eden in his *Observations on Friendly Societies*, 1801, p. 1.

of even the registered societies with the state was the enrol-
ment of their rules by the Clerk of the Peace at Quarter Sessions.
Once enrolled the contact ended, for no returns were made. Thus
the only official sources likely to give an overall picture of the
position in 1815 are the Reports of particular Parliamentary Committees. According to the Report of the Select Committee on the
Poor Laws of 1818, there were 925,429 members of friendly
societies in 1815.[1] Since this figure was obtained from the returns
of overseers of the poor, it would not have been confined to the
membership of registered societies only. The first appendix to
the 4th Report of the Royal Commission in 1874 assumed that it
was so restricted when it compared this figure of 925,429 with the
number of members listed in the returns from registered societies
in 1872—1,857,896—and remarked that this was 'barely more
than double the figure of 1815; results which, considering the
general progress of the country, and especially of its working
classes, do not appear altogether satisfactory'.[2] If this figure of
925,429 members be accepted as the most reliable assessment of
the strength of friendly societies available for 1815—and it seems
approximately correct when compared with Eden's estimate of
648,000 in 1801 or with the poor law return of 704,000 in 1803—
then to get some idea of the numerical growth of the friendly
society movement during these sixty years one should compare it
with the estimated total membership of about 4,000,000 given for
1872. In the period from 1815 to the Royal Commission, there
was, therefore, a fourfold increase in the total membership of
friendly societies.

[1] Report of the Select Committee on the Poor Laws, 1818, Appendix II.
There is here a summary of the returns made by the overseers of the poor giving
the number of members of friendly societies at Easter, 1813, Easter, 1814, and
25 March, 1815, as 821,319; 838,728 and 925,429 respectively. Under the heading
'Observations' it adds: 'The number of persons belonging to friendly societies
appears to be, for the last three years, nearly 8½ in the 100 of the resident population.'
[2] R.C.F.S., 4th Report, 1874, Appendix I.

LOCAL SOCIETIES

In 1815 virtually all friendly societies were local in their organisation; large and county societies had not appeared at all and the affiliated orders were just beginning to struggle into existence. The first of them to be established was the Manchester Unity of Oddfellows whose first Corresponding Secretary was appointed in 1816. The local societies provided such social security—and much of the social life—as their members were able to afford. A typical local society of these years was the Amicable Society of Patrington in the East Riding. This was founded in 1792 with the customary triple aim of providing insurance against sickness and funeral expenses and of bringing members socially into closer contact with each other. Thirty years after its foundation it was flourishing sufficiently to re-issue its articles in 1822;[1] these provided among other things 'that when a member is sick, lame or blind, and rendered incapable of working . . . he shall be allowed eight shillings per week during his inability to work' and 'that upon the death of every free member, notice must be given to the stewards, who, at the next monthly meeting, shall pay to the widow or executor ten pounds . . .' This society sought to encourage conviviality by including in its articles provision whereby each member should pay threepence towards the cost of refreshment at each meeting. Such an arrangement was usual but it did not always appear in the rules.

If it is accepted that these local societies had a membership of just under a million in 1815, it is probable that quite as many still belonged to those societies classed by the Royal Commission as 'Local Town Societies' and 'Local Village and Country Societies' in the 1870s. In 1871 the acting Registrar in speaking of these local societies and of the affiliated orders said 'they would probably be the two large divisions in which to class all friendly societies'.[2] It was societies of this class in particular which continued throughout this period to avoid registration and to persist in abstaining

---

[1] Articles of the Amicable Society at Patrington, Hedon, 1822.

[2] Evidence of A. K. Stephenson before the Royal Commission, 30 January, 1871, q. 602.

from all contact with agents of the state; in the words of the acting Registrar 'there are a great many friendly societies which are neither registered nor have their rules deposited'.[1] There are no definite figures for the total membership of these societies in 1875, but the reports from the Assistant Commissioners showed that they remained numerous and well supported in many districts.[2] Relatively, however, they had declined from the position of containing virtually all members of friendly societies to containing perhaps a quarter to a third of the membership.

The main feature of the organisation of these small societies throughout this period was their complete independence. 'Each is perfectly independent of the other, there is no head authority attempting to exercise any jurisdiction over any group. Each society has its own funds and is governed by its own rules, which are registered separately.' [3] Their self-governing nature and complete independence remained one of their strongest recommendations to their members. Here was an organisation which could be adapted in any way to meet the needs of individuals as they arose; naturally the limits to such adaptability which registration and compliance with a legal interpretation of their functions involved was often not acceptable. If a majority of the members wanted to spend part of their contributions on an annual feast they were not prepared to put themselves in the position where agents of the government might try to prevent them from doing so.

Most of these small societies were formed around ale houses and seldom had more than a hundred members, often far fewer. In the earlier part of this period the managing committee and the officials were usually chosen by rotation.[4] Lindfield Friendly Society dated from 1757 and was governed by four stewards who were changed by pairs every half-year. 'It shall be a fair succession, beginning with the first subscribers to these present Articles, and

---

[1] Evidence of A. K. Stephenson before the Royal Commission, 30 January, 1871, q. 613.

[2] Stanley, p. 25. Young, pp. 10 ff.

[3] Evidence of A. K. Stephenson before the Royal Commission, 30 January, 1871, q. 603.

[4] This practice was also found among the early trade unions.—Webb, *Industrial Democracy*, 1902, p. 7.

so on, until it hath gone through the whole society . . . And if any person whose turn it is to serve shall refuse, he shall forfeit Ten Shillings and Six Pence.' [1] The Friendly Society of Joiners elected by ballot their president while choosing their stewards by rotation among those members of at least two years' standing.[2] The Friendly Society of All Trades at Newburn chose all their officers by rotation half-yearly.[3] The main exception to the provision of appointment by rotation was the office of secretary, which could obviously not be shared in turn by all regardless of their literacy. Sometimes an outsider was appointed as clerk and there was also some provision for payment of a small fee or honorarium to the secretary in some societies. But, even so, it often remained difficult to fill the position with a suitable person, and even among those societies which were registered, the completion of the annual returns left much to be desired and indicated that many local societies had no one competent to act as secretary.[4] Sir George Young in his Report, after contemplating these and other shortcomings, commented that 'as an organisation of thrift it [the local club] has never been a healthy plant, and the improvements which it seems capable of effecting for itself, without extraneous aid, fall far short of what is peremptorily needed'.[5]

It was this lack of education which was often blamed for the failure of these local societies to accept sound actuarial principles in the conduct of their affairs. 'There still exists, however, among the agricultural population a profound ignorance and consequent distrust even of the simplest economic results now established as rules for carrying on a sick and death benefit society without financial mishap,' [6] wrote Sir George Young and he went on to advocate the dissemination of 'simple, practical instructions for the

---

[1] Articles of a Friendly Society meeting at the sign of the Tiger, Lindfield, 1757, Article V.

[2] Rules and Regulations to be observed by the Friendly Society of Joiners, Newcastle, 1821, Rule VI.

[3] Articles, Rules and Orders of the Friendly Society of All Trades, Newburn, 1825, Rule VII.

[4] Evidence of A. K. Stephenson before the Roya Commission, 30 January 1871.

[5] Young, p. 16.   [6] Ibid., p. 17.

compilation of rules and arrangement of account books suited for a village benefit club, and of tables which, though they must be considered provisional, can be recommended without risk of error beyond some trifling divergence on the safe side'. It is hard to believe that such publications would have had any more effect than those which had already been published at different times since 1815. The nature of the local club did not really change in these years; it was not lack of advice but an unwillingness to heed it which led to financial troubles in many local clubs. It was very easy—and indeed obvious—for the Royal Commissioners and middle-class inquirers in general to mistake the aim of those who joined such societies. Certainly they sought insurance against particular contingencies, but they were seeking much more than this, they were seeking those social and convivial activities which membership was expected to afford. The frequency with which the Registrar, Tidd Pratt, had to reiterate his admonitions to societies which attempted to register rules concerning these activities of itself gives some idea of the important part they played in the life of local societies throughout this period.

Among the local societies in towns, the greater density of population led to the formation of societies of special composition during this period—societies with some religious or moral principle as their mainspring. One of the most numerous of these special groups of local societies was the Sunday School type. E. L. Stanley in 1874 wrote of them, 'They are first of all for the sake of the children attending these schools, and are apt to grow into sick clubs for adults who have formerly been attendants as pupils or teachers. They are naturally held at the school and the management is in the hands of those who conduct the school. The contributions are as a rule very low, and an actuary would be surprised how they get on at all. But they manage to succeed very often to a wonderful extent. For they are very cheaply managed and the members are, of course, among the most steady, provident and respectable.' He gave a number of examples of such societies —'The Baptist Sunday School Sick and Burial Society' with 321 members, 'The Independent Methodist Sunday School Society' with 602 members, 'The Oldham Sunday School Union Friendly

Sick and Burial Society' with 178 members.[1] Other local societies
were established on temperance principles or by members of a
particular church or by groups of immigrants. An example of a
combination of the two latter was the 'Guild of Saint Mary and
Saint Joseph, Bristol', a society of 80 members founded in 1868
by a Father Dykes for the benefit of the Irish Roman Catholic
population of Bristol.[2]

The appearance of these local societies based upon some ethical
or religious principle was one of the most striking developments
among local societies during this period. The growth of these
'specialised' local clubs seems to have come only as the towns
grew in size and travelling facilities improved, that is to say when
enough people of a like persuasion were able to meet together
without too much difficulty. The Sunday School societies, for
example, were very common in the towns of East Lancashire.[3]
There were but few of them outside the counties of Lancashire,
Cheshire and Yorkshire. In Lancashire there were 54 registered
societies with 11,359 members, in Yorkshire 7 societies with 421
members and in Cheshire 3 societies with 129 members.[4]

Local societies in general were widely distributed throughout
this period. It is possible to obtain some idea of their distribution
in 1815 from the poor law returns.[5] The parish officers were required to include in their reports particulars relating to the number of members of friendly societies in their districts at Easter
1813, Easter 1814 and on 25 March, 1815. The question they were
asked was, 'What is the number of members in friendly societies
which hold their usual meetings in your parish or place, including
those members not belonging to your parish or place as well as
those belonging to it?'

In the Abstract of Answers and Returns where the parish
officers' replies were printed, there is this official comment on the
answers to this particular question, 'The Returns, in replying to
this question, appear to be very incorrect, many hundreds of them

[1] Stanley, p. 101.   [2] Young, p. 14.
[3] R.C.F.S., 4th Report, 1874, para. 212.   [4] Ibid., para. 216.
[5] Abstract of Answers and Returns relative to the expense and maintenance of
the Poor in England, 1818. The figures for London were issued separately, 1817.

having been forwarded without any answer to it, in the first instance, and after being returned for correction, were again sent back very imperfect; and, in many, noticing only one member in such society, having apparently mistaken the question as applying to the number of societies instead of members; and many of the parish officers have observed that the stewards or clerks of the societies have absolutely refused to give any account of the number of members contained in such societies.' The difficulty which parish officers experienced in some places in getting information is understandable since at the time there were alleged friendly societies which were really trade unions evading the Combination Acts,[1] while hostility towards the agents of the government and

TABLE 2

The number of members of friendly societies in the counties of England on 25 March, 1815
(figures from the Abstract of Answers from Poor Law overseers, 1818)

County	No. of Members	County	No. of Members
Bedford	3,850	Norfolk	14,080
Berks	3,953	Northants	10,424
Bucks	6,434	Northumberland	10,367
Cambridge	4,739	Notts	19,421
Cheshire	22,292	Oxford	6,150
Cornwall	22,941	Rutland	1,375
Cumberland	9,947	Shropshire	24,774
Derby	23,034	Somerset	26,428
Devon	53,022	Southampton	11,611
Dorset	6,209	Staffs	42,305
Durham	13,525	Suffolk	13,814
Essex	20,531	Surrey	26,530
Gloucester	26,066	Sussex	4,958
Hereford	2,870	Warwick	26,856
Herts	10,928	Westmorland	1,052
Hunts	2,509	Wiltshire	16,240
Kent	17,538	Worcs	13,641
Lancs	147,029	Yorks—E. Riding	11,941
Leics	17,217	„ N. Riding	9,697
Lincs	8,755	„ W. Riding	80,684
Middlesex	67,186	London	52,312
Monmouth	8,404		

[1] A. Aspinall, *Early English Trade Unions*, 1949, p. xxiv. 'The unions could easily shelter under the title of friendly societies, and hold their meetings under cover of the rules allowed to these clubs in pursuance of the Friendly Society Acts.'

suspicion of the government's intentions even in genuine friendly societies remained a serious obstacle to official registration until the latter part of the century.[1] Many of the parish officers may well have guessed the strength of those societies in their midst which refused to reveal their numbers and such guesses might often have been exaggerated. Thus there were probably many members who were not enumerated in these returns but the figures there given may be too large in other cases. In spite of these difficulties, Table 2 based on these returns does give a general picture of the distribution of the local societies in the English counties in 1815.

A Select Committee of the House of Lords on the Poor Laws in its Report of 2 September, 1831, gave the following ratios of the number of persons in friendly societies for every 100 of the population at the 1821 census in the following counties:[2]

Bedford	$5\frac{1}{4}$	Middlesex	$6\frac{1}{2}$
Berks	3	Monmouth	13
Bucks	5	Norfolk	$4\frac{1}{2}$
Cambridge	$4\frac{1}{2}$	Northants	7
Cheshire	$8\frac{1}{2}$	Northumberland	7
Cornwall	10	Notts	$11\frac{1}{2}$
Cumberland	$7\frac{1}{2}$	Oxford	5
Derby	8	Rutland	8
Devon	$12\frac{1}{2}$	Shropshire	$12\frac{1}{2}$
Dorset	5	Somerset	7
Durham	$7\frac{1}{2}$	Southampton	$4\frac{1}{2}$
Essex	$7\frac{1}{2}$	Staffs	14
Gloucester	9	Suffolk	6
Hereford	3	Surrey	$6\frac{1}{2}$
Herts	$9\frac{1}{2}$	Sussex	$2\frac{1}{2}$
Hunts	6	Warwick	$10\frac{1}{2}$
Kent	4	Westmorland	3
Lancs	17	Wiltshire	8
Leics	10	Worcs	$8\frac{1}{2}$
Lincs	$3\frac{1}{2}$	Yorkshire	$8\frac{1}{10}$

On the basis of the figures in these two tables Lancashire had the largest absolute number of members of local societies and a far

[1] Smart, *Economic Annals of the Nineteenth Century*, 1910, vol. I, p. 708, tells how in 1819 a rumour that the government was going to seize friendly societies' funds to pay the national debt caused the break-up of some societies in Lancashire.

[2] Report of the Select Committee of the House of Lords on the Poor Laws, 1831.

higher proportion of its population had joined them. Other counties where ten per cent or more of the population were to be found in local friendly societies in 1815 included Cornwall, Devon, Leicestershire, Monmouth, Nottingham, Shropshire, Staffordshire and Warwick. The presence of Cornwall and Devon among those counties where support for local societies was strong is interesting because the affiliated societies were late in making real progress there. This may be accounted for partly by their remoteness from the centres of the Oddfellows and Foresters in Lancashire and Yorkshire and partly by the relative decline in the importance of the local industries in the south-western counties —such as the manufacture of serge in Devon—during the nineteenth century.[1]

The counties where three per cent or fewer were members of local societies were Berkshire, Hereford, Sussex and Westmorland while Cambridgeshire, Kent, Norfolk and Lincolnshire all had fewer than five per cent of their population in societies. The main difference between this second group of eight counties and the first group of nine appears to have been the presence of some sort of industry in the first group and its absence in the second. Friendly society development in general seems to have taken place most rapidly in the most highly industrialised areas where the working people were both better able to afford to make provision for sickness and where, possibly, the need for such provision was greater than among those who worked on the land. It is dangerous to base too many generalisations on figures such as these since, while they provide a rough guide, they may not be accurate in detail. The picture of friendly society activity which Eden drew in his *State of the Poor* in 1797 in the various towns and counties certainly does not conflict with the impression derived from these tables. The description of friendly societies in Preston, 'they have an annual festival every Whit-Monday, and parade through the town after divine service accompanied by bands of music, with

[1] The relative stagnation in these two counties is shown by the population figures between 1811 and 1871; the population of Devon increased from 382,778 to 600,814 or by 57 per cent, that of Cornwall from 220,525 to 362,098 or by 64 per cent, while the population of England and Wales rose from 10,164,256 in 1811 to 22,704,108 in 1871, an increase of 125 per cent.

the flags of different companies', contrasts strongly with his reports from Sussex, in which county the existence of only one
society was mentioned.

The small local societies remained widely distributed throughout the country in 1875. The Assistant Commissioners found such
clubs in all the districts they visited. But it is impossible to reduce
to tabular form any summary of the position at this time for lack
of exact evidence concerning the number of societies or of members in particular districts. Moreover the group was less homo-
geneous by this date. The largest of local societies were by now
larger in numbers than some of those societies classified by the
Commissioners as 'Large Ordinary Societies' and were scarcely
distinguishable 'except in point of extension';[1] such was the
Cannon Street Adult Male Provident Institution of Birmingham
which had 7,733 members in 1872.[2] At the other extremity were
the small village clubs with as few as 20 members continuing
their actuarially unsound lives around the village inn. The
majority of the former group were to be found in the manufacturing cities of the North and Midlands while the latter remained one
of the features of the villages of the southern half of England.[3]

Sir George Young found the village clubs of Buckinghamshire,
Hampshire, Sussex and Devonshire below average while Cambridge, Norfolk, Suffolk, Essex and Lincolnshire appeared to have
a number of very sound local clubs. There were special features in
particular districts. In Bedfordshire and Buckinghamshire there
were a number of local societies for women only which had met
with an unusual degree of success due to the financial independence
which the women were able to gain by plaiting straw at home. A
Mr. Clark was secretary of the Union Female Friendly Society at
Luton in 1872 and he said of the society 'that the members (300 or
so) are chiefly residents in the town, not many in the villages
around. Most of them are unmarried, girls earning wages at
straw-plaiting; but when they marry they don't drop the club.'[4]

[1] R.C.F.S., 4th Report, 1874, para. 207.   [2] Registrar's Report, 1872, Appendix.
[3] Reports from the Assistant Commissioners for Northern and Southern
England, 1874.
[4] Report on the Union Female Friendly Society printed as an appendix to
the Report by Sir G. Young, p. 133.

THE AFFILIATED ORDERS

'The affiliated societies as the clubs of highest organisation among those invented by working men to suit their own wants, and at the present day greatly surpassing all others in popularity, deserve the first place which is assigned to them.' This was the conclusion of Sir George Young in his Report to the Royal Commissioners and was quoted with approval by them in their final Report.[1] The most striking development between 1815 and 1875 was undoubtedly the growth of such societies as the Oddfellows, the Foresters, the Druids, the Shepherds and the like, so that the Commissioners found 34 of these orders with more than 1,000 members each.[2] The total membership of the 34 societies about 1872 was 1,252,275, but among them two orders stood out, the Independent Order of Oddfellows, Manchester Unity, with 426,663 members and the Ancient Order of Foresters with 388,872 members,[3] in other words, approximately two-thirds of the members of the affiliated orders belonged to one of these two giants. Mr. Neison junior in 1877 estimated the total number of affiliated orders at 75 including all the various small groups which at some time had broken away from the main society.[4] In calculating the total number of people who were members of affiliated societies, there should, perhaps, be some allowance made for double membership on the part of those who wished to increase their allowance when sick by joining two societies. Such double membership would be confined to the better-off working men in the towns and must have accounted for only a small proportion of the total strength, but it is not possible to give a definite figure.

The first of the affiliated societies to grow was the Oddfellows and in many ways the development of the Manchester Unity formed the pattern which other societies followed to a greater or lesser degree. Numerous orders of Oddfellows came into existence, but the principal group was the Manchester Unity, most of the others being dissident parties which had broken away at some

---

[1] R.C.F.S., 4th Report, 1874, para. 94.   [2] Ibid., para. 108.

[3] These totals are for England and Wales only.

[4] F. G. P. Neison, 'Some Statistics of the Affiliated Orders, 1877'. A paper read before the Statistical Society.

time. There are numerous myths and legends which find the origin of the Oddfellows among the Romans or other ancient peoples,[1] but the first record relating to the formation of a union of lodges in the Manchester district is a volume entitled 'Minutes and other Documents of the Grand Committees of the Independent Order of Oddfellows connected with the Manchester Unity from the year 1814'. The 'Abercrombie' lodge at Manchester came into existence about 1810, and it appears to have opened other lodges so that by 1814 it was known as 'No. 1 Lodge' and the other lodges were apparently willing to accept its leadership. According to the preface of the volume referred to above, in 1814 'the various lodges first began to form general committees of all lodges in the Manchester district for the purpose of affording each other mutual support, protection and advice'.[2] Within twenty years or so the system of organisation was developed which lasted without any important modification to 1875. In 1816 the first corresponding secretary of the order, Thomas Hignett, was appointed[3] and he came to act as a sort of chief administrative officer for the whole Unity.

The individual lodges, however, did not become mere branches of the central organisation, they maintained full control over their own sick funds and management expenses, but about this time a central funeral fund was established for the Manchester district and contributions and burial monies were paid into and drawn from this central fund for all members of the Manchester lodges. As the number of lodges increased and they spread to other parts of the country, so the district organisation was extended and the pattern established at Manchester of a lodge sick fund and a district funeral fund was adopted generally. Until 1827 the central government of the Order had been in the hands of the Grand Committee, a body elected by lodges of the Manchester district, but after 1827 a Board of Directors was set up which took over

---

[1] Some account of these is given at the beginning of the *History of Oddfellowship: Its Origin, Tradition and Objects* by James Spry, 1867. See also the first chapter of *A Century of Oddfellowship* by R. W. Moffrey, 1910, where there is also a brief discussion of the meaning of the word 'Oddfellow'.

[2] Printed in *Oddfellows' Magazine*, 1891, p. 41.

[3] J. Spry, *History of Oddfellowship*, 1867, p. 5.

the tasks of the committee. The Board of Directors itself was chosen by the Annual Moveable Committee, a body composed of delegates from all the districts, which had first met at Manchester in 1822. The district committees themselves consisted of representatives elected by the lodges. The organisation was thus divided into three parts, the Unity, the district and the lodge. In cases of dispute, an aggrieved member could appeal from the lodge to the district; if his appeal were rejected at that level he could take his case to the central authority. The Annual Moveable Committee from 1841 appointed a special committee of 18 to meet quarterly in Manchester for the purpose of hearing appeals.[1]

There was considerable friction at times between the central authority and the lodges and much of this trouble arose over rates of contribution and of benefits in connection with sickness funds. The inadequacy of contributions to cover proposed benefits was the commonest cause of the collapse of local friendly societies and of individual lodges of the large orders in the early days. The Annual Moveable Committee of 1844 called for returns from lodges of funds and membership figures with the object of having sound tables drawn up. According to Hardwick in his *Manual*, many members feared that the Directors were trying to get possession of the separate lodge funds or that they were going to 'sell the information to the government'.[2] Consequently a number of lodges failed to make the returns required and were suspended. In 1845 certain financial reforms were adopted by the Annual Moveable Committee and the lodges were instructed to carry them out. A considerable number again objected and a struggle ensued. Hardwick wrote, 'It ended in what is termed the "national split", or the formation of a separate society with the title of "National Independent Order of Oddfellows". The great bulk of the Manchester Unity, however, adhered to the law and to the executive.' [3] By the end of this period the National Inde-

---

[1] Much information concerning the constitutional development of the Order may be gathered from J. Burn, *An Historical Sketch of the I.O.O.F.M.U.*, 1845, as well as from Spry, *A History of Oddfellowship*, 1867.

[2] C. Hardwick, *A Manual for Patrons and Members of Friendly Societies*, 1859, p. 40.

[3] Ibid., p. 40.

pendent Order of Oddfellows numbered rather more than 35,000.
The outcome of this particular dispute was the loss of many members but a considerable strengthening of the financial position of
the Order since those who remained accepted the proposals of the
Directors.

The happenings of the 1840s naturally prevent the membership
figures for the Manchester Unity from telling a straightforward
story of expansion. The figures themselves before about 1850 must
be considered as estimates rather than as precise enumerations.
The reluctance of many lodges to make regular returns and the
genuine inability of members to keep books and to fill in forms
inevitably affected the totals. Moreover a dishonest Corresponding Secretary refused to accept his dismissal from the Order and
the Unity lost most of its records up to 1848 through his refusal to
hand them over to the successor who was appointed.

In 1832 the Manchester Unity claimed to have 561 lodges and
31,000 members. The report of a sub-committee presented to the
Annual Moveable Committee at Glasgow in 1838 claimed 1,200
lodges and 90,000 members. 'In 1842, according to the "memorial
for the opinion of counsel", the Order consisted of upwards of
3,500 lodges, enumerating in the aggregate 220,000 members.' [1]
The increase between 1832 and 1842 was thus very rapid. Owing
to the disputes within the Order, the number of members showed
no significant advance for about a decade after which a steady increase began once more as is shown by the table on page 30.
By this time the closer internal administration of the Order was
beginning to work more smoothly and the returns from the
lodges were sufficiently regular and accurate to enable reliable
figures to be published annually.

The distribution of the Manchester Unity's strength in England
can be described briefly enough at the opening of this period. It
was then merely struggling into existence and consisted of no more
than a union of local lodges in the Manchester area—not very
easily distinguishable to an outsider from the old 'free-and-easy'
Oddfellows' clubs. By 1845, half-way through this period, there
were lodges affiliated to the Order in every county in England,

[1] Ibid., p. 39.

TABLE 3

The total membership of the Manchester Unity of Oddfellows, 1848–76

Year	No. of Members	Year	No. of Members
1848	249,261	1862	335,145
1849	234,490	1863	342,953
1850	224,878	1864	358,556
1851	229,040	1865	373,509
1852	225,194	1866	387,990
1853	225,001	1867	405,255
1854	231,228	1868	417,422
1855	239,783	1869	425,095
1856	251,008	1870	434,100
1857	262,883	1871	442,575
1858	276,254	1872	458,159
1859	287,575	1873	470,043
1860	305,241	1874	481,630
1861	316,215	1875	496,529
		1876	508,013

The information in this table is based on 'A List of the Lodges comprising the I.O.O.F. (M.U.)', an annual publication. The figures given are for the total membership and they include those Oddfellows resident in Scotland, Ireland and some of the colonies who were members of this Unity. On 1 January, 1876, these members numbered 51,936.

One of the more remarkable features of the affiliated orders was the anxiety of members emigrating overseas to maintain their membership, and the number in the colonies grew rapidly from about 1860.

although nearly half of the lodges were in the counties of Lancashire and Yorkshire and its strength was concentrated overwhelmingly in the industrial areas—as may be seen from the table which follows. No attempt has been made to show the number of members of the Manchester Unity in each county in 1845 because the figures given in the early 'Lists' may well have been estimates and it was admitted that during the crisis of the 1840s some secretaries were refusing to supply the Unity with accurate figures.[1]

This table illustrates the spread of the Order in the more agricultural counties of the South and West mostly after 1845. A more surprising feature of the table is that there appears to have been a decline in the number of lodges in many of the districts where the Oddfellows were first established. There were fewer lodges by 1875 in such counties as Cheshire, Derbyshire, Lancashire,

[1] Hardwick, op. cit., p. 40.

TABLE 4

The number of lodges of the Manchester Unity of Oddfellows in each English county in 1845 and in 1875

County	1845	1875	County	1845	1875
Bedford	23	26	Lincolnshire	105	78
Berkshire	25	16	Middlesex	87	135
Buckingham	13	23	Monmouth	45	84
Cambridge	20	32	Norfolk	48	96
Cheshire	142	123	Northants	43	47
Cornwall	2	26	Northumberland	93	47
Cumberland	44	45	Nottingham	69	56
Derbyshire	134	122	Oxfordshire	15	16
Devon	40	56	Rutland	5	4
Dorset	3	31	Shropshire	78	79
Durham	97	111	Somerset	31	24
Essex	17	32	Staffordshire	160	123
Gloucester	74	54	Suffolk	21	52
Hampshire	15	53	Surrey	32	72
Hereford	19	13	Sussex	16	49
Hertford	25	23	Warwicks	141	98
Huntingdon	10	8	Westmorland	21	17
Kent	22	78	Wiltshire	26	39
Lancashire	737	507	Worcestershire	91	53
Leicester	74	82	Yorkshire	600	444

Information in this table is based on the Lists of Lodges for 1845-6 and 1875-6, but the totals for counties have been corrected since the List shows lodges as existing in the county in which the district office happened to be situated whereas the actual addresses show that they were frequently in another county.

Lincolnshire, Northumberland, Nottingham, Stafford, Warwick, Worcester and Yorkshire. There were two main reasons for this reduction in the number of lodges. The first was the constitutional crisis of the years following 1845 in the Manchester Unity. The attempt to impose stronger central control led to secessions from the Unity by groups of old-established lodges in industrial areas which had managed their own affairs in the past and were not willing to accept any outside direction. These malcontents joined other unities of Oddfellows or even formed one of their own as when lodges containing nearly 16,000 members formed the 'National Independent Order of Oddfellows' after the Glasgow A.M.C. split of 1845. The main strength of the other unities in the 1850s lay in the counties showing a decline in the number of lodges attached to the Manchester Unity. The second reason for

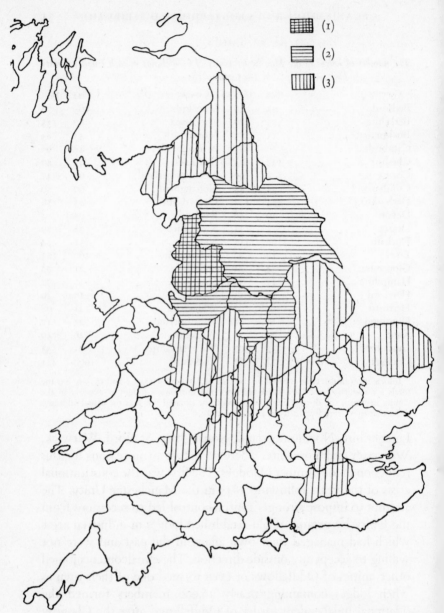

The period of foundation of M.U.O.F. lodges active in 1875.

Counties with more than 25 foundations by 1825—(1)
by 1835—(2)
by 1845—(3)

reductions in the number of lodges was the inadequate rate of contributions charged and the consequent exhaustion of funds and collapse of the lodge. This, again, usually occurred in those counties where Oddfellowship had gained many adherents before 1845 when individual lodges still arranged their own contribution and benefit terms and when little actuarial information was available. By the end of this period about 1,900 lodges had been founded which no longer existed in the order,[1] and the great majority of these had been in the counties listed above.

The total membership of the Manchester Unity more than doubled between 1845 and 1875, going from an approximate 248,000[2] to 496,529. Much of this increase took place in the counties where the Order was spreading for the first time but new lodges were still being established even in those districts where secessions were heavy. It is possible to estimate the whereabouts of this continued growth from the table which follows and which analyses the dates of foundation of the various lodges listed as being active and affiliated to the Manchester Unity in 1875. In this table the dates of foundation of individual lodges were taken from the List of Lodges for 1875–6 in most cases, but where no date of foundation was given for a particular lodge in that List, it was usually possible to trace it in an earlier one. Some lodges have been assigned to counties other than those in which the Order listed them for the reasons explained above.

The decade immediately preceding the constitutional troubles and the secessions saw the most rapid growth of the Order and nearly half of the English lodges active in 1875 were founded between 1835 and 1845 (1,470 of 3,074). This was a difficult period for working men in many industrial districts and it witnessed the rapid growth of a number of working-class organisations of self-help or of self-defence, including the Chartist and Primitive Methodist movements as well as the Manchester Unity.[3]

This table confirms the impression that it was the lodges which had administered their own affairs entirely for many years and

---

[1] Stanley, p. 5.   [2] Hardwick, op. cit., p. 41.
[3] The effect of the Poor Law on the rate of growth of the affiliated orders—and especially on that of the M.U.O.F.—is discussed below in chapter VIII.

TABLE 5

The period in which the lodges of the Manchester Unity which were active on January 1st, 1875, were founded

County	Pre-1825	'25-35	'35-45	'45-55	'55-65	'65-75	Total
			Number of Lodges established:				
Bedford	—	—	15	3	5	3	26
Berks	—	—	6	1	5	4	16
Bucks	—	—	15	4	3	1	23
Cambs	—	—	16	4	6	6	32
Cheshire	7	32	60	8	8	8	123
Cornwall	—	—	1	5	13	7	26
Cumber'd	—	—	32	1	6	5	44
Derby	7	26	58	1	2	3	97
Devon	—	—	11	6	28	11	56
Dorset	—	—	2	8	17	4	31
Durham	—	3	49	5	32	22	111
Essex	—	—	13	14	2	3	32
Glos	1	3	31	6	5	8	54
Hants	—	—	15	21	6	11	53
Hereford	—	—	9	1	—	3	13
Herts	—	—	14	2	3	4	23
Hunts	—	—	8	—	—	—	8
Kent	—	—	24	15	17	22	78
Lancs	62	145	244	16	21	19	507
Leics	1	9	50	7	8	7	82
Lincs	1	1	54	7	10	5	78
Middx	1	—	75	20	19	20	135
Monmouth	—	9	27	3	15	30	84
Norfolk	—	—	40	32	16	8	96
Northants	—	1	35	5	3	3	47
North'd	—	1	28	—	9	9	47
Notts	3	22	24	3	4	—	56
Oxford	—	—	5	1	2	8	16
Rutland	—	—	4	—	—	—	4
Salop	2	5	40	10	11	11	79
Somerset	—	1	13	1	4	5	24
Staffs	5	15	73	6	10	14	123
Suffolk	—	—	20	17	9	6	52
Surrey	1	1	31	10	15	14	72
Sussex	2	—	9	23	4	11	49
Warwick	—	4	81	1	6	6	98
Westm'd	1	4	10	1	—	1	17
Wilts	—	2	14	3	3	17	39
Worcs	1	6	23	10	2	11	53
Yorks	19	165	191	16	29	24	444
TOTALS	114	455	1,470	297	358	354	3,048
					Add 26 undated lodges		26
					English lodges		3,074

The 26 undated lodges are made up of 1 lodge in Cumberland and 25 lodges in Derbyshire whose dates of foundation cannot be traced.

which had built up a strong local tradition which were most likely to have seceded about 1845, for most of the secessions occurred in the counties with the largest number of foundations before 1835, namely Cheshire, Derbyshire, Lancashire, Nottingham, Stafford and Yorkshire. Moreover in estimating the number of secessions or dissolutions in each county, the new foundations must be taken into account. For example, the loss in Lancashire was not of 230 lodges (737 in 1845 minus 507 in 1875) but 286 since there were 56 new foundations.

The very late arrival of the Manchester Unity in any strength in the south-western counties is apparent from this table. Of 113 lodges in Cornwall, Devon and Dorset in 1875 only 14 had been founded by 1845, while a high proportion of lodges in the remaining South Coast counties of Hampshire, Sussex and Kent were also founded after 1845. The explanation of this late development is not merely a matter of distance from the centre of the movement—although this no doubt played a part—but also the difficulty which those working as agricultural labourers must have had in paying contributions on the scale usual in Oddfellows' lodges.[1]

There was a considerable growth in the average membership of lodges between 1845 and 1875 in all parts of the country and it was this feature as well as the foundation of new lodges which accounted for the increased total membership of the Order.[2] The total number of members in 1845 was given as 229,928 for England;[3] this figure would give an average membership for each lodge of about 70 members. Using figures from the same List, the average lodge in Lancashire had 87 members, in Yorkshire 75 members, in Somerset 65 members, in Cambridgeshire 47 members and in Oxfordshire 42 members. The average number of members of the 40 lodges in Devonshire was only 34 in 1845, only 11 of these survived until 1875; this number of dissolutions would seem to have provided an example for those who spoke of the financial unsoundness of small lodges and of the importance of increasing their average membership. It was not until after 1855

---

[1] Young, p. 2.   [2] The size of lodges is analysed in Appendix D, below.
[3] List of Lodges, I.O.O.F.M.U., 1845–6.

that the Manchester Unity secured a reliable foothold in Devonshire and began to make progress that was lasting; the 40 lodges
with only 1,357 members of 1845 had increased to 56 lodges (45
new foundations) with 6,369 members, giving an average membership per lodge of 114 in 1875.[1] The national average by 1875
was 132 members per lodge, the average for Lancashire 122, for
Yorkshire 132, for Hampshire 193, and for the North London
District 141. There was a noticeable increase in the average size of
lodges in all counties between 1845 and 1875 and this was particularly marked in the more rural counties. The general result
was to improve the actuarial soundness of the lodges.

In many respects the growth of the Ancient Order of Foresters
resembled that of the Manchester Unity of Oddfellows. It traced
its ancestry back to ancient times and, according to myth, Adam
was the first Forester. In 1834 the 'Perseverance' (Leeds) Court of
the Royal Foresters claimed 'despotic' powers over the other
courts of that order. The Manchester district called a convention
of courts opposed to the power of the Perseverance Court which
met at Rochdale on August 4th, 5th and 6th and the delegates
present formed the Ancient Order of Foresters. Within three
months 294 courts had transferred their allegiance and in 1835,
when the first High Court meeting of the Ancient Order was held
at Salford, there were supposed to be 363 courts with a membership of 16,510. In 1837 the first court in the London area was
opened and in 1841 the first permanent secretary was appointed.
Internal dissensions led to the appearance of a rival executive in
York in 1847, and in 1848 43 courts had to be suspended—this,
combined with the effects of the current trade depression, ex-
plains the fall in membership for 1849.[2]

The central government of the Foresters was in the hands of a
'High Chief Ranger' who presided over an executive council after
the manner of the Oddfellows' Grand Master and Board of
Directors, while the annual High Court Meeting corresponded to

[1] List of Lodges, I.O.O.F.M.U., 1875-6. The totals have been corrected to
allow for the ex-county lodges listed as being in Devonshire. Figures for other
counties which follow are based upon the same source.

[2] Many of these particulars were given in 'An Historical Sketch of the Order'
which was published in the Annual Directory of the A.O.F. for 1890.

the Annual Moveable Committee except that the Foresters' delegates represented courts and not districts. Like a number of other
contemporary working-class organisations, the Foresters had no
permanent headquarters; the seat of government was moved
every year and the central authority for the year tended to be
chosen from the locality. The advantage of this system was that
no 'clique' ever appeared to gain control of the society for its own
purposes while, on the other hand, 'the Order loses the benefit of
the continued services of the most experienced men'.[1] The system
was undoubtedly the main reason for the weaker central government which the Foresters had in comparison with that of the Manchester Unity. E. L. Stanley found that the legislators changed
each year and became less well known and thus less respected than
their opposite numbers in the Manchester Unity; '. . . the moveable and variable character of the Foresters' executive council
makes it impossible for the Order to trust them with the powers
that might well be given to such a body as the Board of Directors
of the Manchester Unity'.[2]

The actual business efficiency of the Foresters also suffered.
When the younger Neison undertook to investigate the sickness
and mortality experience of the Foresters for the first time he encountered considerable difficulty. 'To tabulate properly these facts
occupied a large staff for a considerable period, and the task was
materially augmented by the necessity under the Society's rules of
the removal of its offices each year to a different centre, a portion
of the work thus being performed in Sheffield, Dublin and
Northampton. These removals not only involved much loss of
valuable time, but necessitated also on each occasion the re-
engagement and fresh training of almost a new staff.'[3]

At the lower level the Foresters' court corresponded to the Oddfellows' lodge; but in spite of a similarity of name, the intermediate unit, known to both societies as the district, was hardly a
geographical unit among the Foresters in the sense that it was
among the Oddfellows. Foresters' courts in the same town might

[1] R.C.F.S., 4th Report, 1874, para. 147.   [2] Stanley, p. 197.
[3] F. G. P. Neison, *Rates of Mortality and Sickness in the Ancient Order of Foresters*,
1882, p. 9.

well have belonged to different districts owing to the degree of overlapping which prevailed, while a number of courts remained entirely outside the district organisation. Sir George Young wrote of this 'The greater laxity among the Foresters in enforcing the complete organisation of their order as an affiliated society, of which this is an instance, has preserved them from the numerous heavy secessions which have been experienced in the Oddfellows, Manchester Unity. For this advantage they have, however, paid dearly, in their much inferior financial position.' [1] Speaking of the organisation of the Foresters, he said elsewhere that they were 'in most respects half a generation behind the Oddfellows, Manchester Unity' and the Royal Commission appeared to agree with this judgement.

As can be seen from Table 6, within eleven years of its foundation the Ancient Order of Foresters had gained 65,909 members

TABLE 6

The growth of the Ancient Order of Foresters, 1845–76

Date	No. of Members	Date	No. of Members
Jan. 1, 1845	65,909	Jan. 1, 1861	189,584
„ 1846	76,990	„ 1862	207,993
„ 1847	83,493	„ 1863	228,026
„ 1848	84,472	Dec. 1, 1863	250,703
„ 1849	80,490	„ 1864	277,746
„ 1850	80,089	„ 1865	301,077
„ 1851	84,348	„ 1866	321,253
„ 1852	89,875	„ 1867	336,791
„ 1853	94,323	„ 1868	349,022
„ 1854	100,556	„ 1869	361,735
„ 1855	105,753	„ 1870	376,663
„ 1856	114,020	„ 1871	396,244
„ 1857	125,423	„ 1872	421,988
„ 1858	135,001	„ 1873	466,888
„ 1859	148,562	„ 1874	468,495
„ 1860	168,576	Jan. 1, 1876	491,196

The information in this table is based on the Foresters' Directory which was published annually. The totals given include members in Scotland, Ireland and overseas; there were very few of these latter before 1860. On 1 January, 1876, there were 50,929 of these members of whom 22,303 resided in Scotland and Ireland and the remainder overseas.

[1] R.C.F.S., 4th Report, 1874, para. 149.

and thus become strong in numbers much more quickly than the Oddfellows, who had taken twice as long to attain such a membership. This was probably due to the changed circumstances of the 1830s which—as was noticed above—was also the period of most rapid expansion of the Oddfellows. Another great burst of expansion seems to have occurred after 1856 and this may well have been due to the spread of the Foresters among agricultural labourers, some of whose village clubs became courts of the Order.[1]

One peculiarity of the Foresters was that the Order contained within itself another order called the Ancient Order of Shepherds (not in any way connected with the Loyal Order of Ancient Shepherds, Ashton Unity). The aim of this inner order was to enable Foresters to insure for additional benefits if they so desired, thus all Shepherds were also Foresters. The lodges of this inner order were called sanctuaries and their funds were kept separate from the funds of the local court. The first complete return of the sanctuaries showed that in 1853 there were 175; this number steadily increased so that in 1871 there were 577 sanctuaries with 21,159 members.[2]

In one sense it is easier to trace the spread of the Foresters in the various counties because its development was much more even than that of the Manchester Unity. Not only was the central control weaker so that no attempt was made to enforce on individual courts a scale of contributions before the 1870s, but even then the rule requiring this contained an 'escape' clause for courts unwilling to adopt the centrally prescribed scales.[3] Consequently there was not the same story of secessions by groups of courts in the areas where the Order had been long established and the table which follows conveys a straightforward story of expansion in most parts of the country.

This table is based on the figures given in the annual Directories published by the Order which began as a comparatively primitive

[1] Stanley, p. 9.
[2] Figures for the number of sanctuaries from 1853 were given in the relevant Foresters' Directories.
[3] Stanley, p. 2.

D

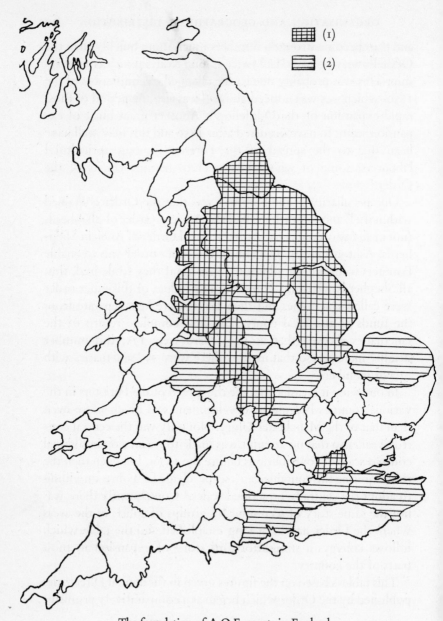

The foundation of A.O.F. courts in England.

Counties with more than 25 courts by 1845—(1)
by 1855—(2)

list in 1841.[1] In these early Directories the courts were shown in ✕
the order in which they had been opened, but as the number grew
and the Directories were needed as works of reference an arrangement by districts and counties was adopted for the first time in
1845. Unfortunately the district organisation did not lend itself to
fitting inside of county boundaries, consequently the totals shown
here for the various counties are not the same as the totals shown
in the summaries at the back of the Directories. The meeting
places of individual courts have been checked so that where necessary courts could be removed from the county under which they
were listed and put in their own county. A few examples make
clear the need for this re-arrangement. Under Lincolnshire in the
1855 Directory were shown 3 courts in Nottinghamshire, 1 in
Huntingdonshire, 2 in Leicestershire, 6 in Northampton, 1 in
Yorkshire, 1 in Cambridgeshire and 1 in Rutland; 13 Cheshire
courts had strayed into the list for Lancashire while no fewer than
141 courts in the Middlesex list for 1865 were really situated in
Essex, Surrey, Kent, Berkshire and Hertfordshire. The membership totals in the Directories for each county were also based on
district organisation, consequently they do not give the real
number of Foresters in each county.

As with the Manchester Unity, the Ancient Order of Foresters
had its main strength in Lancashire and Yorkshire to begin with.
In 1845 it only numbered half as many courts in these counties as
the Manchester Unity had lodges, but by 1875 the latter's lead had
become less pronounced. The counties giving the Foresters least
support up to 1845 were largely the same as those which showed
least interest in the Oddfellows, the counties along the South Coast
and those where there was little industrial development including
Dorset, Hampshire, Sussex, Suffolk, Essex, Oxfordshire and
others. Thus in the period up to 1845 the distribution of membership of the Oddfellows and Foresters was broadly similar, bearing
in mind that the Foresters had started later and were less numerous

---

[1] A Directory was published for the Ancient Order of Foresters by the Leeds
High Court in 1835 which showed 24 districts and 392 courts, but considerable
difficulty was said to have been experienced in obtaining particulars for it and
the regular series of Directories only began to appear six years later.

TABLE 7

The number of courts of the Ancient Order of Foresters in each English county at ten-year intervals, 1845–75

County	1845	1855	1865	1875
Bedford . . .	6	15	22	34
Berkshire . .	—	—	8	10
Buckingham . .	4	11	19	21
Cambridge . .	6	7	13	14
Cheshire . . .	117	126	134	144
Cornwall . . .	—	—	27	21
Cumberland . .	17	15	8	21
Derbyshire . .	20	30	45	48
Devon . . .	—	—	56	85
Dorset . . .	—	1	14	22
Durham . . .	69	48	106	136
Essex . . .	—	10	31	45
Gloucester . .	8	24	78	113
Hampshire . .	3	32	65	88
Hereford . .	1	1	11	12
Hertford . . .	—	6	13	16
Huntingdon . .	6	7	6	7
Kent . . .	5	28	116	170
Lancashire . .	332	326	384	357
Leicester . . .	10	9	32	47
Lincoln . . .	116	96	100	90
Middlesex . .	78	136	363	466
Monmouth . .	—	11	30	55
Norfolk . . .	17	42	84	94
Northants . .	17	28	46	52
Northumberland .	13	12	39	69
Nottingham . .	19	16	28	35
Oxford . . .	—	1	5	8
Rutland . . .	2	3	4	3
Shropshire . .	11	27	58	79
Somerset . .	4	9	23	43
Stafford . . .	35	63	170	221
Suffolk . . .	—	14	15	54
Surrey . . .	7	41	118	151
Sussex . . .	—	22	60	82
Warwick . .	35	35	51	76
Westmorland . .	6	8	8	7
Wiltshire . .	1	7	13	25
Worcester . . .	—	10	43	72
Yorkshire . .	383	377	401	370

These figures are based on the returns given in the relevant Directories of the Ancient Order of Foresters with modifications as explained in the text.

Some courts in Welsh and Scottish counties were members of English districts and were shown as English courts in the Directories. These have been excluded from this table.

at that time. However, Table 7 indicates that significant differences in distribution arose during the period 1847 to 1875.

The most remarkable feature of Table 7 is the rapid spread of the Foresters in the southern and western counties which had been slow hitherto to embrace the affiliated orders. The Manchester Unity showed considerable gains in these counties during the third quarter of the nineteenth century, but its gains were not nearly so sweeping as those of the Foresters. The counties showing the greatest expansion in these years were Cornwall, Devon, Dorset, Essex, Hampshire, Hereford, Kent, Somerset, Suffolk, Surrey and Sussex. Many of the new courts in these counties were established in small market towns and were probably supported by the craftsmen and working people engaged in the various trades of the town, yet the addresses given in the Directories also show many courts in purely agricultural villages. The Foresters gained the support of far more agricultural workers than did their main rivals because their terms were better suited to the labourers' pockets.

In 1877 F. G. P. Neison read a paper to the Statistical Society[1] in the course of which he produced tables showing the membership of the Manchester Unity and of the Foresters in each county of England from 1863 and 1848 respectively, these being the years from which statistics were available. The figures for individual counties are a good deal less useful than they might have been because Neison took the statistics furnished by the societies at their face value without attempting to correct the error which arose in the official figures given by both orders—especially serious in the Foresters—because of their habit of listing all courts and lodges as being in the same county as the headquarters of the district through which they were affiliated. That this can lead—and in Neison's paper did lead—to false conclusions was shown by his remarks on Dorset, where he said of Forestry that, 'it appears to have died out about 1850 and not to have taken root again until 1867'. This was far from what really happened. The first Foresters' court in the

[1] F. G. P. Neison, 'Some Statistics of the Affiliated Orders of Friendly Societies (Oddfellows and Foresters)', read before the Statistical Society on 16 January, 1877.

county was founded at Poole in 1845 or 1846; by 1860 there was a second court at Poole and courts in Weymouth, Dorchester, Blandford, Shaftesbury, Cerne Abbas and Portland; by 1865 there were fourteen courts in the county—three at Weymouth, two at Poole, and one in Bridport, Dorchester, Blandford, Shaftesbury, Cerne Abbas, Portland, Wareham, Wimborne and Verwood. These courts appeared in the various Directories issued by the Foresters at the time but there was no Dorset district before

TABLE 8

The growth of membership of the Ancient Order of Foresters in the regions of England, 1848–76

Region	Number of Members at:			
	1 Jan. '48	1 Jan. '58	1 Dec. '67	1 Jan. '76
South-East (Surrey, Sussex, Kent, Hants, Berks) . . .	2,338	8,390	34,078	50,630
South Midland (Northants, Hunts, Beds, Cambs, Oxon, Herts, Bucks, Middx) . . .	10,219	23,330	77,396	108,585
Eastern (Essex, Suffolk, Norfolk)	1,316	5,587	14,342	22,648
South-West (Wilts, Dorset, Devon, Cornwall, Somerset) .	786	1,338	13,076	21,367
West Midland (Monmouth, Staffs, Hereford, Salop, Warwick, Worcs, Gloucester)	5,612	12,902	42,196	65,464
North Midland (Leics, Lincs, Rutland, Derby, Notts) . . .	8,731	10,987	19,473	26,611
Yorkshire	20,139	25,794	34,429	37,683
North-Western (Lancs, Cheshire) . .	26,986	33,779	47,076	51,591
Northern (Durham, Cumberland, Northumberland, Westmorland) . . .	4,371	7,274	22,285	32,382

1867, consequently many of them were entered as Hampshire courts and some even appeared in the Middlesex list. In spite of these deficiencies as far as the reliability of Neison's county figures and tables are concerned, the totals derived from the county figures when grouped into the regions then used by the General Register Office for births, marriages and deaths do give a more or less reliable picture of the regional distribution of the membership of these two orders since many of the county boundaries obviously no longer matter. Tables 8 and 9 are based on Neison's

TABLE 9

The growth of membership of the Manchester Unity of Oddfellows in the regions of England, 1863–76

Region	Number of Members (at 1 Jan.):			
	1863	1868	1873	1876
South-East (Surrey, Sussex, Kent, Hants, Berks) . . .	21,634	30,413	36,338	39,489
South Midland (Northants, Hunts, Beds, Cambs, Oxon, Herts, Bucks, Middx) . . .	30,195	39,053	44,352	48,019
Eastern (Essex, Suffolk, Norfolk)	16,685	19,674	23,105	25,066
South-West (Wilts, Dorset, Devon, Cornwall, Somerset) .	11,251	16,742	21,264	23,883
West Midland (Monmouth, Staffs, Hereford, Salop, Warwick, Worcs, Gloucester)	42,328	50,778	59,156	64,179
North Midland (Leics, Lincs, Rutland, Derby, Notts) . . .	32,806	38,455	41,116	44,188
Yorkshire	52,054	57,124	59,012	59,381
North-Western (Lancs, Cheshire) . .	72,621	75,160	76,136	77,475
Northern (Durham, Cumberland, Northumberland, Westmorland) . . .	20,018	24,730	28,187	30,995

information and illustrate the rapid progress made by these two orders in the southern regions in the latter half of the period 1815–75, and more especially that of the Foresters in the agricultural regions between 1858 and the end of 1867.

In comparison with the Oddfellows of the Manchester Unity and the Ancient Order of Foresters, the other affiliated orders were of minor importance during this period. Some of them had begun as splinter movements from the M.U.O.F. and the story of their growth in numbers and organisation followed broadly and at a distance of some years the pattern outlined for the two largest societies. None of the other affiliated societies was as well organised as these two by 1875 and virtually all of them still experienced great difficulty in obtaining returns from local secretaries even at the end of this period. In the case of the Loyal Order of Ancient Shepherds, Ashton Unity, the Assistant Commissioner reported in 1874, 'Some returns are made by lodges to the head office but they come in very irregularly and are very carelessly made out. . . . The experience of the head officers was that the chief difficulty they had to contend with was the ignorance of lodge secretaries, especially in the mining districts.' [1] Bearing in mind this limitation on the accuracy of the figures, the five largest affiliated orders after the Manchester Unity and the Foresters had the following membership about 1872 (to the nearest thousand):[2]

Grand United Order of Oddfellows	71,000
Order of Druids	57,000
Loyal Order of Ancient Shepherds (Ashton) . .	46,000
National Order of Oddfellows.	35,000
Nottingham Ancient Imperial Order of Oddfellows .	40,000

Among these smaller orders were some which had some particular ethical or moral principle acting as a guiding force, e.g. the pledge to abstain from alcohol among the Rechabites and the particular beliefs associated with the Rational Sick and Burial Association. G. Cheyney of the Record Department of the Registry of Friendly Societies listed all the affiliated societies in existence in 1877 so far as could be ascertained and found that there

[1] Stanley, p. 15.   [2] Ibid., pp. 11–18.

were 163 of them.[1] Many of these were unregistered and it was almost impossible to ascertain accurately any facts concerning them beyond the knowledge of their existence and, at times, the date of their foundation and registration. This list considerably exceeded Neison's estimate of 75 but clearly many of these would only have come to light as a result of the enthusiastic research of one whose main aim was not actuarial but to obtain a comprehensive list for its own sake. The list named 34 orders of Oddfellows as well as the Manchester Unity, 11 orders of Druids, 10 orders of Ancient Britons, 5 orders of Foresters and 4 orders of Rechabites. The tendency of the affiliated orders to form splinter groups and factions seems to have been in proportion to their enthusiasm for actuarial purity or, perhaps, strong central government. The main interest of these many small affiliated orders lies in the tribute which their mushroom growth paid to the ideals of the few great and well-known orders whose strength and repute were so attractive to working men.

The industrialised counties of the North and Midlands provided most of the membership of these orders. The three main dissentient orders of Oddfellows were most numerous in those districts where there had been many secessions from the Manchester Unity. The third largest affiliated order, the Grand United Order of Oddfellows, possessed little in the way of reliable statistics before 1875; 'the greatest difficulty this and other orders have to contend with is the want of education in the lodge secretaries'.[2] The information which the Assistant Commissioner was able to gather concerning its distribution in November 1870 showed that there were 364 lodges with 21,443 members in Lancashire and 242 lodges and 15,757 members in Yorkshire; there was no comparable concentration in any other county.[3] The second largest dissentient order of Oddfellows was the Nottingham Ancient Imperial; it had no return of the number of its members, but the Assistant Commissioner calculated the approximate membership by averaging each lodge at 70 members. There were

---

[1] C. Walford, *The Insurance Cyclopaedia*, 1870–8, vol. IV, pp. 533 ff., prints this list in full.

[2] Stanley, p. 11.   [3] Ibid., p. 10.

118 lodges in Nottinghamshire, 56 in Leicestershire and between 40 and 50 in Warwickshire, Lincolnshire, Northants, Yorkshire and Derbyshire; 162 lodges were scattered over the rest of the country, only 27 of them in Lancashire.[1]

The National Independent Order of Oddfellows, formed as a result of the 1845 split in the Manchester Unity, was the third largest of the dissentient orders of Oddfellows. According to its Directory for 1871 the Order had 34,364 members, of whom 32,788 lived in Lancashire and Yorkshire.[2] These three orders of Oddfellows must have maintained a considerable popular appeal in their localities to have built up a combined membership of over 30,000 in Yorkshire, more than 40,000 in Lancashire and large followings in other northern and Midland counties. The other smaller groups of Oddfellows, such as the British United Oddfellows and the Bolton Unity of Oddfellows, were largely confined to Lancashire, Yorkshire and the counties about them.

The largest of the remaining orders was the Order of Druids; this was also the largest of the various orders incorporating the word 'Druid' in their title. It had its origin in a splinter movement from the Order of Ancient Druids, but it outgrew its parent body. The membership of the Order in 1871 was distributed as follows:[3]

County	No. of Lodges	No. of Members
Lancashire	581	33,721
Yorkshire	168	9,870
Cheshire	73	3,940
Derbyshire.	23	2,155
Durham	38	2,134
Northumberland . . .	22	906
Middlesex	16	605
Staffordshire . . .	10	521
Worcestershire . . .	10	397
Lincolnshire . . .	4	321
Warwickshire	3	205
Shropshire	4	168
Leicestershire . . .	1	110
Nottinghamshire . . .	1	51
Herefordshire	1	47

[1] Stanley, p. 18.
[2] Walford, *The Insurance Cyclopaedia*, 1870–8, vol. IV, p. 449.
[3] Ibid., p. 432.

The original society, the Order of Ancient Druids, had its headquarters in London and by 1872 it had a total of 19,317 members.[1] According to its Directory, the Order's membership was distributed as shown below. It will be seen that while its headquarters was at Clerkenwell, yet its main strength was in Yorkshire. The management of the head office was almost nominal, concerning little besides the granting of dispensations for new lodges and regalia.

County	No. of Lodges	No. of Members
Yorkshire	111	7,829
Kent	17	1,580
Leicestershire	21	1,420
Warwickshire	18	1,283
Lincolnshire	18	1,036
Derbyshire	10	869
Nottinghamshire . . .	13	698
Cumberland	4	650
Lancashire	6	535
Hampshire	12	527
Middlesex	12	433
Essex	4	304
Gloucestershire . . .	11	299
8 other counties . . .	25	1,521

The last order of noteworthy size was the Loyal Order of Ancient Shepherds, Ashton Unity, who had about 46,000 members in 1871. No returns of this Unity's membership were issued but the Assistant Commissioner published in his Report such figures as he could obtain. Their main strength lay, as usual, in Lancashire and Yorkshire.[2]

County	No. of Lodges	No. of Members
Lancashire	261	17,573
Yorkshire	101	7,098
Gloucestershire . . .	80	4,107
Cheshire	36	2,354
London	22	913
Derbyshire	8	880

[1] Ibid., p. 432.
[2] Stanley, p. 19.

OTHER FORMS OF FRIENDLY SOCIETY

Ordinary large (or general) societies were defined by the acting Registrar of Friendly Societies in 1871 as being of 'quite a distinct class, and may be described, perhaps, as doing business over the counter. They really are offices for life insurance and sickness, but in which there is no connection or personal acquaintance between the members as there is in the ordinary friendly society.' [1] The idea that these were societies doing business over the counter must not be taken to mean that they were local societies; the largest among them carried out business on a national scale from their headquarters in London. This was pointed out in his Report by the Assistant Commissioner for the southern counties when he wrote, 'The Hearts of Oak and the Royal Standard are examples of Societies of the most completely centralised type, having no agencies or recognised agents out of London. Their members transmit their contributions by post-office order, and receive sick pay and other benefits in the same manner.' [2]

The control of these societies was usually in the hands of a managing committee which reported to an annual general meeting. The reason which defenders of these societies gave for their form of management was that it was cheaper to run a society in this manner than it would have been if some measure of popular control were brought into its government. 'They have their governing bodies of directors and manager, just like any ordinary insurance society would have.' [3]

The appeal of these societies was to a very different section of the community from that to which the affiliated orders or local clubs appealed. Sir George Young commented that 'Their members are mostly of a higher degree of respectability, artisans, tradesmen, domestic servants, and others, who, as has often been said to me, dislike the nonsense and mixed company of the club nights, and look for an investment of their savings on purely

[1] Evidence of A. K. Stephenson (acting Registrar) before the Royal Commission, 30 January, 1871, q. 568.
[2] Young, p. 5.
[3] Evidence of A. K. Stephenson before the Royal Commission, q. 571.

business principles'.[1] It was very difficult for ordinary working men to join even if they had sought to do so. The Hearts of Oak, for instance, would only admit those whose weekly wage was at least 22s., and the rules contained a long list of excluded trades with the final insuring phrase 'or any other occupation which the committee may conceive dangerous or injurious to health'.[2] Thus the large ordinary friendly societies stood to some degree apart from the class of organisations usually implied by the term 'friendly society'—they were simply insurance businesses and as a matter of deliberate policy avoided all those social manifestations of the 'friendly' spirit which working-men members thought to be so important.

The actual number of large ordinary societies in existence at the close of this period is uncertain; the acting Registrar was unable to give a closer estimate than between '50 and 100, which is, perhaps, the outside number, 30 being the lowest that would come within this definition'.[3] The six main societies were the Royal Standard, the United Kingdom, the United Patriots, the London Friendly, the Royal Oak and the Hearts of Oak. In 1871 these societies had between them 46,000 members. In 1815 no societies of this type had existed, the earliest of them—the Royal Standard—being founded in 1828.

The largest of these societies by 1872 was the Hearts of Oak. It was founded in 1841 and by 1872 it had 32,837 members. The governing body consisted of a committee of 40 members of whom 10 were replaced every three months at quarterly meetings. Voting by proxy was not permitted, thus control of the elections was in the hands of those members who lived in London and who attended the meetings.[4] This society's strength lay mainly in the London area. The Secretary, in 1872, said, 'We call ourselves a London Society and I should estimate that from 16,000 to 18,000 of the total number of members would be found within the metropolitan postal district.'[5] He stated that the society had no

[1] Young, p. 7.   [2] Quoted in the R.C.F.S., 4th Report, 1874, para. 165.
[3] Evidence of A. K. Stephenson before the Royal Commission, q. 586.
[4] Evidence of T. Marshall before the Royal Commission, 10 April, 1872, qq. 24,268 ff.
[5] Ibid., q. 24,272.

recognised agencies in the provinces although in the rules there was a reference to members' agents 'but they are simply members appointed by their fellow members to act as go-between between themselves and us. They receive the sick pay and hand it to them, thus avoiding the necessity of money-orders to each separate member and they occasionally receive the quarterly contributions and send them up in one cheque.'[1] These self-appointed agents were at Deptford, Poplar, Chatham and Ashford and their presence seems to indicate that, outside the London area, Chatham and Ashford had considerable numbers in membership with the Hearts of Oak. The combined membership of the other five large ordinary societies listed above did not equal that of the Hearts of Oak. Most of their members were in the London area, the remainder of their following being widely scattered. Sir G. Young found a number of members of the United Patriots, for instance, in Bath, Bristol, High Wycombe and Exeter.[2]

The so-called county societies were distinguished not by their geographic pecularity but by their mode of management. 'With these may be classed all societies in which the management is wholly or in great part in the hands of honorary members deriving no benefit from its funds. . . . The name 'County Societies' embodies the attempt to systematise, on the basis of county divisions, the benevolent exertions to which this class of society is due; and some have been founded in pursuance of resolutions taken by the magistrates at Quarter Sessions, as a means of improving the condition of those classes which are in part dependent on the rates and with the hope of eventually superseding the poor law by their means.'[3] Thus the origin of these societies lay in the 'interested philanthropy' of the nineteenth century. They were not founded by working men as were the orders or the local clubs, nor were they run by those they were intended to benefit.

The membership of these societies consisted of two groups—the honorary members and the benefit members. Rule 2 of the Hampshire Friendly Society stated that 'The Society shall consist

---

[1] Evidence of T. Marshall before the Royal Commission, 10 April, 1872, q. 24,272.

[2] Young, p. 7.   [3] Ibid., p. 8.

of benefit and honorary members . . .' Rule 7 stated: 'The
Society shall be under the management of a central board, which
shall consist of the following officers: the president, the vice-
president and eight trustees, who shall be honorary members;
twelve directors, not less than six of whom shall be benefit members; the chairmen of district committees and the representative
or member from each district.' [1] The preponderance of the honorary members in the management was thus assured, for the local
representatives also tended to be gentry and clergy and in this
respect the Hampshire Friendly Society was typical of county
societies. Another society of the same type was the Herefordshire
Friendly Society. The Bishop of Hereford was Patron, Earl
Somers was president 'and names well-known in the county
appear among the list of Vice-presidents, Trustees, Directors etc.' [2]
Honorary membership cost a benefaction of £5 or an annual
donation of ten shillings. As the Registrar said in his evidence
before the Royal Commission in 1871, they 'are managed by
some of the leading gentlemen in any county, or by the clergy'.[3]

The county societies strictly defined as those covering the area
of a whole county were only eleven in number in 1872. They had
begun to grow soon after the Manchester Unity had appeared in
the North and their development was steady but not spectacular.
The first to be founded was the Essex Provident in 1818; it was
followed by county societies for Hampshire in 1825, Wiltshire
and Kent in 1828, Rutland in 1832, Herefordshire in 1838, Cambridgeshire in 1842, Dorset in 1847, Nottinghamshire in 1850,
Shropshire in 1851 and Berkshire in 1872. By 1872 the membership of these societies was given in the Registrar's Report for that
year as 29,197.

In addition to these better-known county societies there were a
number of smaller societies run on the same principles, that is to
say, with the assistance or under the control of country gentry and
clergy. These often covered the area of a hundred or sometimes
of the poor law union. The total membership of these societies

[1] The Rules and Regulations of Hampshire Friendly Society, 1825.
[2] F. C. Morgan, *Friendly Societies in Herefordshire*, 1949, p. 12.
[3] Evidence of A. K. Stephenson before the Royal Commission, q. 594.

was never great in the nineteenth century and the Royal Commission estimated that it was probably not far in excess of 60,000.[1]

This class of society was largely confined to the southern half of the country and was entirely missing from the industrial districts. E. L. Stanley, whose task it was to prepare a detailed report on the counties of Cheshire, Derbyshire, Lancashire, Leicestershire, Lincolnshire, Nottinghamshire, Shropshire, Staffordshire, Warwickshire, Worcestershire and Yorkshire, mentioned only two county

TABLE 10

The membership of county societies at the end of 1871 or the beginning of 1872

Name of Society	No. of Members
Town and County of Cambridge	384
Dorset Friendly	2,732
Essex Provident	9,315
Hampshire Friendly	6,322
Herefordshire Friendly	1,088
County of Kent	850
Nottingham County	103
County of Rutland General	196
Shropshire Provident	916
Wiltshire Friendly	7,130
South Bucks Friendly	900
North Devon and South Molton Provident	411
East Gloucestershire Provident	330
West Gloucestershire Friendly	938
West Middlesex Provident	159
North Somerset	955
North Staffordshire Provident	1,188
West Suffolk Friendly	871
West Surrey General Benefit	927
Aldham and United Parishes	2,094
Loes, Hoxne, Thredding and Plomesgate Hundreds	219
Tendring Hundred Benefit	933
Margaret Roothing and District Friendly	572
Stoke and Melford Union Association	1,338
Stoke Holycross Benevolent	588
Dunmow Friendly	1,128
Windsor Royal United Benefit	698
Benefit Society of the Hundreds of Lodden and Clavering	132

All particulars in this table are based upon the Appendix to the Registrar's Report for 1872 or the Report of the Royal Commission, 1874.

[1] R.C.F.S., 4th Report, 1874, footnote to para. 159.

societies, in Nottinghamshire and Shropshire, neither of which had attracted much support. On the other hand, Sir G. Young as Assistant Commissioner for the southern half of England found such societies fairly widespread, although obviously lacking popular appeal. The actual particulars of the membership and distribution of the main societies in this class at the end of this period—so far as they are ascertainable—are given in Table 10.

Societies formed by workmen of a particular factory or workshop for protection against sickness or funeral expenses were referred to by the Royal Commission as 'particular trade societies'. Included in this class were local and non-local societies associated with a particular form of employment or with the employees of a particular company. Many such societies when founded and controlled entirely by the workmen themselves very soon grew into trade unions and concerned themselves with building up funds for such purposes as the insurance of members against unemployment in times of trade depression or for use as strike funds when involved in a contest with their employer. It is easy to see why any form of association among men with the interests that fellow employees have in common should come in course of time to put such matters before insurance against ill-health or death. When trade was poor and the members of such an association could not get enough to eat it was obvious that a common fund accumulated ostensibly for some other purpose must be used to provide them with some sort of regular 'dole' until trade improved. Similarly, if such a group of men became involved in a contest with their employers about which they felt keenly, they would tend to throw into the contest all the resources which they possessed—for whatever purpose such resources might originally have been accumulated. In these ways many of the friendly societies in particular trades grew into trade unions as the activities of the latter came to be at least tolerated by the law.[1] Sir George

---

[1] R.C.F.S., 4th Report, 1874, para. 252.

In a note on p. 23 of their *History of Trade Unionism*, S. and B. Webb wrote of local sick clubs, '. . . in some cases, for various reasons . . . the sick and burial club was confined to men of a particular trade. This kind of society almost inevitably became a trade union.' The Glasgow Journeymen Coopers and the Newcastle Shoemakers were cited as examples.

E

Young in his Report remarked of such societies, 'Many such clubs which still remain on the Register have converted themselves into trade unions or branches of a trade union and ceased to recognise the fact that they were formerly registered. Of this the Carpenters' Friendly Union in Bristol is an instance. It is now a branch of the Carpenters' Union, a society with branches in various parts of the country, some of which amalgamated their funds and became the Amalgamated Society of Carpenters and Joiners, one of the most powerful of the better-known trade unions. The Secretary is unaware that it was ever registered, and, indeed, was puzzled to account for the fact that it appears on the Register.'[1]

For these reasons there was no significant growth of societies of this type during this period. Where societies with their membership confined to a single occupation did exist and were important, they were usually supported by the contributions of employers and membership was often compulsory in such cases; this state of affairs was familiar in the pit clubs of the coal industry and in a number of railway friendly societies. 'In all these one great difficulty is continually recurring in various forms—that the society is of necessity the society of the master and not of the men. By its means the shop establishes a hold on the services of the workman who cannot withdraw without sacrificing the benefit of his contributions; and, on the other hand, the workman has no compensating hold, and it is hard to see how any such hold can be given him, on the employment offered by the shop.'[2] Numerous examples of this were cited including the pit club at Easton colliery and the railway shop club called the Bristol and Exeter Railway Labourers' Annual Benefit Club.

The number of voluntary friendly societies which could be described as being confined to particular trades showed a tendency to diminish. 'The fact is that with the growth of knowledge and experience the number of these special friendly societies, formed of members engaged in one trade "or of one class of persons united under the same circumstances, or living under the same

[1] Young, p. 19.
[2] Ibid., p. 20.

conditions", which Mr. Tomkins states to be "exceedingly small" at present, must go on diminishing.'[1]

Dividing societies had always been confined to one locality; no such society ever succeeded in becoming national or even regional because of its necessarily temporary nature. In a sense they were forerunners of even the local friendly societies and it seems probable that they decreased in size during this period, certainly their relative importance declined greatly. They were really clubs whose members divided up the greater part of any fund which had been accumulated at the end of each year—or sometimes at the end of every two or five years.[2] The fact that they offered a dividend as well as sick and funeral pay accounted for their popularity. The advance of actuarial knowledge and the growth of the affiliated orders dealt them severe blows, as did the pressure of the Registrar who ultimately refused to grant them the benefits of registration on the grounds that they were not permanent societies.[3] The hostility of 'Authority' in general to such clubs was shown by the remarks which the Royal Commission quoted with evident approval from the evidence of 'a witness with great experience' who said '. . . that the lower class of labourers, who cannot generally join the affiliated orders, commonly betake themselves to such clubs; that they impede the work of an ordinary friendly society, lead to direct evil, and pauperise the population'.[4]

These societies were found mainly in certain limited areas by 1870. There were quite a number of them among the agricultural labourers of the South and East who were not in a position to pay the higher premiums demanded by the affiliated orders and who were strongly attracted by the prospect of a dividend. There were numerous 'Slate Clubs', 'Birmingham Clubs' and 'Tontines' in industrial districts—notably East London, Liverpool, and the West Riding. It appears that sharing-out clubs in industrial districts were often regarded not as a substitute for membership of a permanent society but as a supplement, as a way of saving a little

[1] R.C.F.S., 4th Report, 1874, para. 254.
[2] Evidence of A. K. Stephenson before the Royal Commission, 30 January, 1871, q. 632.
[3] Young, p. 21.   [4] R.C.F.S., 4th Report, 1874, para. 300.

extra for Christmas while at the same time providing additional insurance against ill-health during the year.[1] Sir George Young gave several examples of such clubs in the southern and eastern counties while E. L. Stanley gave further examples from the industrial regions.[2]

'Collecting societies and burial societies generally' fulfilled functions covered by what had been entirely local societies in 1815. By 1875 some of these had become national in their scope; the best known was probably the Royal Liver Friendly Society. The strong appeal which these societies evidently possessed seems to have rested upon the dread of working people for the pauper funeral of the nineteenth century. Many who could not afford to insure themselves against both sickness and death in a normal friendly society nevertheless insured against the expenses of their funerals by subscribing to a so-called friendly society which existed solely for that purpose. It should, perhaps, be borne in mind that in the 1870s there were still some collecting societies which offered insurance against sickness as well as funeral expenses—the Royal Liver Society itself still published sickness tables—but the position at that time was best summarised in the words of the Royal Commission's Report: 'The great bulk of collecting societies are burial societies; the great bulk of burial societies are collecting societies.'[3] The general practice of these societies was to collect the subscriptions by means of regular collections from house to house so that the larger of them partook rather more of the nature of industrial assurance companies than of friendly societies in the usual sense of the term. 'Though working under the Friendly Societies' Acts, [they] are really insurance offices, started without any capital and under the control of no shareholders, and conducted principally for the benefit of the office-holders, and only incidentally for that of the assured.'[4]

The two largest burial societies were the Royal Liver Friendly Society with about 600,000 members in 1875 and the Liverpool Victoria Legal Society with about 200,000 members at that date. The latter usually spent some 40 per cent of its total income in

---

[1] Stanley, p. 88.   [2] Young, p. 22, Stanley, p. 88.
[3] R.C.F.S., 4th Report, 1874, para. 411.   [4] Stanley, p. 27.

management expenses, while in the year ending in June, 1871, the Royal Liver collected into its burial fund £176,053, of which it spent £67,088 on management. The headquarters of most of the large burial societies were at Liverpool and the business seems to have thrived more fully in Lancashire than in most other parts of the country.

The only burial societies which really had something of the character of friendly societies—in the usual sense of that term— were the local burial societies. Some of these still survived in 1875; they had constituted the sole form of burial society in 1815. They were organised in various ways. In some there were no regular contributions but only levies to help the family of a deceased member to pay for the funeral. In others the organisation had become more advanced and a regular contribution was paid and a fund maintained out of which to pay stated benefits. The Chatham Royal Dockyard ran entirely on the collection of levies when required while the Devonport Equitable Benefit Society founded in 1830 had an accumulated fund of £10,993 by 1871 working on the principle of regular contributions. The financial stability of local burial clubs was much less reliable than that of local sick clubs. 'The burial club which survives a generation is an exception,' Sir George Young claimed.

Widows' funds or local annuity societies had declined greatly in numbers by the time the Royal Commission examined the situation in England. Quite a number of these societies had been founded in the first half of the nineteenth century and may have been connected with attempts to get the government of the day to sponsor parochial annuity associations. The return furnished to Parliament in 1852 of the friendly societies in England and Wales[1] included a separate list of annuity societies; this showed that 40 of these societies were registered. Evidence taken by the Royal Commission seemed to indicate that most of the existing annuity societies were unregistered because of the legal requirement for registered societies which offered annuities (i.e. the production of an actuarial certificate); the Commissioners also felt that the Post

[1] Abstract of returns respecting Friendly Societies in England and Wales during the five years ending 31 December, 1850 (1852).

Office scheme for granting annuities had contributed to the reduction in the number of societies of this type. 'There is, however, a compact group of annuity societies proper in the West of England, since the Registrar's Report for 1872 enumerates in Devon 10 with £223,260 funds and 1,363 members. The only other body returned as a society for granting annuities is the Nottingham and Nottinghamshire Annuity Society with £784 funds and 865 members. This would bring the total funds for eleven societies to £224,144 and the total membership to 2,228.' [1] The number of registered annuity societies had thus declined in twenty years to virtually a quarter of the earlier figure.

There remains one form of organisation which was really as much a savings bank as a friendly society—the deposit friendly society. In common with county societies this was not the invention of working men seeking to alleviate their lot, but the product of the philanthropic energy of the clergy and county gentry. The originator of this system was the Reverend Samuel Best who in 1831 founded the Abbots Ann Provident Society in accordance with the principles that came to be associated with this kind of society. In expounding the scheme in his 'Parochial Manual', Best wrote: 'Let the mind in the outset be divested of the idea of a common fund or club. The Society is rather a savings bank than a club. A member's money is, and remains, his own, and under his own control, under such limitations only as are necessary for the protection of all. Each member has his own fund, and at his own disposal, if circumstances should require it, to appropriate as he may think fit.' The main difference between this and ordinary friendly societies was the building up of a deposit account for each member. When a member was sick a certain proportion of his sick benefit had to be taken from his own account and this was supplemented from the society's sick fund. The size of the supplement depended upon the class of membership of the individual, those frequently suffering ill-health would receive a smaller subsidy. The society also paid a doctor to give such treatment to members as they might need. The weakness of this system from the member's point of view was that his sick benefit

[1] R.C.F.S., 4th Report, 1874, para. 587.

could not last indefinitely—the length of time for which he could draw depended on how soon his own deposit was used up. This weakness was the main argument used against these societies by their rivals.[1] The system did not achieve great popularity before 1875 in spite of its achievements later.[2] However, the scheme was adopted in modified forms by some of the county type of societies in various districts including the Nottingham County Society and the Surrey Deposit Society which was founded in 1868 and which changed its name to the National Deposit Society in 1871. It was probably due to the lack of a convivial element as much as to the limitations of its sickness insurance schemes that the deposit type of society failed to gain wider support before 1875.

The Royal Commission placed societies for females in a class apart from other societies but admitted that, strictly speaking, these societies did not form a distinct class of their own at all but were simply a group which could be divided into as many classes as societies for males; there were female versions of affiliated orders, female village and town clubs and female burial societies. The Commission reproduced a table showing the societies which made returns in 1872 to have 22,691 members and that 17 counties of England and Wales appeared to have no friendly societies for women—except, of course, those which were unregistered and of which there is no accurate record.[3] The main limitation on the formation and activities of female societies was the fact that women were not usually the bread-winners of families, a housewife could hardly insure against loss of earnings when sick; moreover in the days of large families and frequent pregnancies the economic cost of sickness insurance for a married woman was apt to be high.[4]

---

[1] *Foresters' Miscellany* for April, 1873, has an example of this in an article attacking deposit societies on these grounds.

[2] W. Beveridge, *Voluntary Action*, 1948, ch. I, gives some account of the later progress of deposit societies.

[3] R.C.F.S., 4th Report, 1874, paras. 590 and 591.

[4] When women were permitted to join mixed societies, there was often a rule forbidding payments during pregnancy. In the Herefordshire Friendly Society it was laid down that no payment was to be made to a mother during the month following childbirth.—F. C. Morgan, op. cit., p. 12.

In the women's societies the number of lapsed members was considerable, for as soon as there was financial difficulty within a family, the woman's subscription to her friendly society became an object for economy. Sir George Young found a number of female friendly societies thriving in Bedfordshire and Hertfordshire where many women were engaged in straw-plaiting. 'In the straw-plaiting districts the success of female friendly societies is evidently to be ascribed to the fact that a large part of the female population are in receipt of good wages.' [1] Female friendly societies could only thrive where there was a good deal of regular employment for women and stable employment for their husbands—the latter was vital or her membership would lapse while the whole of the wife's earnings were used to tide over her husband's period of unemployment.

Female societies had a long history. Eden found a number in the 1790s.[2] These were composed of married women with the specific aim of providing for the 'lying-in-month'. As late as 1875 female societies often met in public houses and it was customary to set aside a fixed sum to be spent on liquor at each meeting. In fact, in spite of their long history, the Royal Commission found against women's societies and quoted with approval Sir George Young's recommendation that the proper provision for a working-class woman was the man's own club which should include a subscription for medical aid to the whole family. 'In conclusion, if the absolute prohibition of any sort of club is defensible, that of women's clubs meeting in public houses has most to be said for it.' [3]

FRIENDLY SOCIETY DEVELOPMENT IN TWO CONTRASTING COUNTIES, LANCASHIRE AND DORSET, AND IN LONDON

In order to envisage the pattern of friendly society activity in any particular county during this period, one must bear in mind all of these different classes of society which have been noticed

[1] Young, p. 30.
[2] F. M. Eden, *Observations on Friendly Societies*, 1801, p. 21.
[3] R.C.F.S., 4th Report, 1874, para. 609.

above, for by 1875 all of the main classes were represented in most of the counties of England. This pattern becomes clearer from studying more closely particular counties or districts.

In friendly society matters it was the county of Lancashire which usually established the precedent that other counties were later to follow. In 1815 it was one of the most populous of counties and perhaps the most highly industrialised. Moreover its population was increasing rapidly—even more rapidly than that of Middlesex—throughout this period. In 1811 its inhabitants numbered 828,309, by 1871 the population had increased to 2,819,495.[1] That the rapid progress of the industrial revolution and the growth of towns and population led to much misery among those classes of the people least able to protect themselves is a commonplace; the reactions of these classes through the development of trade unions and working-class political movements have also become an accepted part of the history of the last century and a half. But perhaps the wretchedness of the individual is greatest when he is alone in his misery; if many are suffering together there is a certain sense of strength to be gained from being one of many, but the pains of sickness or death of their very nature cannot be relieved even in this fashion. It was to help them in times like these that the working people of Lancashire led the way in the development of friendly societies. Social and economic conditions in that county made the need urgent earlier and more widespread than elsewhere, and, at the same time, made possible the growth of organisations to meet the need. The story of the local societies to begin with, followed by the growth of the affiliated orders, is, in its outline, similar to what was to happen in other parts of the country, but it happened first in Lancashire.

No one will ever know for certain how many local societies there were in Lancashire in 1815, but the number of members returned by the poor law officers in that year was 147,029,[2] far more than in any other single county of England although it may well be below the real number. About this time, the first affiliated

[1] Figures taken from the Census returns for 1811 and 1871.
[2] Abstract of Answers and Returns relative to the maintenance of the Poor in England, 1818.

order was beginning to evolve in the Manchester district and it was the Oddfellows of that town who first worked out this form of friendly society. By 1845 the newly founded List of Lodges claimed 737 M.U.O.F. lodges in Lancashire and 64,605 members.[1] The Directory of the Ancient Order of Foresters listed 332 courts of that order in the county for the same year.

The second half of this period, from 1845 to 1875, was a time of consolidation for the affiliated orders in Lancashire. The lodges and courts became larger and their finances and administration became much stronger while the actual number of lodges declined (from 737 to 507) and of courts grew only slowly (from 332 to 357). The average membership of lodges of the Manchester Unity in Lancashire increased from 87 in 1845 to 122 in 1875.[2] At the same time many new affiliated orders were spreading in the county; some of them were other unities of Oddfellows which had been formed or joined by lodges which had seceded from the Manchester Unity after 1845.

According to the Report of the Registrar, in 1872 there were 633,053 members of registered friendly societies which had made returns from Lancashire. In that year the Registrar sent forms to 2,863 registered societies in the county but only 1,695 were filled up and returned.[3] Thus the total number of members of all societies, registered and unregistered, may have been somewhere near a million, certainly it must have been well above the 633,053 in the 1,695 societies which made a return. The Assistant Commissioner who visited the county drew up the table opposite to show the strength of the various affiliated orders there in 1872.[4]

Apart from these affiliated orders and the still numerous local societies, a large number of the remaining 633,053 members listed by the Registrar belonged to burial societies which, except in a legal sense, were hardly friendly societies but were rather life insurance offices. The Registrar's figures also included the Sunday School societies of East Lancashire which have been referred to above.

[1] List of Lodges of the I.O.O.F.M.U., 1845–6.
[2] Based on the lodge membership figures given in the relevant List of Lodges.
[3] Appendix to Registrar's Report for 1872.   [4] Stanley, p. 79.

The friendly society movement generally avoided entanglement in party politics; this was especially true of the larger orders although it did not prevent them from pressing for legislative or other governmental action when it suited their interests. But in Lancashire there were a few examples of small orders which owed their existence to political issues. The Orangemen were such an order and they were quite numerous in Preston; their Grand Master told the Assistant Commissioner in 1872 that they would

Affiliated orders in Lancashire about 1872

Order	Lodges	No. of Members
I.O.O.F.M.U.	513	61,049
A.O.F.	364	29,479
G.U.O.O.F.	364	21,443
O.D.	581	33,721
L.O.A.S.A.U.	261	17,573
N.A.I.U.O.O.F. . . .	27	1,620
N.I.O.O.F.	259	19,474
U.O.F.G.	130	8,490
A.N.U.O.O.F.B.U. . . .	172	9,714
U.A.O.D.	6	535
Rational Association . .	—	1,260
Order of Mechanics. . .	71	3,540
Rechabites	64	3,260
Locomotive Engineers . .	10	813
Order of Catholic Brothers .	23	1,524
Orangemen	Numbers uncertain	
TOTALS	2,845	213,495

expel a member if he 'voted for a Liberal member of Parliament', moreover 'if the wife of a member became a Roman Catholic, they would expel the husband'.[1] To offset the influence of the Orangemen, there was a United Order of Catholic Brethren of 1,524 members in Preston and Blackburn whose rules went beyond the usual ground traversed by friendly society regulations. Rule I placed the Order 'under the special patronage of the Blessed Virgin'. On 25 March each year a special mass was celebrated in each district of the Order and their families were

[1] Ibid., p. 107.

recommended to recite daily the Angelus Domini for the welfare of the Order and the conversion of England.

The existence of these warring bands led to incidents on feast days which did not fit into the usually peaceful and harmonious public displays of the larger orders. The Orangemen, in an attempt to guard against provoking the Catholics, did not order party tunes to be played by their bands on feast days. 'The musicians are warned that if any breakage of instruments results from their playing a party tune, they must bear the loss themselves. However they are not safe even then, for on one occasion an Irishman with no ear for music asked what tune they were playing, and on being falsely told by some wag that it was "Croppies lie down", he was through the big drum in a moment.' [1]

A county which contrasted strongly in the social and economic sense with Lancashire was Dorset. Friendly societies developed much later here. The traditional social pattern had been less disturbed and the need for the societies and for the affiliated orders was much less strongly felt. The population increased much more slowly, from 144,499 in 1821 to 195,537 persons in 1871.[2] The number of members of friendly societies given in the Returns of 1815 was 6,209.

The affiliated orders only came to the county long after they were well established in the northern industrial regions. In 1845 there were no Foresters' courts and only three lodges of the Manchester Unity were recorded in the List of Lodges based on the position at 1 January, 1845. In 1875 there were 31 lodges and 22 courts.[3] Four Oddfellows' lodges and four Foresters' courts were unregistered in 1872 whereas in Lancashire about 100 Oddfellows' (M.U.) lodges and 168 Foresters' courts were not registered or did not return the forms required in 1872.[4] It was usually in the older lodges and courts that the tradition of hostility or at

[1] Stanley, p. 107.

[2] Census returns for 1821 and 1871. This was an increase of only 35 per cent against the national increase of 125 per cent.

[3] List of Lodges of the I.O.O.F.M.U., 1845–6 and 1875–6. Directories of the A.O.F. for 1845 and 1875.

[4] These figures are based on a comparison of the entries in the relevant Directories of the orders with those in the Appendix to the Registrar's Report for 1872.

least of non-co-operation with the state lingered; there were very few of such lodges or courts in Dorset, hence the Registrar's figures for that county give a far more complete picture of the friendly society movement there than they do in Lancashire.

The Registrar gave the total number of members for Dorset in 1872 as 11,130. Apart from the lodges of the Manchester Unity and the courts of the Foresters, two sanctuaries of Shepherds and one United Sisters Benefit Society branch were registered along with 38 ordinary societies. These 38 included the Dorset County Friendly Society with its 2,372 members.[1] This was one of the largest and more successful of the county class of societies and its existence and comparative success afforded yet another point of contrast between industrial Lancashire and rural Dorset. There was no room for societies conducted by honorary members in the northern county, but among the people of Dorset such a society appealed so strongly that its membership in the county exceeded that of the Foresters. The Registrar's list of local societies in Dorset also serves to illustrate that it was mostly in the villages of the south that the local clubs still predominated. Their addresses were in such places as Fordington, Melbury Abbas, Lytchett Maltravers, Stour Provost and Motcombe, while most of the lodges of the Manchester Unity in Dorset were in the towns including Bere Regis, Weymouth, Poole, Blandford and Wareham.

Conditions in London were in some ways unlike those in any other county. The greater diversity of occupations than in most provincial areas, the rapid expansion of population and the fact that it was the capital, all had their effect on the development of friendly societies. An initial difficulty in considering the situation in London lies in defining the area that the term should include. Here it is understood to cover the City of London and the County of Middlesex as it existed in 1875. The number of members of friendly societies in this area according to the returns of 1815 was 119,498[2] while the population in the Census of 1821 was 1,144,531. By 1871 the Census figure showed that the population

[1] Appendix to the Registrar's Report for 1872.
[2] Abstract of Answers and Returns relative to the maintenance of the Poor in England, 1818. The figures for the City of London were published separately, 1817.

had increased to 2,539,765 and the local societies had been to some extent replaced and partly added to by a greater variety of forms of friendly society than in any other district. According to the forms received back by the Registrar (909 out of 1,281 sent out —a higher proportion than in most districts) there were 153,545 members of registered friendly societies in 1872.[1] These were distributed over the following societies: 292 Foresters' courts, 113 Manchester Unity lodges, 38 lodges of the London Unity of Oddfellows, 5 Nottingham Ancient Imperial Oddfellows' lodges, 3 Grand United Oddfellows' lodges, 10 Druids' lodges, 90 sanctuaries of Shepherds, 2 tents of Rechabites, 10 lodges of the Improved Order of Old Friends and 3 lodges of both the Comical Fellows and Sons of the Phoenix. There were also 13 burial and female societies and 360 single societies ranging from large ordinary societies such as the Hearts of Oak returning 32,837 members to small local clubs of fewer than twenty.

The affiliated orders spread later in London than in Lancashire or Yorkshire; the large increase in their membership came about ten to twenty years later than in the two northern counties, the Manchester Unity of Oddfellows expanding rapidly in the 1840s and the Foresters in the 1850s. Because of the difficulty of defining the limits of 'London', the figures given for the total number of members and of lodges in the various directories often seem contradictory. In his Report the Assistant Commissioner for London stated that the Foresters were by far the most popular order in London by 1872, and by adding various courts in the Essex, Surrey and Kent suburbs to those of the London United District, the East London District and the City of London District, he obtained a total of 613 courts with 76,213 members. He added, however, that 'several courts belong to [the London United] district which are not situated in London, but in distant places, such as Reading or in Hampshire, in the Isle of Jersey, in Dorsetshire, in Devonshire. Altogether more than 100 courts with more than 11,000 members are outside Middlesex and beyond the suburbs of London.'[2]

[1] These figures and those which follow are from the Appendix to the Registrar's Report for 1872.
[2] Stanley, p. 127.

The Manchester Unity was the second largest order in London and in the four districts which it defined as London districts it claimed a membership of 22,968 in 184 lodges at the beginning of 1874.[1] None of the other orders could really be compared with these two from the point of view of the size of its following in the capital, but there were 38 registered lodges of the London Unity of Oddfellows. There were Oddfellows' clubs in London before the foundation of the Manchester Unity but they were convivial clubs only and any personal relief was given in the form of charity. In 1842 a table of contributions and benefits was drawn up and recommended for use in these clubs which by now had formed themselves into the London Unity. In 1871 they claimed to have a total of 65 lodges and 2,477 members in London as well as some 4,000 adherents in other parts of the country.[2]

The six principal ordinary large societies have been discussed above.[3] They were a feature of the London scene probably because like other centralised institutions they tended to establish themselves in the capital. They had all been founded in the first half of the century; the dates of their foundations were the Royal Standard, 1828; the Royal Oak, 1837; United Kingdom, 1839; Hearts of Oak, 1841; United Patriots, 1843; the London Society, 1824.

There were a relatively larger number of societies limited to members of a special trade in London than elsewhere and some of these had special funds from which to pay relief to those out of work, an example of this being the Trade Society of Lithographic Printers founded in 1833.[4] In the East End and Bethnal Green areas there were a considerable number of dividing societies called Birmingham Clubs which divided a part of their funds among members at the end of the year, usually keeping enough capital in hand to ensure that the society itself did not expire at each division. Finally there were a group of old societies which traced their origin to the arrival in this country of the Huguenots at the time of their persecution by Louis XIV. These

---

[1] List of Lodges, I.O.O.F.M.U., 1874-5.
[2] C. Walford, op. cit., vol. IV, p. 409.
[3] Supra, pp. 50 ff.   [4] Stanley, p. 130.

included the Society of Lintot, founded in 1708, the Norman Society, founded in 1703, and the Friendly Benefit Society, founded in 1687 as the Society of Parisians. In 1872 the societies still had a considerable number of members with French names.[1]

[1] W. Waller, *Early Huguenot Friendly Societies*, 1901.

CHAPTER THREE

THE LOCAL SOCIETIES AND AFFILIATED ORDERS

SOCIAL COMPOSITION OF THE MEMBERSHIP AND LEADERSHIP

THE MEMBERS

F^ROM the point of view of their membership, the local societies can be divided into two broad groups, those whose members followed the same occupation and those with a mixed membership. The relative importance of local societies diminished throughout this period and the societies of the first group often had a far more transient existence than those of the second.

In 1815 and for the earlier part of the period trade unions as such were at least frowned upon by 'authority' and were unable to lead an open existence, on the other hand friendly societies were not only permitted but granted certain legal privileges if they registered. Consequently many of the early one-trade societies might well have called themselves trade unions had circumstances been different. As it was they did the work of unions as well as of friendly societies and this often led to their collapse since the funds accumulated to meet sickness and death benefit were spent on strikes. Such was the fate of a number of local societies whose members were miners in Northumberland and Durham as the result of a strike in 1844 when the friendly societies were broken up and the accumulated funds divided among the members to sustain them in their strike.[1] Small local societies whose members followed the same occupation were quite widespread in 1815, but because of their involvement in trade conflicts they never became an important segment of the friendly societies' movement.

The local societies which survived, and in their own way

[1] Report of the Commissioner on the state of the Population in Mining Districts, 1846, p. 8.

flourished, were those with a mixed or a predominantly agricultural membership. It was never likely in such cases that a majority of the members would favour devoting the funds of the society to strike purposes. The membership of such societies obviously depended on the nature of local industry. In the analysis of societies in Sheffield in 1843 printed by G. C. Holland,[1] none of the seven societies there analysed had a majority of its members following the same trade; the Prince of Wales drew its members from 34 trades, the Fitzwilliam from 21 trades, the Bethel from 30 trades, the Church of England from 13 trades, the Birmingham Reform Society from 11 trades, the Revolution from 51 trades and the Tradesmen's Society drew its members from 26 trades. Most of these societies of a mixed membership had been established for some years and seem to have been thriving concerns; the Prince of Wales Society was founded in 1790, the Fitzwilliam in 1822, the Bethel in 1828, the Birmingham Reform in 1835, the Revolution in 1788 and the Tradesmen's in 1761. The total number following the main trades in these societies included 276 cutlers, 107 grinders, 91 manufacturers, 73 file-makers, 73 clerks, 62 silversmiths, 59 scissorsmiths, 55 labourers, 51 carpenters, 39 forgemen, 36 miners, 35 white metalsmiths, 32 razor makers, 29 sawmakers, 29 shoemakers and 25 butchers. There were also 63 other occupations, none of which had a following of more than 20 members.[2]

There was much less variety than this in the occupations followed by the members of rural local societies where agricultural labourers usually predominated.

Since the most striking development in the history of friendly societies during the nineteenth century was undoubtedly the emergence of the affiliated orders, the question naturally arises as to whether they had a special appeal for certain classes and occupations, at least to begin with, and, if so, which ones. There is a surprising lack of reliable evidence bearing on the occupations of members of the affiliated orders. The information came to be regarded as valuable by the actuaries, but even where it was in-

[1] G. C. Holland, *The Vital Statistics of Sheffield*, 1843, pp. 211–13.
[2] Ibid.

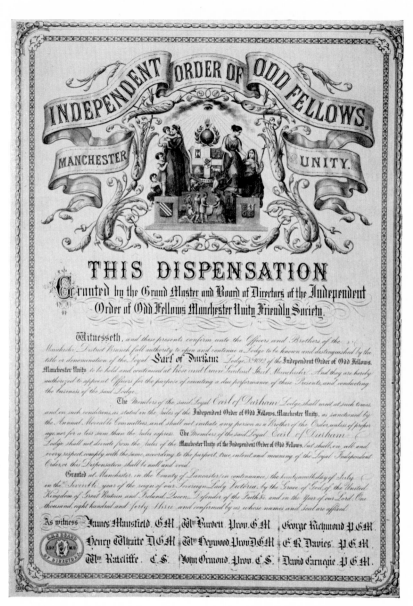

Dispensation granted to open and continue the Earl of Durham Lodge
No. 1012, 1843.

cluded in returns, the orders seem to have made little use of it until after this period and the returns themselves are no more. When he carried out the first thorough valuation of the Ancient Order of Foresters, the results of which were published in 1882, Neison sorted his information not by occupations, but by districts—rural, town or city respectively—'the idea being that a rough division of this character would partially take into account not only the density of the population, but also the influence of occupation, it being presumed that agricultural and most of the healthier out-door pursuits would be found located in the rural districts, whilst on the contrary, the principal unhealthy avocations would exist in large towns and cities. Until accurate research has been made into the value of life in every important occupation . . . some such rough approximation of the facts must be made as is here done.' [1] Thus even in the 1880s the Foresters still lacked any occupational analysis of their Order.

The only affiliated order to have made much progress in collecting information concerning the occupations of its members in this period was the Manchester Unity of Oddfellows. In 1850 the Corresponding Secretary published the results of his survey of the returns for the years 1846 to 1848 which had been specially called for. He classified the experience of members during those years in part by occupation, distinguishing the twenty-six principal occupations undertaken by members. Table 11 is based upon these returns.

This table accounts for 62·45 per cent of the total membership, the remaining 37·55 per cent being engaged in sundry occupations or not accounted for in the returns. The largest single class shown here, the rural labourers, may easily be misinterpreted since the term did not necessarily mean agricultural labourer. It seems to have meant any member classed as a labourer within the class of

---

[1] F. G. P. Neison, *The Rates of Mortality and Sickness of the A.O.F. Friendly Society*, 1882, p. 49.

The Royal Commission tried without success to find the occupations of members of the orders. Question 38 of the questionnaire for affiliated orders asked 'To what class of society do your members belong?' The answers were not helpful, 'All classes' being a typical reply. It seems that the officers of the orders themselves after did not know and therefore could not be very helpful.

TABLE II

The principal occupations of members of the Manchester Unity of Oddfellows,
1846-8

Occupation	Per cent of Order	Approx. number
Baker	·98	2,450
Blacksmith	3·8	9,500
Bricklayer	1·8	4,500
Butcher	1·2	3,000
Carpenter and joiner . .	6·0	15,000
Clerk	1·4	3,500
Cooper	·35	875
Domestic servant . .	2·61	5,175
Dyer	·54	1,350
Hatter	·58	1,450
Labourer (town) . .	6·8	17,160
Labourer (rural) . .	8·7	21,800
Millwright	·39	975
Mill operative . . .	2·17	5,435
Miner	4·93	12,325
Plumber	1·89	4,725
Potter	·41	1,025
Printer and compositor . .	·78	1,950
Sawyer	·66	1,650
Shoemaker	3·9	9,750
Spinner	1·82	4,550
Stonemason . . .	2·96	7,400
Tailor	3·4	8,500
Weaver	3·0	7,500
Wheelwright . . .	·74	1,850
Woolcomber . . .	·68	1,700
TOTALS	62·45	155,095

The percentages in this table are from H. Ratcliffe, *Observations on the Rate of Mortality and Sickness in the I.O.O.F.M.U.*, 1850, pp. 39-60.

The approximate number in each trade has been calculated by applying this percentage in each case to the average total membership for the years 1846-8, which was, in round figures, 250,000. The actual membership on 1 January, 1848, was 249,261 according to the Report of the Corresponding Secretary issued in April, 1849.

rural lodges, which were defined as lodges 'held in any township, village or locality, the inhabitants of which numbered less than five thousand'.[1] Thus 'rural labourer' apparently included labourers who did not work on farms as well as those who did and there

[1] H. Ratcliffe, *Observations on the Rate of Mortality and Sickness in the I.O.O.F.M.U.*, 1850, p. 13.

may well have been many of the former in small industrial towns with a total population of less than 5,000.

A comparison of the percentage of the Manchester Unity's membership which followed the occupations listed above with the percentage of the employed male population of England and Wales in the same occupations as given by the Census of 1851 shows fairly clearly the type of trades in which the affiliated orders made their strongest appeal to working men up to the middle of

TABLE 12

The percentages of members of the Manchester Unity in particular occupations in 1846-8 with the national percentage of occupied males as stated in the Census of 1851

Occupation	Per cent of M.U.O.F.	Per cent of occupied males
Woollen and cotton manufacture	8·21	5·68
Blacksmith	3·8	1·6
Bricklayer	1·8	1·15
Butcher	1·2	1·03
Carpenter and joiner . .	6·0	2·68
Miner	4·93	3·03
Plumber and painter . .	1·89	·81
Printer and compositor . .	·78	·40
Shoemaker	3·9	3·63
Stonemason	2·96	1·32
Tailor	3·4	1·9
'Rural labourers' (M.U.O.F.) .	8·7	—
Agricultural labourer, Farm servant, shepherd . . .	—	24·5

The percentages of gainfully occupied males in England and Wales have been calculated from Summary Table XXV of the Census Report for 1851—Population Tables II, vol. I.

the nineteenth century. It is not possible to do this for all of the twenty-six occupations listed by the Manchester Unity since the Census return used different classifications in some cases. As different classifications were used for the various grades in the textile industries, these have been combined in Table 12 under the heading 'Woollen and cotton manufacture'.

Perhaps the most obvious conclusion to be drawn from the Manchester Unity's figures is that up to 1850 the Unity recruited most strongly among those working men who formed the better-paid groups of that time. Textiles, mining, printing and various

trades connected with building seem to have provided the Oddfellows with much of their membership. That textiles and building provided a fair proportion of the membership of the Manchester Unity in its earliest days would appear to be confirmed by
its strength even before it became known on a national scale in the
industrial districts of the North—especially in Lancashire and the
West Riding.

TABLE 13

The number of travellers in the M.U.O.F. 1848–72

Period				No. of cards issued	Amount paid to travellers
1848–52	.	.	.	4,721	£4,468
1853–7 .	.	.	.	2,500	£1,619
1858–62	.	.	.	3,797	£3,590
1863–7 .	.	.	.	2,864	£2,406
1868–72	.	.	.	2,204	£1,750
TOTALS 1848–72		.	.	16,086	£13,833

This table is based on information from F. G. P. Neison, 'Some Statistics of the Affiliated
Orders,' *Journal of the Statistical Society*, vol. XL, 1877.

The affiliated orders originated among these better-paid occupations and their contributions and benefits were consequently
designed to suit the pocket and the needs of this class of working
man. The contributions and benefits were higher in the Oddfellows than was usual among the local societies. While seven shillings a week was the customary sick pay among local societies, the
Manchester Unity seldom paid less than ten shillings.[1]

Apart from the rate of sick benefit, the provision made by the
affiliated orders for the movement of their members from one
part of the country to another—whether by travelling allowances
or clearances—shows that the industrial occupations in which
'tramping' was widespread must have been reasonably well represented among the orders. Apart from town and rural labourers,
the most numerous particular occupations shown in the member-

[1] Some instances at St. Helens in the 1840s are given in T. C. Barker and
J. R. Harris, *A Merseyside Town in the Industrial Revolution, St. Helens 1750–1900*,
1954, pp. 260–1.

ship figures for the Manchester Unity in 1846–8 were carpenters, miners, shoemakers, blacksmiths and tailors in that order. All of these, with the exception of the miners, were groups of men who practised the custom of tramping.[1] When a member of the Manchester Unity set out in search of some employment, he first had to obtain a card from his lodge recommending him to other districts and showing that he was 'in benefit'; in the Foresters a somewhat similar document was called a licence.[2] Table 13 gives some particulars of the number of cards issued and of the amount paid in relief to travellers by the Manchester Unity between 1848 and 1872.

The actual number of payments made in the years 1863–7 was 44,278 while in the years 1868–72 it amounted to 50,218.

As distinct from the question of tramping, the general mobility of labour in the nineteenth century meant that societies whose membership was largely among the industrial working men would have to make provision for permanent transfers on the part of members from one part of the country to another. This the affiliated orders attempted in two ways, by a system of 'clearances' and by permitting one lodge or court to act as a collecting agency for another. If a member took his clearance from his lodge or court it meant that he had met all his liabilities to date and could present himself with his clearance certificate to a lodge or court in the district to which he was moving. There were certain limitations on this right and members seem at times to have preferred to remain in membership with their first lodge or court and to have chosen to remit their contributions to it and to receive their benefits from it. This they were able to do provided that the local lodge or court acted as the agent so that in time of sickness the visitor from the local lodge would see that the beneficiary was in fact unwell and thus protect lodge funds.[3]

In these ways the affiliated orders met the needs of a highly mobile industrial proletariat and their growth and the consequent

[1] Article by E. J. Hobsbawm in the *Economic History Review*, 1951, p. 299 (vol. III, 2nd Series).

[2] Details of the proceedure governing travelling and clearances in the M.U.O.F. and the A.O.F. are set out in Appendix A.

[3] Details of the arrangements are in Appendix A.

diminution in the relative importance of the local societies may
well have been due in part to the latter's inferiority in this respect.
The local friendly society was suited to those whose lives were
static, of its very nature it could not meet the needs of the worker
who was mobile. Most societies prevented men over forty from
joining since it was the contributions of the first half of the working life which were intended to pay for the benefits required during the sickness expected in a man's later years. The member of a
local society who had to move to find work virtually lost all his
subscriptions, the Oddfellow or the Forester could 'take his benefits with him'—even to many parts of the colonies.

The impression that the affiliated orders originated and throve
among relatively better-paid workers, thrown together in large
numbers, is really confirmed by the geographical distribution of
the Oddfellows and Foresters in the nineteenth century. The Manchester Unity first became widespread in Lancashire, Cheshire,
Derbyshire and the West Riding or the earlier industrial region;
the next notable phase of growth was in the counties of Durham,
Northumberland and Monmouth as the development of industry
brought relatively well-paid immigrant workers to those districts.
The orders spread more steadily in the less industrialised areas.[1]

Before leaving the question of the composition of the affiliated
orders, it would be wrong not to point out that the composition
of the individual lodges and courts within the orders must have
been determined by some of the factors which decided the composition of the local societies and their membership did not by any
means correspond with national averages. This was an important
point for the solvency of an order rested upon the solvency of
each of its lodges since they administered their own sickness benefits. The financial position of miners' lodges was often especially
difficult for miners had a higher rate of sickness than any of the
other trades and in the mining communities there were not
enough men following other occupations to counterbalance their
preponderance in the lodges. In 1862 the Corresponding Secretary of the Manchester Unity wrote 'Miners form 5·76 of the
general class of lives, and if each society had this number per cent

[1] Distribution tables on pp. 34 and 42.

of miners and colliers forming a portion thereof, the general tables might give a sufficient amount of contribution; but, as it is a well-known fact, that there are societies in certain localities, in which they form a greater percentage than the one named, it is absolutely necessary, for future safety, that a higher rate of contribution should be paid for similar benefits than in societies which do not include so high a rate per cent of this class of member.' [1]

In spite of their attractions, certain classes of working men tended to form their own societies or at least to remain outside of the affiliated orders for various reasons. The largest group of these was the agricultural labourers. In the table on page 75 rural labourers were shown to form 8·7 per cent of the Manchester Unity in 1846–8 while the Census of 1851 showed that 24·5 per cent of gainfully occupied males were engaged in one of the farming occupations. The term 'rural labourer' included many others besides farm labourers according to the definition given by the Corresponding Secretary of the Manchester Unity, consequently the lack of proportion between the number of agricultural labourers in the Oddfellows with the number in the country generally was far more marked than even this table seems to indicate. There were various reasons as to why this was so.

It was improbable that a man working on a farm had been a migrant to the village himself or that his father had been. Migration, in so far as it affected the countryside, had been away from it to the towns. The disadvantage, therefore, which the local club had for the town workman was not as obvious to the country labourer who continued to support it. He had never tried to move from one place to another and to transfer his membership from one club to another whereas it was probable that the townsman— or his father—had had personal experience of moving and of the difficulty which a man might have in trying to join a friendly society when he was no longer young.

Another factor which delayed the recruitment of farm labourers to the affiliated orders was the influence of the country gentry as shown in the 'county' type of friendly society which was 'almost

[1] H. Ratcliffe, *Observations on the Rates of Mortality and Sickness in the I.O.O.F.M.U.*, 1862, p. 54.

peculiar to the agricultural population of the South and East'.[1] Those labourers who were dissatisfied with the local village clubs were sometimes attracted to these societies which claimed to be run on sound financial lines and which were managed by the leading men of the district. Thus the position which might have been occupied by the lodges or courts of the affiliated orders came to be occupied to some extent by the county societies.

In different parts of the country various local factors may have delayed the entry of the agricultural labourer into the orders. In the course of his inquiries in Northumberland in 1872, the Assistant Commissioner found few friendly societies among the country people because of the annual contract system of hiring labourers whereby the employer was chargeable with the maintenance of the labourers he had hired for the year and was bound to pay them their wages even at the time of ill-health.[2]

But none of these reasons was probably as important as the difference between the money income and requirements in time of sickness of the better-paid occupations among which the affiliated orders grew up and the money incomes and requirements of the farm labourers. The local village societies flourished among them because they charged less than the affiliated orders even if they also paid less in benefit. Sir George Young reported that twelve shillings per week was the usual benefit for which the Oddfellows subscribed in time of sickness and he compared this with the case of a lodge in the Banbury district of the Manchester Unity which had been started for agricultural labourers with a standard rate of sick pay of only seven shillings and sixpence per week.[3] Towards the end of this period there was a considerable expansion of the numbers of lodges and courts of the orders in the rural counties; this was especially true of the Foresters.[4] Some of this expansion may have been due to the spread of the orders among the craftsmen and tradesmen of the small country towns, but there does seem to have been an increase in the number of farm labourers who came to look to the affiliated orders.

---

[1] R.C.F.S., 4th Report, 1874, para. 179.
[2] Report by G. Culley, Assistant Commissioner, 1874, pp. 1, 167 of Appendix.
[3] Young, p. 2.   [4] See distribution tables, pp. 34 and 42.

According to the returns for 1872 for Sussex, there were Foresters' courts at Kirdford (with 39 members), Lavant (58), Nutbourne (68), Peas Pottage (62), Singleton (107), Lower Beeding (133), Bosham (81), Coldwaltham (79), Ditchling (82), Aldingbourne (71), and Graffham (34).[1] Now these were agricultural villages, they were not in any sense trading centres, even for the countryside around them, none of them had a market and none had more than one or two shops. The majority of the members in these courts must have been farm labourers. In 1845 there had been no Foresters' courts in Sussex, in 1865 there were 60.[2] Similar figures can be given for most of the southern counties. The conclusion must be that the orders, and especially the Foresters, were beginning to make progress among the agricultural community from the 1850s. The Foresters probably made more progress than the Oddfellows because they were less exacting than the latter. A local village club found it much easier to become a Foresters' court than to become an Oddfellows' lodge since it was often able at this time (before 1870) to maintain its existing charges and benefits. The Manchester Unity had already begun to advance actuarially and to have more stringent requirements for new lodges.

If it had in fact been mainly the low money income of the farm labourers which had kept them outside the orders earlier, this difficulty was being steadily overcome in two ways during the last fifteen or twenty years of this period. The money wages of the labourers were rising from 1852 until 1855 and again from 1858 until 1873,[3] thus bringing these workers at least nearer to the point at which they could contemplate membership. Secondly, the orders themselves seem to have sought to increase their strength in the southern counties: the Foresters accepted many local clubs as courts while the Manchester Unity was willing to go some way in meeting the special requirements of the farm labourers—as in the Banbury district.

[1] Appendix to the Registrar's Report for 1872, County of Sussex, p. 153.
[2] Figures from the relevant Directories of the A.O.F.
[3] Table of Agricultural Earnings in England and Wales (after Bowley) in J. H. Clapham, *An Economic History of Modern Britain*, vol. II, p. 286.

In spite of these developments, a comparison of Oddfellows' lodges, Foresters' courts and local clubs in predominantly rural areas at the close of this period still shows that the proportion of agricultural labourers in the local clubs was much greater than the proportion in Oddfellows' lodges while the Foresters' courts occupied an intermediate position. The valuation returns published by the Registrar in 1880 showed the membership of registered societies divided into four main classes, viz.: light labour with exposure to the weather, light labour without exposure, heavy labour with exposure, heavy labour without exposure. These returns were incomplete—of the eleven Foresters' courts listed on page 81 only three made the required return—yet they do show that the lodges of the Manchester Unity in Dorset, Huntingdon, Suffolk and Sussex had the highest proportion of members classified as 'light labour without exposure' and the lowest of 'heavy labour with exposure' in all four counties while the local clubs had the highest proportion of members in the category 'heavy labour with exposure' and the smallest proportion engaged in 'light labour without exposure'. Table 14 confirms the impression that the better-off tended to be found in the Manchester Unity and the less well-off turned to the local clubs.

A second large group of workmen whose position has to be considered separately was the miners. Their position was quite different from that of the farm labourers in that it was not a low money wage which made their friendly society provision different from that of the majority of industrial trades. It was really the nature of their occupation and the high rate of sickness which it caused which led to separate and special societies for miners only, and it was during the last fifteen years or so of this period that the growth of separate societies for miners was taking place on a large scale, the very period when the agricultural labourers were being absorbed by the general affiliated orders.

While the miners formed 4·93 per cent of the membership of the Manchester Unity in 1846–8[1] and 5·76 per cent by 1861[2] their

[1] H. Ratcliffe, op. cit., 1850, p. 52.
[2] Ibid., 1862, p. 54.

TABLE 14

The types of occupations followed by members of the M.U.O.F., A.O.F., and the local clubs in the 1870s in four agricultural counties

County	Society	Light WITH exposure	Labour w'OUT	Heavy WITH exposure	Labour w'OUT	Seamen	No. of Members	Per cent. of males over 15 shown as ag. labs. in 1871
DORSET	M.U.O.F.	12·4	41·1	29·5	10·9	6·1	5,090	
	A.O.F.	12·6	39·8	31·7	11·1	4·7	2,882	23·9
	Local clubs	6·0	24·1	63·2	6·6	·1	1,193	
HUNTS	M.U.O.F.	9·9	44·4	31·0	14·7	—	1,032	
	A.O.F.	5·7	22·8	59·2	12·3	—	602	39·9
	Local clubs	—	15·9	83·7	1·4	—	69	
SUFFOLK	M.U.O.F.	11·2	47·7	20·2	17·4	3·5	6,490	
	A.O.F.	8·8	32·4	35·3	16·2	7·3	3,828	29·6
	Local clubs	2·5	16·9	75·2	4·5	·9	4,573	
SUSSEX	M.U.O.F.	11·6	41·0	30·9	11·3	5·2	3,983	
	A.O.F.	11·9	31·9	42·2	10·8	3·2	4,791	28·1
	Local clubs	6·0	17·5	67·1	6·3	3·1	2,074	

NOTES:

(1) Brighton returns have been excluded from Sussex since they include some 5,000 railwaymen whose friendly society headquarters were registered there but many of whom worked and lived outside the county.

(2) The apparent numerical preponderance of the Manchester Unity in some of these counties was not real. It was due to the greater business efficiency of the Order in making returns when compared with the Foresters and the local clubs.

This table is based on the Abstract of Returns of Sickness and Mortality of 1880 and the Census of 1871. The figures for individual societies of the three types have been totalled within each class and converted to percentages to make them comparable. The actual number involved is in column headed 'No. of Members'.

position within the Order was not very satisfactory once the Unity began to try to enforce actuarially sound scales of contribution and benefit. Some lodges came to refuse to admit miners as members while those in which the miner members were a majority came to be principally miners' lodges.[1] The story of what happened among the tin miners of Cornwall was told by James Spry, Corresponding Secretary to the Plymouth District of the M.U.O.F. 'They are a strange race. When they take a thing into their head, they will follow each other all over the district, and nothing can stop them. Thus formerly there was a West Cornwall District, with centre at Hayle, several lodges and some hundreds members. When the first step was taken towards a graduated scale, great discontent ensued; and a great battle in which Mr. Ratcliffe, the Secretary, was ousted for defalcations caused the collapse of all credit in the Society. The lodges began breaking up and seceding, and of all the district only the Truro lodge was left . . . The miners have taken to the Philanthropic now, and we do not in all lodges admit them.'[2] The 'Philanthropic' referred to was the 'Loyal Philanthropic Association' which was the miners' special order in the South-West. By 1872 the Grand Master of the Philanthropic thought it was social feeling which kept the miners out of what he called the 'tradesmens' societies like the Oddfellows and Foresters.[3] Certainly the existence of the affiliated orders never led to the abandonment of colliery clubs by the miners nor did it appear to hinder the emergence of the Miners' Permanent Relief Societies after 1860.

Because of the nature of the miner's work, there seem to have been pit clubs in most areas, although there was no single pattern on which they were all organised. In some areas the owners contributed a certain amount towards the funds, in others they gave nothing; in some districts the miners' contributions were stopped from their wages, but not in others; sometimes the clubs were run on an annual dividing basis and any funds accumulated during a comparatively accident-free year were spent on an outing or given to individual members. In 1831 Lord Durham established a fund for the miners in his pits 'to which his Lordship contributed a large proportion of the sum annually required to meet cases of

[1] Examples of both of these in Derbyshire are in Stanley, p. 153.
[2] Taken from notes of a conversation with Mr. Spry contained in Section M of the Appendix to Young.
[3] Young, p. 83, Appendix.

accident or sickness'. In case of sickness the fund paid seven shillings per week and Lord Durham two shillings and sixpence; in case of accident the fund again paid seven shillings and Lord Durham five shillings. Up to 1844 the average annual charge to Lord Durham was said to be £190.[1]

Examples of something less organised than the 'Lambton Collieries Association' as Lord Durham's fund was called were given by a Mr. Blyth in 1872 when he estimated that every colliery in the North-East had its dividing club, 'they begin in January and continue throughout the year to give a certain amount of relief for a certain payment, and at Christmas or at the New Year they divide the surplus amongst the members'.[2] In these cases there was no permanent fund and any miner working at a colliery where there was no other provision for accident or sickness would clearly find himself in a difficult position if a mining accident injured many of his colleagues at the same time or if there were some epidemic—unless he belonged to some other friendly society as well.

In some areas it had never been easy for a miner to join even a local friendly society when it was largely composed of members of other trades. Where such societies existed in mining areas, they frequently had a rule designed to keep miners out—the dangerous nature of their occupation from the point of view of the club's box had been apparent in such districts long before the actuaries made their calculations. The Tyne Iron Society of Lemington, Northumberland, admitted men of most trades, but in Rule I it was stated that 'No collier shall be admitted'.[3] At Bladon, in Durham, the Friendly Society used the same phrase in its first article.[4] Consequently there were a number of ordinary local societies, not

---

[1] Report of the Commissioner on the State of the Population in Mining Districts, 1846, p. 18.

[2] Evidence before the Royal Commission on Friendly Societies, 1872, q. 27,194. Mr. Blyth was Secretary to the Northumberland and Durham Miners' Permanent Relief Fund.

[3] Articles, Rules, Orders and Regulations of the Tyne Iron Society, Lemington, Rule I, 1826.

[4] Articles, Rules, Orders and Regulations of the Bladon Friendly Society, County Durham, Article I, 1824.

attached to any particular pit or employer, which were confined to miners, such as the Miners' Society of Newcastle which was founded in 1812.[1]

The societies attached to particular pits, largely run by the owner and membership of which was compulsory, seem to have been the most unpopular among the miners themselves. In a pamphlet of 1826, the Miners' Association in the north-eastern coalfield stated that 'We view, therefore, with some jealousy and suspicion a recommendation lately submitted to us from the colliery viewers, or some of them, to institute a general fund for the relief of colliers, their widows and families. We can hardly hope that those who have refused to attend to our complaints or make any reply to our just remonstrances will be prepared to lay aside all partiality and sinister views and interest themselves sincerely in the management and direction of a fund solely for our benefit.' [2] Complaints were often made that such societies were little more than a device by the employer for holding back part of a man's wages, and the Assistant Commissioners in 1872 found them extremely unpopular in the areas where they still existed such as Staffordshire, Worcestershire and some parts of South Lancashire.[3] Even where the management was to some degree in the hands of the members, these societies were hardly friendly societies in the full sense of the term. Wallsend Colliery Relief Fund was founded in 1831, the President was to be John Buddle Esquire and the other officials were to be elected annually[4]— unusual proceedings in a time and district where friendly society officers were chosen by rotation. These clubs were sometimes forbidden to gather in public houses—as was Wilson's Darton Collieries Club near Barnsley which was founded in 1833.[5]

It was only towards the end of this period that a form of friendly

---

[1] Articles, Rules and Regulations of the Miners' Society, Newcastle, 1829.

[2] A Candid Appeal to Coal Owners and Viewers . . . from the Committee of the Colliers' United Association, 1826, p. 3.

[3] Stanley, pp. 89, 172, 173, 174. Further evidence on this point was given by J. M. Ludlow to the Royal Comm. on Labour, 1892, q. 1828.

[4] Rules and Regulations of Wallsend Colliery Relief Fund, 1832, Rules II and III.

[5] Wilson's Darton Collieries Club, Darton, Nr. Barnsley, 1833, Rule VII.

society organisation evolved which was to meet the miners' problem more satisfactorily; this solution took the form of the Miners'
Permanent Relief Societies. The first of these to be established
was the Northumberland and Durham Permanent Relief Fund,
set up in 1862 and numbering about 25,000 members ten years
later.[1] The society had local lodges after the manner of the affiliated orders and a central committee of thirteen of whom ten
were delegates from the lodges and three were 'honorary members' who owed their position to the contribution of the employers
to the Fund, which was originally intended to be twenty per cent
of the total income but which had sunk to 6·9 per cent in 1886.[2]
The pressure exerted by the Miners' Union against compulsory
pit clubs and the Truck Act of 1861 cleared away possible obstacles to the growth of the new permanent societies. By the time
of the Royal Commission there were societies similar to the
Northumberland and Durham in North Staffordshire, in Lancashire and in Cheshire. Others were established later in the West
Riding, in North Wales, in the Midlands, in South Staffordshire
and in Monmouthshire and South Wales.[3] By 1887 these societies
had some 229,000 members out of a total eligible population of
about 500,000 miners.[4]

A final group of working men whose friendly societies stood
outside the general system were the railwaymen. As with the
miners, it was believed that railway service led to more than the
average amount of sickness and the experience of the Midland
Railway Friendly Society suggested that this was about 40 per

[1] Particulars relating to the Fund are from the evidence of A. Blyth, its secretary,
in qq. 27,031 and following of the evidence before the Royal Comm., 1872.
[2] J. F. Wilkinson, *Friendly and Provident Institutions of the Working Classes*,
1888, p. 22.
[3] G. L. Campbell, *Miners' Thrift and Employers' Liability*, 1892, Table A.
[4] Their distribution is shown in this table—based on G. L. Campbell, op. cit.

Northumberland and Durham founded 1862, membership 91,627			
North Staffordshire	,,	1869,	,,	4,172
Lancashire and Cheshire	,,	1872,	,,	41,217
West Riding	,,	1877,	,,	20,610
North Wales	,,	1878,	,,	10,585
Midland Counties	,,	1879,	,,	3,313
Monmouthshire and S. Wales	,,	1881,	,,	42,168
Midland District	,,	1883,	,,	15,882

G

cent in excess of the usual figure.[1] Membership was usually compulsory for all employees of a company and contributions were deducted from the men's wages; powers to enforce this were often taken by the companies in the railway acts under which they operated. Unlike the compulsory pit clubs which disappeared, these railway societies, fortified by special acts of Parliament, continued to flourish after 1875. Apart from the Midland Railway Friendly Society which was founded in 1860, the group included societies attached to the London and South-Western, the London, Brighton and South Coast, the Great Eastern, the Great Western, Bristol and Exeter and the Great Northern companies.[2] The attitude of the railwaymen towards these compulsory societies was shown by J. M. Ludlow (then Registrar of Friendly Societies) in his evidence before the Royal Commission on Labour in 1892. He gave this as one of the causes of friction between employer and employed, stating that 'the men generally chafe very much under that obligation . . . because it compels them virtually to throw up their own societies unless they choose to pay to two different funds at once. That is the main ground on which they dislike it. And then again there is the feeling of fear of forfeiting benefits, or rather the feeling that they are tied to the particular employment by this statutory benefit, which they would forfeit if they leave it.'[3] For a man past middle age it would have been impossible to join some other society if he left or were dismissed by the company, thus the system really gave the employer the power not only to dismiss a man but to inflict a considerable fine on him as well.

THE LEADERS

In the local societies there was no distinction of occupation or social class between the membership and those who acted as leaders of the society for the time being. In most of the earlier societies the office of steward and the other offices were filled by rotation, thus all possibility of any distinction was ruled out.[4]

[1] Stanley, p. 76.   [2] Appendix to the Registrar's Report for 1872.
[3] Evidence before the Royal Comm. on Labour, 1892, qq. 1,758–61.
[4] Supra, pp. 18 ff.

The position in the affiliated orders contrasted strongly with that in the local friendly societies. It is possible to trace the occupations of about seventy leading figures in the Manchester Unity during this period who were considered to have rendered sufficiently outstanding service to the Order to merit the publication of short 'portraits' in the *Oddfellows' Magazine*, and of these not more than five could be described as employees—taking the term to include government or local government officials. The occupations of these men are set out in detail in Appendix B. A similar situation existed in the Ancient Order of Foresters. Through the *Foresters' Miscellany* the occupations of thirty-nine leading Foresters have been traced and only seven of these could be described as employees. In general, an examination of the social background of the leading figures in the two principal affiliated orders serves to emphasise the importance of the part played by self-made men and members of the 'middle class' in building up and managing these great societies.

These leading men of both orders followed a great variety of occupations and included farmers, doctors and literary men as well as a large proportion of small and not-so-small business men. The only feature which most of them had in common was their freedom to organise their own time. If they wanted to take two or three days off from business to attend a meeting of the Board of Directors in Manchester or a district meeting, then they were able to do so. Most of the duties which the Grand Master of the Manchester Unity or his deputy or the Provincial Grand Masters had to perform carried no financial reward; the only leading official in the Order who was remunerated was the Corresponding Secretary.[1] The position was similar in the Foresters. It would have been very difficult in these circumstances for an employed man who was not in some unusually favoured position to accept the highest offices in the orders. It was probably the question of time involved in these duties rather than the financial difficulty which excluded most working-class members. If it had been mainly a financial difficulty, the orders could have overcome this by offering their members some compensation for loss of earnings.

[1] J. Burn, *Historical Sketch of the Manchester Unity*, 1846, p. 121.

The amount of time which a Grand Master or a Past Grand Master of the Manchester Unity might be called upon to devote to the Order was shown by the activities of Thomas Armitt in 1825 and 1826. His period of office as Grand Master expired in 1825 and it was as Past Grand Master that he undertook these duties. He was appointed by the Manchester Quarterly Committee in June 1825 to visit various lodges in the South of England and to furnish them with copies of a new lecture, known as the Patriarchal Degree. His itinerary was: July 4, Chester; July 5, Newcastle (Staffs); July 6, Wolverhampton; July 9, Birmingham; then to Worcester and Cheltenham and by July 12 to Brighton; the return journey lay through London and the East Midlands and took from the 13th to the 21st of July when he finally arrived back in Manchester after a total absence of 18 days.[1] In the following February Armitt was again travelling round various lodges, this time in Lancashire and Yorkshire, for 12 days.[2] All this was, of course, additional to the time spent at normal committee and Board meetings.

From the material available, it seems likely that the majority of these business men and tradesmen who led the orders were of humble or comparatively humble origins who had received little or nothing in the way of formal education but who had managed to make themselves prosperous by seizing the opportunities which must certainly have been numerous in the expanding industrial towns before 1875. They were self-made men who had also met with good fortune. Thomas Armitt, for instance, who was Grand Master from 1823 to 1825, was born in 1774. His father died when he was nine years old and his mother was left to manage a large family. Thomas was put to work on a farm. He seems to have been increasingly dissatisfied with his lot, 'I found my wages did not increase with my family'—this was after he had married at the age of twenty. His dissatisfaction led him to leave his native village of Rushton Spencer and to make his way to Lancashire where he finally managed to begin in business on his own account as an earthenware dealer in Salford.[3]

[1] *Oddfellows' Magazine*, IV, 1835, pp. 59 ff.
[2] Ibid., pp. 111 ff.   [3] Ibid., p. 57.

Manchester Unity
of the
Independent Order of Odd Fellows
Friendly Society

Officers of the order Trustees
and Board of Directors

Name	Office	Residence
James Charlebot	Grand Master	Southampton
Charles Hardwick	Deputy Grand Master.	Preston, Lancashire
Henry Ratcliffe	Corresponding Secretary	Manchester
Saml Daynes	Past Grand Master	Norwich
James Roe	Past Grand Master	London
John Schofield	Past Grand Master	Bradford Yorkshire
Henry Buck	Provincial Corrg Secy	Birmingham Warwickshire
John Watson	Provincial Corrg Secretary	Durham
Benjamin Sheet	Past Grand Master	Wighsworth Derbyshire
William Alexander	Corr CS	Leeds Yorkshire
William Lightton	Past Provincial G Master	Ton Tyne & Berwick
John Gale	Past Provincial G Master	Liverpool District
Benjn G. Davies	Prov Corresponding Secretary	Merthyr Tydfil Wales.
William Aitken	Trustee	Ashton under Lyne
Thomas Duff	Past Grand Master & Trustee	Liverpool

Manchester
19 February 1857

The success story of Thomas Armitt could have been rivalled
by those of many other distinguished Oddfellows and Foresters
of those days. William Brown, P.P.G.M., was born at Stockport
in 1796 'of poor but honest parents'. His father died when he was
very young leaving a large family and a widow, consequently the
children had to be sent to work as soon as they were capable of
doing so. William Brown's only formal education seems to have
been in first a Wesleyan and, later, an Anglican Sunday School.
He eventually became a shoemaker, only to leave that occupation
to become a broker and accountant, using in these latter pursuits
a good deal of the knowledge that he gained as auditor for the
Stockport district of the Manchester Unity.[1] Edwin Noon was
born in 1820 at Ilkeston in Derbyshire; his father was a machinist
in a hosiery works and died before any of his family had grown up.
At the age of ten he became an apprentice framework knitter's
needle maker and later followed this trade until he was thirty-six;
he became chairman of the trade union. He then went into business on his own and in 1863 had 'an extensive business as an ale
and porter merchant'; by that time he had held various public
offices such as chairman of the board of gas inspectors, chairman
of the highway board, and guardian of the poor. In addition to
being Provincial Grand Master of the Belper district of the Manchester Unity, he was Chief Ranger of the Derbyshire district of
the Ancient Order of Foresters and a freemason.[2] W. N. Waldram
was born in 1814 at Kibworth, Leicestershire, where his father was
a wheelwright. He left his home at eighteen and went to live in
Leicester to take employment in the wool trade. After two years
he gave this up and travelled on the Continent as servant to a
family. On returning to Leicester he went to work for a brewery;
in 1842 he became assistant manager and in 1845 manager of the
brewery. In 1852 he became a partner and in 1863 he took over the
business entirely. As an Oddfellow he had held some sort of
office continuously since 1839, having 'passed three times through
the Noble Grand's chair of his lodge'.[3]

Although the majority of careers seem to be similar to those of

[1] *Oddfellows' Magazine*, VII, 1843, pp. 337–8.
[2] Ibid., New Series, IV, 1863, pp. 65–7.   [3] Ibid., pp. 129–30.

William Brown, Edwin Noon and W. N. Waldram, there were a few well-known Oddfellows who started from a more comfortable background; among these was Bryant Allen, P.P.G.M. He was born in Norwich in 1806 of 'respectable' parents and educated at the Blue Coat School. He was apprenticed to a Quaker who carried on a large business as a dyer. By 1861 it could be said of him that he had himself 'for many years carried on a respectable business as a dyer in Norwich'. He was a noted public figure in Norwich as an active supporter of the Liberal party.[1]

The principal affiliated orders claimed to be free from political or religious bias and in general their claim appears to have been justified, and the 'memoirs' and 'portraits' of leading members of the orders seldom mention a man's political affiliations. Yet it is, perhaps, relevant that in such cases where political views are mentioned, the party to which support was given was—as in the case of Allen—the Liberal party. There is no distinguished Oddfellow or Forester of this period of whom it is recorded that he was prominent as a supporter of the Conservative cause; nor, for that matter, are there any who showed any signs of being attracted by Socialism. A belief in the virtues of free trade, of governmental economy and of leaving people to manage their own affairs without undue interference from the state was typical of those who were in the social position which most of the prominent members of the affiliated orders occupied at this time. There was certainly no feeling of condescension among these men, which undoubtedly was present in those who organised the county societies; they might be more prosperous than some of their brethren in the lodges but they felt in no way different. They were not seeking to 'help the poor' or to 'relieve the rates' or to 'make the working men more prudent'; they looked upon themselves as hard-working individuals whose success was due to personal qualities such as independence and thrift, and their membership of the orders had usually pre-dated the coming of success in business. They probably felt that their membership was one of the factors which had helped them to get on in life.

The officials who were likely to have most influence in the

[1] *Oddfellows' Magazine*, New Series, III, 1861, pp. 65–6.

orders were the principal secretaries, known as the Corresponding Secretary in the Manchester Unity and as the Permanent Secretary in the Ancient Order of Foresters. In the Foresters it was Samuel Shawcross, who became Permanent Secretary in 1843 and who remained in office until after the end of this period, who guided the Foresters during the time when they were becoming a national Order and who really laid down the pattern that the Order was to take. In 1866 it was said of him 'The improved travelling system and the Foresters' Directory—the improved system of book-keeping and numerous other working improvements— owe their origin to him. He has attended 25 consecutive High Court meetings; and out of 1,157 Council meetings, he has been absent from about 10.'[1] Shawcross came from Stockport where his family owned a cotton business.

From 1848 the Corresponding Secretary of the Manchester Unity was Henry Ratcliffe and his influence on the Oddfellows and on the friendly society movement in general was probably greater than that of any other single official. Apart from his organisational work within the Order, he devoted himself to the problem of solvency and of building up a body of data on which to base tables of contributions and benefits. The results of his inquiries he published in 1850, 1862 and 1872. The effect of his work was first felt in his own society, but it was by no means confined to the Manchester Unity since the data which Ratcliffe collected and classified showed friendly societies generally for the first time the extent of the actuarial problems that confronted them and the sort of solutions they would have to apply.[2]

[1] *Foresters' Miscellany*, vol. V, 1866, p. 5.
[2] A fuller account of Ratcliffe's actuarial work is given in the next chapter.

CHAPTER FOUR

THE PROBLEM OF FINANCIAL STABILITY

WHEN the Home Secretary wrote to Sir Stafford Northcote inviting him to become chairman of the proposed Royal Commission on Friendly Societies, he stated in the letter: 'You are aware that the rules of friendly societies are now certified by the Registrar, and their tables for granting annuities are certified by an actuary. This state of the law is not found to prevent societies duly certified from being fraudulently or incompetently managed. Tidd Pratt believed that not 25 out of the 20,000 friendly societies were so managed as to secure them from considerable risk of failure. Under these circumstances Lowe proposed in his bill of the last session that the government should no longer give certificates which were valueless and calculated to mislead. One principal object of inquiry would be whether this course is to be pursued, or whether an attempt should be made by legislation to give security for efficient management; and if so what the legislation should be.' [1] This problem of the financial stability of the friendly societies became the aspect of their work which most attracted the attention of statesmen during this period, and it was this problem, as much as anything else, which caused Gladstone's ministry to initiate a general inquiry into the friendly societies of the nation.[2]

Such concern was, no doubt, justified. The stability of the

---

[1] A copy of this letter is among the miscellaneous papers of J. M. Ludlow, who was secretary of the Commission.

[2] Gladstone had, a few years previously, shown strong feelings on the question of friendly society finance. In the course of a debate on state annuities in the House of Commons on 7 March, 1864, he said, 'I venture to tell the House that this Bill has grown, not out of a consideration of the case of the assurance societies, but out of a consideration of the case of the friendly societies, and of the wholesale error, but not error only, for along with error, deception, fraud and swindling which are perpetrated on the most helpless portion of the community, who find themselves without protection and without defence.'—Hansard, Third Series, CLXXIII, 7 March, 1864.

financial position of his society was of great importance to the individual member although it was not the only thing that mattered. What happened only too often was that a man might join a local club when in his twenties and contribute in the expectation that later in life he would find security in time of sickness or old age. In many cases the club did not last until he was in need of assistance; it might break up when he was only in his forties. If it did, he would have contributed during the best years of his life when he had little to gain from membership in the way of sickness benefit and then find himself unprotected as he approached the age at which illness becomes more frequent. If he were over forty when the club broke up, he would be unable to join another, since even the most primitive clubs usually prevented men from joining who were well on into middle age, and forty was usually accepted as the upper limit for initiation. In other cases the club might have lasted longer but have broken up when a man had reached old age and sickness. The consequences then were even more tragic, inasmuch as he would have contributed for perhaps forty years, yet on trying to claim benefit there would be none and he would have to seek relief from the poor law— relief to which he would have been entitled without paying any premiums! When a club broke up, there always seem to have been plenty of recriminations and accusations of improper management, yet the main reason for financial trouble was usually the simple one of too much benefit for too little contribution.[1]

The fixing of benefits and contributions was largely a matter of local custom combined with an element of competition. Contributions were frequently about 1s. per month while the customary benefit went as high as 10s. per week in towns. If a new society wished to grow and thrive alongside one offering these terms, it would have to try to offer some further inducement, material or otherwise. This sometimes took the form of spending a larger proportion of the contribution in liquor on club night, or it might take the form of offering an indefinite period of sick pay at full benefit instead of a limited period at full pay followed by reduction to half-pay for the remainder of the sickness, which was more

[1] Holland, *Vital Statistics of Sheffield*, 1843, p. 207.

usual. Competition remained strong throughout this period and one of the main causes of the formation of many clubs was the rivalry of small inns, each of which wanted its club and wanted to attract more men to it than its rivals could to theirs.[1] The Royal Commission reported that among the villages of the South of England 'there are hardly any where one or more clubs have not failed at need, and disappointed their members, within the memory of persons now living'.[2]

The members or potential members were clearly not in a position to judge whether a society was sound or not. They would probably have various reasons for joining a particular society and finance would play its part only so far as a society seemed cheap or otherwise when its contributions were considered in relation to the promised benefits. It was equally obvious in 1815 that the full liabilities of a club were not understood by those who managed it. It was partly because of this that the government tried to take a hand in making registered societies more secure when in 1819 it enacted that justices were to refuse registration to any society until its tables and rules had been approved by 'two persons at the least, known to be professional actuaries or persons skilled in calculation'.[3] The main effect of this enactment was to reveal that it was not only the members and managers of local clubs who were not in a position to calculate the liabilities of a friendly society. A Select Committee of the Commons some six years later found this provision 'in principle, of the highest utility' but marred in practice mainly by the lack of data concerning questions of average sickness and mortality. There was no body of actuaries ready and waiting in the counties of England to calculate suitable tables for all the local clubs or to check the tables in use, and the Committee found 'that in many counties, the Bench have been satisfied with the signatures of petty schoolmasters and accountants whose opinion upon the probability of sickness, and the duration of life, is not to be depended upon'.[4] It was not before the middle of the nineteenth century that a reasonable amount of information concerning sickness and death was collected to form the basis of calcu-

[1] Young, p. 16.   [2] R.C.F.S., 4th Report, 1874, para. 227.
[3] 59 Geo. III, c. 128, section 2.   [4] S.C.F.S., 1825, pp. 12–13.

lations of probability. While liabilities could not be properly assessed because the information for making such an assessment was lacking, financial reliability was bound to be a gamble.

Apart from this fundamental difficulty which impeded the establishment of any proper system of contributions and benefits, there were numerous other factors which aggravated the financial condition of the societies. Of these other factors, the one which received most publicity—especially from opponents and would-be advisers of the societies—was the question of management expenses. This term could either refer simply to the secretary's out-of-pocket expenses and the rent of a room once each month, or it could cover the cost of the ceremonies and convivialities which members expected of their club. In the latter case it could amount to a considerable sum and must have helped to undermine the stability of many societies—as it did in the town of Oldham as late as the 1870s. When the Assistant Commissioner visited it he found 230 societies of which virtually all spent their funds partly on convivial practices and neglected the principles of sound management. 'As a natural consequence, nearly all of them are insolvent . . . in the more obvious and painful sense . . . of now failing to pay the benefits they have promised, and either "closing the box", that is repudiating for a varying time their obligations, or at least cutting down their benefits and so making a composition with their creditors.'[1] The Committee of 1825 had found the same trouble fifty years earlier, although by the 1870s it had become less of an abuse in that a separate account for 'management expenses' was now often kept by the societies. In 1825 the Committee reported that meetings were usually held in public houses and added '. . . there is much reason to believe that encroachments also took place upon the common fund, and these were not likely to be checked if the Secretary or Treasurer happened to be the landlord of the house'.[2]

Many of the local societies tended to have their members drawn from the same age-group, thus if the amount which individual members paid in had not been carefully calculated to cover the whole of their liabilities, any deficiency could not be

[1] Stanley, p. 92.　　　　[2] S.C.F.S., p. 7.

covered by contributions from younger members as the average age advanced.[1] There were a number of examples of societies collapsing for this reason in the Poor Law Report of 1834. According to the report from Leeds, 'There are many [friendly societies], but several have been broken up by young men failing to enter and keep up the funds.' At Boroughbridge it was reported that 'There have been several [societies] in the neighbourhood, but they are all broken up, owing to the increase in the claims of the aged, which have deterred the young from entering, owing, in fact, to erroneous calculation', while at Elland '. . . a number of societies have been dissolved because as the members grew older the calls on the fund increased, and no younger members would join'.[2]

Where the club managed to continue recruiting younger members and by this means postponed its day of reckoning, the older members sometimes found themselves in difficulties because they had been so successful in bringing in younger men. Where the younger members found themselves in a majority and saw their contributions going to the support of elderly members they sometimes expelled those who did or would soon require benefits. 'Another material defect was found in the provision made against a fraudulent or inequitable disposition of the funds, or dissolution of the society. . . . It might easily happen that, without any infringement of the law, a club might be dissolved, really to the serious injury of those who had contributed to it for many years.'[3] Once the younger members had brought about the dissolution of the club, they often re-formed themselves into another club, taking care not to admit the older members of the previous one.

Another weakness which was found in societies large and small before the development of an actuarial science—and in many long after its development—was the charging of uniform contributions regardless of the age of entry and regardless of the obvious fact that older men were sick more often. Some attempt was made to

[1] Conversation of S. H. Culley, Secretary of the A.O.F. Exeter district, with Sir G. Young and reprinted in Appendix C to his Report.

[2] Appendix A to the 1st Report from Commissioners on the Poor Laws, 1834, pp. 777, 783, 806.

[3] S.C.F.S., p. 7.

overcome this by imposing an initiation fee which was larger the older a man was, but it was never sufficient to cover in one payment the difference which should have been charged by way of a graduated system of premiums.[1]

The Committee of 1825 pointed to another factor which may have undermined a few societies and, in an incidental manner, it made clear a second difficulty with which the early societies were confronted. The first of these arose out of the working of the Combination Acts. While trade unions were forbidden, a number of genuine friendly societies consisting predominantly of members of one trade quite naturally used their accumulated funds to help the majority of members in industrial action if the need arose.[2]

The final obstacle to the achievement of financial security in the earlier friendly societies lay in the method of procedure which the law prescribed for registered friendly societies to follow in seeking to protect themselves against a dishonest trustee or other official or member. The method of proceeding was by an indictment at common law, and it was suggested that the law would be much easier to enforce if the power were given to any two justices in petty sessions to issue an order freezing the affairs of a society and that any person concerned in a breach of such an order should be punished by summary process.[3]

The improvement of financial stability could only be achieved by setting right abuses and changing the circumstances which permitted or gave rise to them. The principal circumstance was clearly the lack of any reliable tables of contribution and benefit which could be recommended to friendly societies, and this deficiency in its turn could only be remedied by collecting suitable data concerning working men's sickness and mortality from the friendly societies themselves or from some other source. It was absurd to rail against the shortcomings of the societies when there was no scale by which to measure the deficiencies. Consequently during the middle years of the nineteenth century much data on sickness and mortality was collected from the experience of the

[1] F. G. P. Neison, *Observations on Oddfellows and Friendly Societies*, 1846, pp. 13-14.
[2] S.C.F.S., p. 7.   [3] Ibid., p. 21.

societies and for the first time laws of probability were worked out which could be applied to insurance among the working classes. The growth of this part of the actuarial science occurred in response to the needs of the friendly societies and they themselves took an increasingly active part in its development, not only in collecting and providing data, but in the work of analysing the evidence and drawing up tables of probability. The development of the friendly societies between 1815 and 1875 was hampered by the lack of statistics of sickness and mortality, the provision of which was necessary for the development of the societies; on the other hand, the growth of actuarial studies could not have taken place at that time if friendly society insurance against sickness and death had not been developing on such a scale, for the necessary data on which to base the calculations would have been lacking. Thus the growth of an actuarial science between 1825 and 1875 was both a consequence and a cause of the development of friendly societies.

The first attempt at providing tables of probability for sickness in the friendly societies had been made by a Dr. Price in 1789. He based his tables on a theory that in societies consisting of persons under 32, a 48th part will always be sick; from 32 to 42 the proportion sick would increase by a quarter; from 43 to 51 by a half; from 51 to 58 to three-quarters more; and from 58 to 64 to double. This scheme of probability was drawn up for the convenience of Parliament, which had a measure before it at the time concerned with the poor law. The rate of sickness to the age of thirty-two was said to have been based upon observations while the increase in its rate after that age was a matter of hypothesis.[1] In experience the actual rate of sickness shown in the table was found to be much too low, especially in the older age-groups, and the adoption of 'Dr. Price's Tables' by no means assured solvency.[2]

In 1824 the Highland Society issued tables based upon its own experience and that of other benefit societies going back to 1751. Here, again, certain weaknesses soon became apparent since the data on which the tables were based was itself inadequate largely

[1] C. Walford, *Insurance Cyclopaedia*, 1870–8, vol. V, p. 386.
[2] C. Ansell, *A Treatise on Friendly Societies*, 1835.

as a result of the difference in character between Scottish friendly societies and English societies. The Scottish societies were to a considerable extent looked upon as charitable organisations; men did not appeal to them for aid until their own private resources were exhausted, thus the amount of sickness was in fact much greater than that which the Highland Society had paid for. In some of these Scottish societies there was a long waiting period after joining before benefit could be claimed, which sometimes amounted to five years; also periods of sickness had to be of a certain length—it varied from 6 to 14 days—before benefit could be claimed even after five years of membership. Thus the experience on which the Highland Society based its tables was of little use to the English societies in their very different circumstances.[1]

The Select Committee of the House of Commons in 1825 reviewed both of these sets of tables and found them wanting. Of Dr. Price's tables the Committee 'doubted whether the estimate of sickness upon which they are founded is accurate',[2] and of the Highland Society's tables they wrote that they 'certainly do not feel justified in recommending these Scots tables . . . for adoption by any society in England'.[3] This Committee admitted that the necessary data was not available on which to base reliable tables for working-class societies in England and recommended that the matter should be referred to a new committee charged with examining this particular point. In the course of their Report, the Committee of 1825 had favoured the idea of periodical returns from registered societies to the National Debt Office.[4] A new committee reported in 1827 and the recommendation which was to be most important was that these returns should be required at least once in five years and that failure to provide them should be visited by the penalty of depriving registered societies of their right to invest in $4\frac{1}{2}$ per cent debentures.[5]

[1] F. G. P. Neison, 'On our Present Knowledge of the Mortality and Sickness of Members of Friendly Societies', 1873, p. 1. (This was printed as an Appendix to the 3rd Report of the Royal Comm. on Friendly Societies.)
[2] S.C.F.S., p. 18.
[3] Ibid., p. 15. [4] Ibid., p. 19.
[5] Report of the Select Committee of the House of Commons on Laws respecting Friendly Societies, 1827, p. 12.

The outcome of this recommendation was that for the first time an attempt was made to gather the data on which reliable tables could be based. The purpose behind the returns was summarised in the clause of the act of 1829 ordering them to be made, 'and whereas it is desirable for the better security of such societies, that correct calculations of tables of payment and allowances, dependent on the duration of sickness and the probabilities of human life, may be constructed for their assistance; and whereas the present existing data on these subjects have been found imperfect and inefficient; be it therefore enacted, that every such society established or to be established under the authority of this act, shall within three months after the expiration of the month of December, 1835 and so within three months after the expiration of every further period of five years, transmit to the Clerk of the Peace for the county wherein such society is held a return of the rate of sickness and mortality experienced by the said society . . .' [1] The Clerk of the Peace had to transmit these returns to the government. Direct contact between the societies and the government was avoided.

The first set of tables based on data gathered from the experience of English societies was published in 1835.[2] The Society for the Diffusion of Useful Knowledge set itself the task of collecting information from societies covering the period 1823–7. The condition in which most societies kept their books at that time was such as to make it extremely difficult to gather reliable information so that in the end the tables had to be based on the evidence afforded by some 5,000 lives. Among those over the age of fifty the experience was too small to justify the conclusions as to the average amount of sickness likely to be encountered. The work of analysing this information was undertaken by C. Ansell, whose survey of the questions and conclusions was published by the Society for the Diffusion of Useful Knowledge in *A Treatise on Friendly Societies in which the doctrine of interest of money and the doctrine of probability are practically applied*. The publication of this work giving a rate of sickness considerably higher than that of the

[1] 10 Geo. IV, c. 56, section 34.
[2] Ansell, *Treatise on Friendly Societies*, 1835.

Highland Society's tables would, it was hoped, make solvent those societies which adopted Ansell's tables, but in 1846 Neison could write that 'instances occur almost daily of societies breaking down whose contributions approximate to those tables'.[1]

The first reliable sets of tables were those based on the data which Neison obtained from the government's returns under section 34 of 10 Geo. IV, c. 56, for the period 1836–40. The results were published in 1845 in a volume entitled *Contributions to Vital Statistics* and showed a rate of sickness 36 per cent above that of the Highland Society's tables and 19 per cent above that shown by Ansell's.

In 1850 Henry Ratcliffe, the Corresponding Secretary to the Manchester Unity of Oddfellows, published tables based upon the experience of that Order.[2] 'Returns of the most ample kind for the years 1846–7–8 were required from all the lodges composing the Unity; and thus was obtained all the information desirable to be possessed, relative to the sickness and mortality experienced by the members of the Manchester Unity.'[3] This was only the first of the publications of the M.U.O.F. on their rate of sickness and mortality. In 1862 and again in 1872 further collections of tables were published showing the experience of the Order in later periods.

After the publication of Neison's analysis of the government's figures in 1845 and of the Oddfellows' analysis of their own figures it might be thought that the issue of sound tables was, actuarially at least, settled and that it only remained to get the societies to adopt tables akin to those of the Oddfellows or Neison (which were in many ways similar). But in 1853 and 1854 the government published figures produced by Finlaison, Actuary of the National Debt Office, from the returns of the period 1846–50, the same source of data as Neison had used only it was ten years later.[4]

[1] F. G. P. Neison, *Observations on Oddfellow and Friendly Societies*, 1846, p. 7.
[2] H. Ratcliffe, *Observations on the Rate of Mortality and Sickness existing among Friendly Societies*, 1850.
[3] Ibid., from the Preface.
[4] Report and Tables of Sickness and Mortality among members of Friendly Societies as shown by Quinquennial returns to 31 December, 1850, 1853 and further Report of 1854.

H

The rate of sickness shown by Finlaison was much less than that of Neison or the Oddfellows. The cause of the discrepancy lay in the definition of sickness which Finlaison adopted. 'It is clearly to be understood that although separate cases of sickness occurring to the same individual during each year were added together so as to make the return perfectly accurate, yet that nothing but sickness in the true sense of the word, that is, sickness incapacitating from labour, and requiring constant medical treatment, and of limited duration, as contradistinguished from chronic ailment and increpitude, was considered to be sickness.' All cases of slight paralysis, blindness, mental disorders or senile infirmity were 'carefully eliminated'.[1] Thus the societies were now officially recommended to adopt tables of sickness which carefully excluded many of the risks for which members expected relief. To sort out sick members in this fashion and to give relief to those suffering from a disease which the government actuary included in his tables but not to those with illnesses which were excluded was obviously absurd. Yet Tidd Pratt, the Registrar, took steps to recommend these tables to societies by publishing extracts from them in his first annual Report as Registrar and told the societies that 'too little discrimination by far is often used in distinguishing real sickness from the so-called that is often merely an incapacity to labour'.[2] Finlaison's tables confused the issue just when the position was becoming clear and the Royal Commission was to comment that 'There is no doubt that the plan on which these tables were formed has proved unfortunate, and that many societies and even actuaries have made use of the tables without discovering that they were inapplicable to societies which do not limit the benefit to sickness as defined by Mr. Finlaison'.[3]

The position in 1875 was that while a number of reliable general tables had been drawn up—notably those by Neison and Ratcliffe—it had become increasingly apparent that occupation rather than place of residence was the main factor in determining the amount of sick benefit a member might seek from his society

[1] From the Government Actuary's Further Report of 1854, p. 7.
[2] Registrar's Report, 1856, Appendix I, p. 48.
[3] R.C.F.S., 4th Report, 1874, para. 793.

and comparatively few accurate figures were available on this point. The Royal Commission recommended the government to inquire into the sickness experienced by different classes of societies and to prepare tables accordingly. 'Also the rates of sickness prevailing in important trades should be ascertained, and monetary tables—rates of premium and valuation tables—should in like manner be calculated for them.' [1]

Thus as a result of some fifty years of effort on the part of the societies themselves, the actuaries and the government the main obstacle to financial stability was overcome and at last there existed a means of determining reasonably accurately the right relationship between contributions and benefits. Throughout this period some societies showed more anxiety than others to render their finances more secure and the actual adoption of scales of contribution and benefit which would make the societies solvent came about—or did not come about—in accordance with the amount of pressure exerted by popular opinion in different districts. The removal of other factors which tended to undermine the financial stability of the societies had always been a matter of having the will to reform rather than lack of knowledge. As the years passed, the propaganda of those who desired greater security gradually had its effect among members and abuses diminished.

The struggle for reform and solvency dominated the story of the development of the Manchester Unity of Oddfellows in the middle years of the century, for it was this issue which brought about the constitutional conflict between the Order's central government and the claims of the lodges to local autonomy. [2] Before 1844 no attempt was made to persuade the local lodges to adopt any one particular scheme of contributions and benefits. The haphazard process of fixing rates in accordance with local feeling or competition with other societies was almost universal. In 1845 for the customary benefit of 10s. or so per week in sickness, £10 on the death of a member and £6 to £10 on the death of his wife, some lodges were charging 4d., some 5d. and some 6d. per week. [3] Sickness benefit was entirely the responsibility of the

---

[1] Ibid., para. 801.   [2] Supra, p. 28.
[3] Quarterly Report I.O.O.F.M.U., January, 1845.

individual lodges while death grants were chargeable to the funds of the districts to which the lodges contributed according to the size of their membership. Thus if the total amount of sickness suffered by its members was heavy, a lodge might have to 'close the box' or even break up. The leaders of the Unity were aware of the need for improvement; in 1844 it was reported 'that 225 lodges closed in 1843 for want of funds; and that many more, during the same period, applied for help'.[1] In 1844 an attempt was made to obtain figures for sickness experience and financial returns from the lodges; many refused to divulge the information sought and the Directors suspended lodges with 16,000 members between the Annual Moveable Committee at Newcastle in 1844 (when the returns were decided upon) and the next A.M.C. at Glasgow in 1845. At this second meeting a resolution was passed ordering every lodge to establish a separate fund for all expenses other than sickness and funeral benefit; lodges were still to fix their own contributions and benefits but these were to be within the limits of 1s. weekly in sickness and £1 at death in return for each $\frac{1}{2}d.$ of contribution per week.[2] The constitutional consequences of this have already been discussed; the passing by the A.M.C. of this resolution was a considerable victory for the leaders of the Unity in their quest for security, not because the proposals themselves were adequate to ensure financial stability, but rather because they had succeeded for the first time in limiting the financial autonomy of the lodges. In the face of the secessions, the enforcement of the new conditions was difficult, but by 1847 they appear to have been fairly widely accepted.[3]

The inadequacy of the new scales of contribution was soon pointed out by Neison. 'The payment necessary to provide the benefits promised will thus be seen to amount to £1 19s. 5d. to each member yearly, but the actual sum demanded according to the new scale, No. 1, is only £1 2s. 9d., being about 42 per cent less than the terms necessary to enable the Unity to meet its

---

[1] Quarterly Report I.O.O.F.M.U., July, 1844.

[2] R. W. Moffrey, *A Century of Oddfellowship*, 1910, p. 55.

[3] C. Hardwick, *Manual for Patrons and Members of Friendly Societies*, 1859, p. 84.

engagements.'[1] Neison's criticism was intended to be helpful and certainly the evidence which he collected concerning the solvency of the Oddfellows must have provided the Directors of the Order with some useful arguments when they were dealing with the lodges which objected even to their modest and actuarially inadequate reforms. In Manchester itself in 1846 there were six lodges which had been established on an average for twelve years; they contained 530 members and their total accumulated funds were only £91 13s. 6d. which was less than one-twelfth of the initiation fees that the members must have paid on joining the lodges.[2] Just as the Manchester Unity had been the first of the affiliated orders to become a nation-wide organisation, so it was the first to feel the full effects of the increased burden on the sick funds of a high average age among its members and to discover the practical consequences of not building up sufficient funds when members were young to meet their liabilities when they grew older.

The question of age of entry and the amount that could be accumulated from a man's contributions before he became subject to the illnesses of old age was a matter which had received insufficient attention so far. The contributions were not graduated according to the age at which a man began to pay, nor were the initiation fees graded steeply enough to overcome this deficiency. The actual deficit which this involved in the case of an average member was calculated in 1846 as an annual loss of 4s. 8d. in the case of a member first joining at twenty, an annual loss of 14s. 1d. for those entering at thirty and an annual loss of £1 5s. 6d. for those first joining at forty.[3]

No further financial reform could be attempted by the Directors before 1853. In that year the Annual Moveable Committee assembled at Preston and adopted for the first time graduated scales of contribution based on age of entry. In addition to the minimum scales recommended in 1845, it added payments ranging from 6d. to 7s. 6d. per annum while the initiation fee was reduced to a minimum of 5s., rising to £1. Clearances were also

[1] F. G. P. Neison, *Observations on Oddfellow and Friendly Societies*, 1846, p. 15.
[2] Ibid., p. 19.   [3] Ibid., p. 27.

regulated at this time. While one of the advantages of the affiliated orders was that when a man moved from one district to another he could keep his membership by simply transferring to another lodge, in the case of an elderly man this could be something of a liability for the receiving lodge. Henceforth an entrance fee of from 1s. 6d. to £1 was imposed and a maximum age of forty-five years after which lodges were not to be compelled to receive transferred members.[1] The figures adopted at Preston were based on the experience of the Unity for the years 1846–8 as published by Ratcliffe.[2] The new scales were not immediately adopted in all lodges; the A.M.C. itself had not recommended that any attempt should be made to compel existing members to contribute in accordance with them. But although it was some time before the full effect of these reforms was felt, after 1853 the battle for reform had in fact been won.

The length of time that had inevitably to pass before all lodges and districts would attain solvency was shown by the investigations of the Royal Commission twenty years later when insolvent lodges and lodges not fulfilling the financial requirements of the Unity were still to be found in different parts of the country. The Commissioners wrote 'of the total number of lodges [3,168] valued, 813 or nearly 26 per cent appear to have a surplus, the rest a deficiency'; the overall deficiency of the Order was then calculated at £1,343,446 16s. 5d. The deficit was worst in the counties where the Order had established itself earliest and where most progress had been made before the introduction of reformed rates of contribution. The average deficiency of £3 12s. 3d. per member rose to £5 12s. 7d. for Lancashire and to £5 9s. 4d. for Yorkshire.[3]

On the whole the Commission found in favour of the Manchester Unity, stating that 'it stands, moreover, foremost among the orders through the successive steps which it has taken towards the attainment of financial security'.[4] In spite of its apparent actuarial deficiencies even after reform had gained a hold in the

[1] R. W. Moffrey, *A Century of Oddfellowship*, 1910, p. 66.
[2] H. Ratcliffe, *Observations on the Rate of Mortality and Sickness existing among Friendly Societies*, 1850.
[3] R.C.F.S., 4th Report, 1874, para. 140.   [4] Ibid., 139.

Order, the Manchester Unity was never overtaken by disaster for two reasons to which the actuaries seem to have paid little regard. In the first place there were a large number of lapsed members whose contributions had been paid during the years of their vigour and who lost their claim on the funds of the society later through failing to maintain their contributions. Neison made no allowance for the benefit which accrued to the Unity through lapsed policies. The importance of this factor may be judged from these figures given by the Corresponding Secretary in his report on the financial position of the Preston district in 1858, 'If reference be made to the last number of the Magazine, it will be seen that during the last ten years no fewer than 69,307 members have left the society, being at the rate of an average of 2·6 per cent per annum; and during the same period the deaths have only been 26,500 or about 1 per cent per annum.' [1] The second saving factor was that the orders were not simply insurance companies but fraternities, and when the funds were exhausted it was not unknown for a levy to be imposed on all the members of a lodge, for a collection to be taken or for aid to be given by another lodge or by the Unity itself.

Once the proper balance between contributions and benefits in accordance with the laws of probability of sickness and mortality had been made known as a result of the work of such men as Ratcliffe and Neison, the acceptance of financial reform spread slowly through most other affiliated orders, but in none had it gone so far as it had in the Manchester Unity by 1875. The Ancient Order of Foresters had expanded rapidly in the twenty years before 1875 and its average age was lower than that of the Oddfellows, consequently the problem of heavy sickness in old age had its impact on the courts of that Order at a later date. The Foresters, moreover, had not built up such a strong central government as the Oddfellows of the Manchester Unity and it was not possible to proceed with reform either as early or as rapidly as in the latter Order. The Foresters first attempted to adopt the principle of graduated contributions in the 1850s, but a relapse followed although a number of courts voluntarily maintained the

[1] Hardwick, *Manual for Patrons and Members of Friendly Societies*, 1859, p. 84.

improvement.[1] In 1871 the High Court adopted a resolution that courts should accept a graduated scale of contributions for new members and, in spite of an attempt to set aside this recommendation at the High Court meeting at York the next year, the first resolution was maintained—although it was ignored by many courts.[2]

The Foresters were much later than the Oddfellows in collecting data from their courts on which to base their tables. In 1873 a report on the sickness experience of the Order in 1870 was published, but Neison, who compiled it, wrote that 'It will be gathered from one or two of my observations that I do not think much reliance is to be placed in the figures appearing in this report as to the Foresters' sickness experience. This arises, as clearly stated, from the manner of filling up the returns.'[3] This illustrated once more the difficulty which was experienced in finding suitable men to act as local secretaries in the societies as well as the dislike felt at what some considered to be interference on the part of the central authority in the affairs of the courts. The first comprehensive survey of mortality and sickness experience among the Foresters was made as a result of a resolution taken at the High Court meeting in 1878. The survey was to cover the years 1871–5 and the Executive Council directed the Secretary to 'consult with F. G. P. Neison Esq. as to the best mode of proceeding, and that F. G. P. Neison Esq. be retained to complete the analysis and deductions from such Sickness and Mortality Experience upon the Schedules being prepared'. This work was completed and published in 1882.[4]

None of the remaining smaller affiliated orders—with two special exceptions—had got as far even as the Foresters in this

[1] Hardwick, *Manual for Patrons and Members of Friendly Societies*, 1859, p. 84.

[2] It was only in 1885 that drastic action was finally taken to enforce the graduated scales. In that year the Executive Council at Leeds suspended 52 courts and 5,000 members for failing to implement the decision of 1871.—Chief Registrar's Report for 1889, p. 34.

[3] F. G. P. Neison, Report upon the Sickness Experience of the A.O.F. for the Year 1870, presented to the Executive Council, 1873, p. 10.

[4] F. G. P. Neison, *The Rates of Mortality and Sickness of the Ancient Order of Foresters' Friendly Society*, 1882.

matter. Before financial reform of an Order could be attempted there had to be some central government in the society which could gather the necessary data, ascertain what the position really was, and then make the necessary proposals to correct whatever deficiency might have become apparent; some of the orders still lacked any real central authority capable of undertaking this. In the 1870s the Order of Druids and the Ancient Shepherds of the Ashton Unity were discussing proposals for a graduated scale of contributions; the Bolton Unity of Oddfellows were collecting the necessary information from their lodges and some of the other small orders were also attempting to bring about a reform in their organisation preparatory to financial reform—or so they claimed.[1]

The third largest society in 1875 was the Grand United Order of Oddfellows, and while this Order had not adopted a graduated scale, it had begun to insist on financial returns. This society, in common with the others, was driven to some sort of reform by its own difficulties in the 1850s and 1860s. The following paragraph from a Preston newspaper in 1859 throws some light on these difficulties.

'Grand United Order of Oddfellows.

'The quarterly meeting of delegates from lodges in the Preston district took place on Saturday night last at the George the Third Inn, Brook Street, when, after meeting the demands of different lodges, which were rather unusually heavy through so many deaths, a resolution was read from the North Star lodge, No. 213, requesting the committee to establish a separate fund to be called "The Embarrassed Lodge Fund" for the relief of any lodge or lodges whose sick funds may become exhausted through long runs of sickness. After considerable discussion on the subject, it was resolved, "that, through the vast amount of sickness at present to be met by the different lodges, this meeting considers it unwise to extract additional levies from either lodges or members".'[2]

The two special exceptions to the general rule among the smaller affiliated societies were the Rational Sick and Burial

[1] R.C.F.S., 4th Report, 1874, para. 157.   [2] *Preston Chronicle*, 19 March, 1859.

Association and the Independent Order of Rechabites. Neither of these could really be considered typical among the affiliated orders in view of the limited nature of their appeal and their membership was hardly typical. The Rational Society adopted a graduated scale in 1861, the Rechabites adopted their graduated scale in 1871, but as early as 1839 the latter had separated their management from sickness funds and in 1842 they appointed a committee to draw up a fixed scale for sick and funeral funds to be adopted by all tents in the Order, instead of permitting each tent to continue making its own regulations in financial matters.[1]

The problem of the financial stability of friendly societies had attracted the attention of the government first when the only form of society at all widely known was still the small local club and the legislation of 1819 had been directed to the case of such clubs. The development of actuarial knowledge during these years was of less value to such clubs than to the affiliated orders for a number of reasons. There was difficulty in applying tables based on the probability of the 'average' amount of sickness among working men to particular small groups of men who composed these local clubs; what is true of the average may well not be true of the particular group; the larger the group, the more likely it is to correspond to what has been ascertained as the 'average'. Moreover the men who ran these local clubs were seldom skilled in adapting tables of sickness to the needs of their society even when such 'safe' tables had become available. Thus the quest for greater financial reliability became one of the main reasons for the decline in the importance of the local societies and for the increasing measure of support which the large affiliated orders were able to attract. The Committee of the House of Lords on Friendly Societies in 1848 noticed this process going on at that time and commented that 'While the small bodies are decaying or sinking into neglect, the affiliated bodies are growing rapidly in strength, and extending their branches into every part of the kingdom'.[2]

In spite of the disadvantages of the small societies, it was true

[1] *Jubilee Record of the Independent Order of Rechabites*, 1885, pp. 15-21.
[2] Report of a Select Committee of the House of Lords on Provident Associations, 1848, p. 4.

that many survived and flourished for many years. In 1843 there were found to be ten of these societies in Sheffield which were still thriving, having been founded between 1740 and 1794, although these appear to have been exceptional for it was reported at the same time that 'the insolvency of such clubs, after they have existed for twenty or thirty-five years, is of frequent occurrence'.[1] In 1871 a Mr. Tompkins of the Registrar's office wrote an account of a number of small local societies which had been in existence for considerable periods, his object being to show that societies without a great number of members could attain stability.[2] Yet while making due allowance for exceptions, the general picture during the latter part of this period was of some small clubs being absorbed as lodges or courts of the affiliated orders and of others breaking up through financial instability.[3]

The county type of societies were not faced with this problem of financial stability to the same extent as the affiliated orders or the local societies; founded by magistrates and gentry, they were semi-charitable institutions in that the subscriptions from honorary members helped them to pay their benefits. Also, since they were not 'popular' foundations, there was not the same incentive to lower subscriptions and to raise benefits among their managers as in other societies. The ordinary large societies were also less worried by the problem of stability since they, too, were hardly under popular management but resembled insurance companies and their appeal was to a limited section of the community, thus there was not the same pressure to keep the charges low and the benefits relatively high. Their stability had been assured, in a sense, since their managers were making their living out of them and would certainly not offer tables which involved paying more than they were likely to receive.

As the friendly societies developed in the years following the Napoleonic wars, the problem of financial stability was bound to become more acute and more noticeable to politicians and to the

[1] Holland, *Vital Statistics of Sheffield*, p. 206.
[2] H. Tompkins, *An Account of Some Remarkable Friendly Societies*, undated (about 1871).
[3] Stanley, p. 25.

public. The fall of an insolvent local club might have caused some distress among its members, but it would hardly have caused a national outcry; the collapse of such an organisation as the Manchester Unity of Oddfellows or the Ancient Order of Foresters through bankruptcy would have been a national disaster and would certainly have caused a public outcry. Thus the growth of the friendly society movement was enough of itself to account for the actuarial research, the governmental inquiries and the movement for reform in the bigger societies during this period.

CHAPTER FIVE

CEREMONIES AND CONVIVIALITIES

IN most types of society there was some sort of social activity which was organised alongside that insurance against sickness and death which—at least in the eyes of the government—constituted the 'raison d'être' of friendly societies in general. These social activities were at their liveliest in the local clubs and local lodges or courts of the affiliated orders, while in the latter they became merged in a whole collection of mysterious forms and ceremonies in which the mythology of 'Oddfellowship' or 'Forestry' flourished.

The pattern of friendly society convivialities for the individual member was really set by the local clubs. The idea of paying a regular premium for insurance against sickness and funeral expenses simply did not appeal strongly enough to working men of the late eighteenth or nineteenth centuries for it to be possible to run the societies as purely insurance businesses. The monthly meeting at which the 'premium' was paid had to be made attractive in some way, and membership was further enhanced by the addition of an annual—or sometimes half-yearly—feast. These appear to have been the least that a member demanded of his friendly society. In some places there were other attractions such as a 'club day' which would include a procession and a funfair; occasionally sports meetings were arranged and there were excursions.

The minimum requirements of monthly meetings and a regular feast were usually provided for in the rules of the society. In the Articles of the 'Friendly Society, Meeting at Thomas Finch's at the sign of the Tiger in Lindfield' drawn up about 1757 the first article provided for the regular monthly meeting, 'That a society shall meet at the house of Thomas Finch, at the sign of the Tiger in Lindfield-town, in the county of Sussex, the first Monday in every month, or where the majority shall think fit to keep the common stock. And their hours of meeting shall be from seven to nine in the evening, from Lady-day to Michaelmas, and from six to eight from Michaelmas to Lady-day'. Article XI stated 'That there shall be two feasts every year, and those feasts be holden on the first Thursday in July and January, and whenever the same shall be kept, each member shall pay one shilling: [that is to say] sixpence for their dinner, and sixpence for liquor'.[1] According to the rules of the Friendly Society founded at Campsall in the West Riding in 1795, 'This society shall hold its meetings in the town of Campsall aforesaid, and at the house of William Crowcroft, innkeeper, at the aforesaid place during the will and pleasure of this society on the first Thursday in every month, and the hours of meeting shall be during the months of November, December, January and February from six o'clock in the evening till eight; and from seven o'clock in the evening till nine, during the other months.' Here again provision was made for a feast 'Upon Whitsun Tuesday the day appointed for the anniversary or feast-day of this society in every year, each member belonging to the same shall pay one shilling and eightpence towards the feast, which shall be held at the house where this society always hold their monthly meetings'.[2] In the North and in the South the same sort of provision for at least a minimum of convivial activity may be found in these early local clubs. Such provision was almost universal and a final example may be taken from the rules of the Friendly Brothers who from 1808 met at the Duke's Head in Great Peter Street, Westminster, and whose members were to gather at that inn 'every fourth Tuesday throughout the year, as in the calendar, between the hours of eight and ten in the evening, from Lady-day to Michaelmas, and between the hours of seven and nine from Michaelmas to Lady-day'. It was also provided that 'to commemorate the institution of this society, and to promote the unity of its members, such of them as may be so disposed, with others whom they may invite, shall once a year,

---

[1] Articles agreed upon by a Friendly Society, Meeting at Thomas Finch's at the sign of the Tiger, in Lindfield, in the County of Sussex, London, 1757.

[2] Rules and Orders of the Friendly Society held at Campsall in the West Riding of the County of York, Doncaster, 1796.

on the meeting night of the month of August, sup together at such time and place as shall be appointed by the stewards chosen for that purpose'.[1] From the reports drawn up in connection with the Royal Commission, it is evident that in the 1870s the individual member still expected at least the regular monthly celebration and the annual feast from his local society or, by that time, his local lodge.

The convivial element was encouraged by the custom of holding friendly society meetings in public houses. It appeared that the local inn was the only suitable place for a number of men to meet together and it also seems that the innkeepers themselves did much to promote the formation of clubs meeting on their premises with an eye to the business which would result. The monthly meeting was certainly far more than the mere attendance of a collector who would receive contributions for two hours at a local inn; the conclusion of the official meeting after two hours did not necessarily mean an end to the revelry. The local club or lodge often paid no rent as such for the room in which they met, but undertook to buy a certain amount of liquor each lodge night—sometimes paid for by way of an extra levy on the members and sometimes out of the club's funds. The practice of using the club's funds to purchase liquor was strongly condemned by the actuaries, the clergy, the government and all those who gave advice, as it were, from above. Registration was refused to any societies which made formal provision in their rules for such payments, yet the Royal Commissioners' inquiries showed that the custom was still widespread among the unregistered societies and that even among the registered such expenditure had come to be entered as an expense of the management fund. Stanley wrote in his Report, 'One of the great causes of insolvency in the East Lancashire societies has been their mixing up of their funds and spending a good deal of them in drink, which they falsely enter as rent of room.'[2] Among

---

[1] Rules and Orders to be observed by the members of a Benefit Society called the Friendly Brothers, held at the Duke's Head, Great Peter Street, Westminster, Southwark, 1810.

[2] Stanley, p. 87.

unregistered societies Stanley gave a number of examples of some
paying their rent in 'lodge liquor' in the Nottingham district; at
Plumtree there were two such, '1. A sick club, unregistered,
founded in 1828, with 89 members and £450 invested in six
houses; they bring in £26 a year gross rent; they have 1½d. a
member lodge liquor and £5 or £6 yearly from the box for a
feast. 2. Another unregistered sick club . . . there is six shillings
worth of lodge liquor every lodge night; five shillings worth for
a committee and one shilling a head of liquor at the feast . . .' [1]

Such a waste of money and such apparently unthrifty behaviour
was frowned upon by the Royal Commission, but the Commissioners had to admit that 'It must not be overlooked that the
objection to the law [concerning registration] being too strict—
especially with reference to public house meetings and liquor payments in lieu of rent—is urged by many societies of a respectable
and improving character . . .' [2] From the point of view of many
societies, these practices were essential if they were to hold their
membership, mere insurance had not a strong enough appeal.
Many much stronger denunciations of the very custom of meeting at public houses than the mild rebuke administered by
the Royal Commission had come from other parties at earlier
times. A fairly typical example was the denunciation written by
J. W. Cunningham, Vicar of Harrow, in 1817:

'I will take the liberty of stating the general constitution of
these societies as they now exist:

'1. In the first place, they meet for all business of the Society at
a public house.

'2. They thus meet once every month and once or twice, in
addition, every year.

'3. They subscribe generally two shillings per month to the
club, out of which sixpence is to be spent in liquor for the benefit
of the publican whose house they frequent.

'4. Whatever be the number present, the sixpences of the whole
club are to be thus spent: so that if the night be bad, or any other
obstacle to their meeting arise, ten men may drink the sixpences
of one hundred.

[1] Stanley, p. 51.   [2] R.C.F.S., 4th Report, 1874, para. 72.

'5. In general the publican is the treasurer; and, partly by his rank of life, partly by his habits of business, partly by his influence over the sots in the club, who are his debtors, gains a considerable ascendancy in the Society, which he often employs either to borrow the money in the box for himself, or for some of his friends.

'Now, of course, a Benefit Society thus constituted is pregnant with every possible mischief to society.' [1]

The Reverend Cunningham and those who wrote in similar vein were quite accurate observers and there is no reason to challenge the actual description which he gives of a society in 1817, but those who wrote in this sense seem to have made little or no effort to understand the point of view of the sort of men for whom such societies were intended.[2]

The annual feasts appear to have aroused less hostile comment. The Royal Commission stated that 'The question of feasts rests upon a somewhat different footing. Although instances will be found in the reports of our Assistant Commissioners in which clubs have been broken down by an encroachment on their benefit funds for the purpose of their feasts, there are others in which the giving up of the feast is alleged to have been the breaking down of the club. The importance of this attraction, especially as respects the country population, cannot be denied.' [3] Few societies were in doubt as to the value of the annual feast. Occasionally the rules did permit the members to decide from year to year whether they would have a feast or not, but usually there was no question of not having one. Of the 23 societies described by F. C. Morgan in his *Friendly Societies in Herefordshire*, 21 are said to have had an annual feast. No feast is mentioned in the case of one society whose

---

[1] *A Few Observations on Friendly Societies and their influence on Public Morals*, J. W. Cunningham, 1817.

[2] An apposite comment on the efforts of the act of 1829 to restrict such revelry was contained in the report of Captain Chapman to the Poor Law Commission in 1834 on its effects in parts of Devon. 'The putting an end to merrymaking is, in the opinion of all persons, an unnecessary interference with the enjoyment of the lower orders, and has been the cause of so many societies breaking up.' —Appendix A to the Report of the Poor Law Commission, 1834, p. 445.

[3] R.C.F.S., 4th Report, 1874, para. 72.

rules have not been discovered nor in the case of the Hereford-shire Friendly Society—the county society under the patronage of the bishop.[1]

A society whose members were supposed to decide from year to year was the Friendly Society of Joiners, founded in 1777. In the rules of 1821 it was stated that 'at the last six week's meeting in the year, every member then present shall vote for or against a dinner at the next general meeting, on New-Year's day; and if there be a majority for a dinner, the agrecment for the cost, and the number to provide for, shall be settled in the room at the same time'.[2] The only considerable group of friendly societies not having an annual feast were a number of clubs founded by honorary members. The Bishop's Stortford Friendly Society was set up in 1839 as a result of the efforts of local worthies who became honorary members and according to the rules the annual meeting must have savoured rather of the annual general meeting of a company than anything in the way of a typical friendly society feast.[3] Some of the societies run by honorary members came to introduce an annual feast of some sort in an effort to attract members.

Few descriptions of the actual feast day of a local club can rival that given by Alfred Williams of the annual club day at South Marston in Wiltshire. He wrote: 'What a day the old club anni-versary used to be in the village years ago, before the little society became enfeebled and crippled by other more powerful and national institutions! It was quite the event of the year; Christmas and Easter were nothing to it; it was, in truth, the red-letter day of all, young and old alike. There were about thirty members in the society altogether. These contributed a certain amount per month for sickness, and the club "broke up" every five years; that is to say, the accumulated moneys were shared out to members, only retaining a sum for present needs. The anniversary was held on the second Tuesday in May. This comprised a general assembly at the

---

[1] F. C. Morgan, *Friendly Societies in Herefordshire*, 1949.

[2] Rules and Regulations to be observed by the Friendly Society of Joiners of Newcastle on Tyne, 1821.

[3] Rules for the Bishop's Stortford Friendly Society, 1839.

Burnley, Industry Lodge: a convivial jug, 1819.

inn—the headquarters of the club—a general procession to church, headed by a brass band in the morning, and afterwards a parade of the village, with music and collections for the society's funds, at the manor, the farms and the houses en route. At one o'clock all sat down to a substantial hot dinner of roast beef and other cooked meats and vegetables, provided in the club-room; the band played selections; the foaming ale was brought in in large two-gallon cans; the greatest good nature prevailed. Farmers and all belonging to the gathering; it was no one-sided affair, and a great number of folk attended from the neighbouring villages; all the old people made it their business to come to "Maason Club". The procession was headed by three men bearing blue silk flags with tassels and fringes, a large one first and two smaller ones, one on each side. The members wore regalia, red and blue sashes and rosettes, and walked with blue staffs with gilt heads.

'Jimmy Boulton always carried the big flag. He wore a stout leather belt, with socket in front; the flag-staff fitted into this; if there was a breeze he needed all his strength to maintain it. He was just in his element then; you may imagine how his eyes twinkled with pleasure, and what delight he felt. His old face was redder than ever; his smile was ineffable. How very proud he was of that fringed and tasselled silk! If the wind blew he kept it upright and rigid; if it was calm he would wave it about from side to side, and when the crowd was stationary before the farms, or near the clubroom, he would hold it so low as to touch the people's heads.' [1]

A feature which was present in the rules of many of the local societies was a provision that all the members were to attend the funerals of deceased colleagues. The Campsall Friendly Society had this rule, 'The Master, Wardens, Common Councilmen, and all the members of this society, shall attend the funeral of every free member of the same, who shall die within three miles of Campsall aforesaid, and shall follow the corpse from the house where he lies deceased to the place of interment, in a decent and orderly manner; . . . Any member neglecting to attend as aforesaid, notice having been given him or them of such funeral, shall

[1] Alfred Williams, *A Wiltshire Village*, 1912, pp. 234-5.

forfeit threepence each.' [1] This rule, specifying in detail the duties required and enforcing them by a penalty, was typical of the duty towards dead members enjoined on the living by local societies.

There is no doubt that it was for their social activities, whether these were club night meetings, feasts or funerals (which were usually followed by a supper), quite as much as for the security they were able to afford, that members joined the small local clubs throughout this period. The case of Hitchin Friendly Institution, a local society run by honorary members and found by the Royal Commission to be in a very strong financial position, made this clear. 'The Hitchin Friendly with a constant acknowledged surplus, and able to invest every year more than the whole contributions of its members, had fewer members in 1872 than it had twenty years previously [304 against 311]. On being asked to explain this anomaly, Mr. Hawkins [the Treasurer] wrote as follows: I cannot account for so flourishing a society as the Hitchin Friendly Institution is acknowledged by all the neighbourhood to be, having so few members, unless it be the attraction the public house affords of conviviality, though accompanied by bad management.' [2]

The position in many societies was well summarised in this extract from the notes on a conversation which Sir G. Young had with a Mr. Boult who was secretary to the Holyport United Friendly Benefit Club. 'Mr. Boult does not know the difference in position of a registered and unregistered club, and thinks the rules about arbitration for disputes and greater security as against officials would be by no means sufficient inducement, under the circumstances, to the members generally to give up the feast and monthly beer. "They don't see no good in a club without it, they say."' [3]

The large affiliated orders during this period did not abandon any of these activities; they could hardly have afforded to do so if they were to maintain their membership. After it became possible

[1] Rules and Orders of the Friendly Society held at Campsall in the West Riding of the County of York, 1796, Rule XLII.
[2] R.C.F.S., 4th Report, 1874, para. 247.　　　[3] Young, p. 142.

for them to register in 1851, some of the orders tried to insist on all their branches becoming registered societies. Legally it then became impossible to spend funds on ceremonial or social activities. The standard form of reply which the Registrar sent out in response to inquiries from societies on the application of their funds read as follows:

'Sir,—In answer to yours of . . . , I beg to acquaint you that no portion of the funds of a friendly society can lawfully be applied otherwise than in payment of the benefits granted by the rules, and of the NECESSARY EXPENSES of management.

'Each Society must determine for itself what, under its rules, are necessary expenses.

'Payments for anniversaries, processions, bands, regalia are clearly unnecessary, and therefore unlawful.

'The Registrar will decline to certify any rule purporting to authorise such payments.' [1]

The receipt of one of these letters made the legal position perfectly clear, yet in fact the law was disregarded on this point by the orders; the law was unenforceable because it failed to take into account the views of those who became members of societies. From the point of view of the government, it was difficult to detect this illicit expenditure and still more difficult to take effective legal action to prevent it.

With few exceptions the lodges of the Oddfellows and the courts of the Foresters held their monthly meetings in public houses. Undoubtedly as time went on an increasing number must have paid a genuine room rent to the landlord and paid for any drinks separately, yet the amount of rent agreed even in these cases must have borne some relationship to the profit likely to accrue to the landlord in providing the members with refreshment. In the 1870s the old system of confusing the two and paying for liquor from the funds still prevailed in many places and the reports of the Assistant Commissioners illustrated this. A good deal of light was thrown on the practice by the following extract from an article in the *Oldham Standard* of 27 January, 1872, which gave an account of a meeting held at the town hall where E. L. Stanley as

[1] Printed in the Registrar's Report for 1872.

the Assistant Commissioner for the district addressed a gathering of officials from the Oldham lodges of the Manchester Unity:

'There was another thing which was quite contrary to law and to the rules of the Order and yet that district and that Order was only in this respect acting as the other Orders and societies of the district had done—the spending of an immense quantity of money, and wasting an immense quantity of its resources. He knew they all knew what he was going to say. (Laughter.) He referred to the fiction of room rent, as it was called. They had in the district more than 2,000 members, and about five lodges containing as near as possible one-fourth of the district, paid as rent for the rooms £10 10s. 6d. The other 1,500 odd paid as room rent, but having it back in beer, very nearly £100. Was it right that, whereas they might suppose at the same rate the remainder could be accommodated at the very most for £35, they should be spending £60 in addition out of the funds of the society. If they deliberately made the sick and funeral fund so low that they could not pay the benefits out of it, and the management fund so high because they were going to pay expenses which they did not venture to put in what was called their balance-sheet, because they knew them to be wrong, but inserted in other ways, how did they consider they could hold themselves out to the world as a really honest society? They were spending money that should be devoted to another purpose, and making a false statement in writing as to how they spent it . . . He had spoken plainly to them, because he felt sure in speaking to the friendly societies it was better to do so than to beat about the bush. He had no doubt, as secretaries, many of them had said the same thing to the members of their lodges, and had found it hard work to get them to listen to them.' [1]

In Oldham at this time there were 24 registered Oddfellows' lodges; of these only 5 were complying with the law in this matter. The other 19 lodges still paid for refreshments for the monthly meeting out of the funds and showed it in the accounts as room rent. The local secretaries appeared to know what the law required, but—to judge from the last sentence of this extract—also knew what their members required; thus, pressed from both sides,

[1] *Oldham Standard*, 27 January, 1872, referred to in Stanley's Report.

the usual way out was by suitable entries debiting the management fund with excessive 'rent' payments.

It should, perhaps, be noticed in this connection, that there were affiliated orders founded to meet the needs of groups of people with particular sets of beliefs which sometimes prevented them from following customs otherwise general among the orders. The membership of these societies was usually small, the best-known being the Independent Order of Rechabites whose members in 1873 numbered just over 9,000 or $\frac{1}{52}$nd of the total membership of the Manchester Unity of Oddfellows. The Rechabites quite naturally did not follow the accepted pattern of behaviour. Rule 1 of the General Rules of the Order adopted in 1835 was 'That this Society shall be denominated the Independent Order of Rechabites and shall consist of persons of good moral character, free from lameness or disorder, of any religious persuasion, who shall be members of the Temperance Society, having signed the following pledge:—"I do hereby voluntarily promise to abstain from all intoxicating liquor—such as Brandy, Whiskey, Rum, Gin, Wine, Ale, Porter, Cider, Perry, distilled Peppermint, etc. I will not engage in the traffic of them and in all suitable ways discountenance the use, manufacture and sale of them." ' [1] The social activities of the Rechabites seem to have taken the form of amateur sports meetings, fêtes and similar functions.

In the main affiliated orders the annual feast, far from being abandoned, was considerably enhanced in its importance for members since it was the occasion on which aprons, sashes, banners and various symbols of the good works which were associated with the orders might be publicly displayed. This description of the annual feast day of a lodge at Monmouth in 1828 gives some impression of how much more there was to a feast than simply the meal in many lodges:

'The Waterloo lodge of the Independent Odd Fellows made their annual summer excursion on Monday the 4th (of August) within the celebrated ruins of Ragland Castle, eight miles distant therefrom, the use thereof being kindly granted to them by A. Wyatt Esq., agent to the Duke of Beaufort. The preparations for

[1] *Jubilee Record of the Independent Order of Rechabites, Salford Unity*, 1885, p. 11.

the occasion were conducted with the same spirit-stirring zeal which has ever marked the proceedings of the Waterloo lodge. At six o'clock the merry bells of St Mary's Tower proclaimed, in clamour loud, the commencement of this Odd Fellows' holiday. A little before nine, the full band marched to the lodge house, in the street leading from which to the river the conveyances took their ground. The signal for starting being given, the procession moved off, headed by the band with two cars, and led by the Grand Master of the district in an open chariot-and-four, followed by six other chariots, whilst the rear was brought up by gigs, cars etc., making an aggregate of twenty-five conveyances on its entry into Ragland, besides numerous horsemen, pedestrians etc. At the village of Mitchelltroy, the inhabitants had erected an arch of flowers, and their example was followed at the turn-pike gate near Thloft-y-thloi, and a third rose its aerial bow at the top of the hill leading into Ragland. The brethren and their friends dismounted at the Beaufort Arms Inn (the headquarters for the day), and immediately repaired to the Castle, in the Yellow Tower of which floated the Union Jack. Unanimous was the feeling of admiration on the survey of these far-famed remains of castellated splendour. After a cursory glance, and slight refreshment being partaken of, a procession was formed on the terrace in front of the entrance gateway, and eighty-four brethren walked, in full costume, with the insignia of the Order, through the village, returning to the castle in the same order, amidst the assembled crowds that lined the road. At two o'clock, dinner was announced, to which nearly 200 sat down, under a large tent in the Fountain Court. The cloth being removed, the usual routine of toasts were given, and the pleasures of the evening were enlivened by some excellent singing and recitations composed for the occasion. The tinkling strings of the harp now summoned the votaries of Terpsichore to the pleasures of the mazy dance; and two parties were soon formed on the bowling green, to enjoy this their favourite amusement. The Castle, at this time, presented the most animated appearance; the dancers on the green; tea parties in the tent; the porter's lodge crowded with an attentive audience to the vocal exertions of Mr. and Mrs. Allford, who were professionally en-

gaged; the summits of the South-West and other towers filled
with lovers of the foreign weed and cheerful glass; the broad
shadows of the massy walls relieved by the scattered smiling
groups employed in exploring the widely extended ruins, adding
to the general picturesque effect of the scene, whilst the music of
the band stationed in the Fountain Court reverberated through
"the proud baronial pile", devoted to ruin by the iron hand of
Cromwell—these were amidst the sources of enjoyment to the
numerous visitors, on whom the shades of evening stole with but
too rapid strides, to interrupt the pleasures of the day.' [1]

This description gives something of the atmosphere which
members sought in the convivial and ceremonial functions of their
friendly societies. There was very little organised entertainment
as men have since come to know it, there were no annual holidays,
thus the colour and amusement without which life was so dull and
tedious were furnished on the monthly club nights or the feast
days. In this account there are also signs of a rather more elaborate
and almost ritualistic approach than was present in the ordinary
local clubs, for the brethren processed 'in full costume, with the
insignia of the Order', it would probably not be too much to
claim that the affiliated or secret orders added the ceremonial to
the convivial element already present in local societies.

The reasons for the growth of a whole body of secret rites and
symbols along with the growth of a myth of Oddfellowship or
Forestry were varied. There was undoubtedly some conscious
imitation of the masonic pattern among the Oddfellows. An
article in the *Oddfellows' Magazine* for 1829 stated that 'The Order
of Oddfellows was originally instituted on Masonic principles, the
object of which is to cement more firmly the bonds of social feeling and sympathetic intercourse between man and man'.[2] The
masons appeared to do two things, to enjoy a fair measure of
prosperity and to stick together, surrounding their activities and
contacts with a good deal of secrecy. There was in fact a close
connection with the masons in the early years of the Manchester
Unity. The Grand Committee of the Unity on 15 March, 1815,
resolved 'that in consequence of information received from the

[1] *Oddfellows' Magazine*, I, 1829, p. 68.   [2] Ibid., p. 146.

Masonic Grand Lodge, John Wood never be admitted into our Order'. On 25 September, 1816, the Committee recorded that they had been in touch with the masons concerning one of the brethren and had agreed that he was not worthy of membership in any society.[1]

The most important reason for the growth of a distinctive ritual in the different orders was the desire to be unique in some way, not to be as other men were, to have something which no one else could possibly possess; consequently care was taken to ensure that a great part of it remained secret. The aim was to make an Odd-fellow working in a cotton mill in Accrington feel that he had more in common with an Oddfellow working in Portsmouth Dockyard than he had with another Accrington cotton worker who was not an Oddfellow. Hence the whole series of signs and passwords (changed regularly) by which an Oddfellow travelling far from his home district might gain admission to a strange lodge.[2] Finally the effect of these rites was to encourage the myths of Forestry or Oddfellowship to flourish; they became far more to many members than merely societies for insurance against sickness and funeral expenses, they became ways of life.

The ceremonies and rites of the affiliated orders found only a slight reflection in their printed rules, the reason being that if secrecy were to be preserved concerning them they could only be referred to in general terms. The Foresters had what might be called an enforcing clause which stated that 'No court, district or member shall be allowed to use any regalia but that recognised by the Order, and the second degree of Ancient Shepherds, as laid down by the Lecture Books of the two Orders, but that banners and flags be allowed to be used'.[3] The detailed provisions in these

---

[1] Minutes and other Documents of the Grand Committees of the I.O.O.F.M.U., from January, 1814, to December, 1828.

[2] Some examples of passwords from the Minutes of the Grand Committee in 1816 were 'Daniel in the Lion's Den' (May), 'Benjamin—youngest son of Israel' (Sept.), 'Barnabas—son of consolation' (Oct.). In 1821 a new type appeared with 'Relieve distressed brethren' in June.

[3] General Laws of the Ancient Order of Foresters, Rule 101, of 1865 edition. The Ancient Shepherds here referred to was the inner Order of the Foresters and should not be confused with the Loyal Order of Ancient Shepherds (Ashton Unity).

matters lay concealed in the lecture books and were revealed only to the initiated. Similar provision was made in the General Laws of the Oddfellows (M.U.) where detailed instructions were given in the rules as to the keeping of the lecture books:

'That the lecture book and supplement shall be kept in a box with two locks, in the desk of some safe place; the Noble Grand shall keep one key, and any Past Grand appointed by the lodge shall keep the other.

'That no officer or other member shall be allowed to take the lecture books or supplement out of the lodge, under the penalty of two pounds two shillings, which shall be paid into the district fund.

'That lodges occupying lodge rooms in outbuildings, shall remove the box containing the lecture book and supplement into some safe apartment in the house where the lodge is held.' [1]

Fines, suspensions and expulsions were among the penalties prescribed by both Oddfellows and Foresters for members who copied or divulged signs and secrets from the lecture books. The rules of both orders contained sanctions to enforce secrecy in the matter of the password. In the Foresters this was covered by Rule 75: 'That should any brother make known to any person not duly and legally initiated a member of this Order, any of its secrets, and most especially the grip, pass-word, sign, counter-sign or travelling password, he shall be for ever expelled . . .'

In spite of the secrecy which shrouded these activities, it is possible to gather from various sources the main elements of the larger orders' ceremonies. The Manchester Unity of Oddfellows had a number of mystical emblems, the earliest and most important being the Emblem of the Order as it was called. This emblem consisted of a number of figures on a large and dominating base. A large panel on the base represented Britannia, attended by Europe, Asia and Africa, bestowing the Grand Charter on the U.S.A.; on either side were the Royal Arms and the Arms of the City of Manchester. Above this base were the figures of faith, hope and charity along with the shield of the Order; such symbols

[1] Laws for the government of the Independent Order of Oddfellows, Manchester Unity, Rules 257, 258, 259 of 1855 edition.

as an hour-glass, crossed keys, a bee-hive, a terrestrial globe, a lamb and, above them all, the all-seeing eye—or 'the Omniscient Eye of the Great Creator'. Each of these had its meaning to the initiated: the hour-glass symbolised fleeting time while the crossed keys stood for knowledge and security.

In the *Oddfellows' Magazine* for 1829 a lecture on the emblems was printed in question and answer form. The reader was told that the wise members would endeavour to understand all the symbols in the emblem and that there were both philosophical and theological explanations. The explanation given of the eye was that 'the natural eye of man is the medium of the most exquisite pleasure and delight to the mind of that man who has any knowledge of the work of an infinite and almighty Being, the Creator of the Universe; as the organ of sight is the most perfect of our senses, with it we take a view of all things around us, and it gives us a correct image of the different objects placed at such a distance from us, that all attempts to reach them are impossible. Besides, it has the property of being charmed with the mean of its own enjoyment, viewing things the longest without being satisfied. This emblem also reminds us of the Eye of Providence, or the wisdom, power and goodness of the great Jehovah. It is surrounded with rays of light, to intimate that crimes committed under the darkest covers, are naked and open to his view . . . The grand purpose of this emblem is to show to all officers and brothers, that an unerring providence attends all their ways, pries into all their secrets, records all their thoughts and actions on pages more durable than brass; from this we may see the necessity of acting continually as under the inspecting eye of the Great Judge of heaven and earth.' [1] This lecture continued by taking each symbol in turn and attaching to it a quasi-theological or philosophical significance. It was to such beliefs as these that opponents were referring when they accused the orders of 'magic' and 'mummery'.

In reading accounts of friendly society functions in this period, one often encounters references to the costume worn and to the regalia. The Nottingham Oddfellows in 1835 specified what costumes the members of a lodge should wear. The chairman or

[1] *Oddfellows' Magazine*, I, 1829, p. 26.

Grand Imperial was to have a scarlet robe with a crimson cord terminating in tassels of the same colour, a velvet collar in crimson trimmed with yellow silk or gold lace and a velvet turban cap of crimson. The Vice-Grand was to have a blue robe, belt and collar trimmed with white silk or silver lace and a light blue cap. The Imperial Father was to wear a black gown and belt with scarlet facing and a scarlet collar and a black hat. The Secretary was to have a green robe faced with scarlet, collar and turban cap to match. The Treasurer and Wardens were to have collars and caps like the Secretary's. Members were to wear green velvet turban caps and collars of the same material bordered with white. Sashes of various prescribed colours might also be worn by past officers of the lodge. 'For funeral regalia, the grand lodge supply a silk velvet pall and scarfs at a moderate charge.' In hot weather it was permissible to wear appropriate medals indicating rank and status within the lodge in place of these different robes.[1] All the secret orders had costumes which indicated membership and the office held—or once held—within the society, but the actual details of the costume naturally varied from one order to another.

Some of the earliest resolutions of the Grand Committee of the Manchester Unity were concerned with regalia and ceremonial. The first resolution preserved in its Minutes was 'That every brother provide himself with an apron at his own expense', the second was 'That each member subscribe one shilling towards purchasing funeral regalia'. In 1815 it was decided 'That the death supporters carry drawn swords and be attired in caps and gowns', and 'That none but death supporters and tylers walk in caps and gowns during the procession'. It was further resolved 'That every brother appear in a white napkin and white stockings; also a white apron with the following binding:—Past and Present Grands, scarlet sash with mazarine blue rosette on the shoulder and tied with mazarine blue; mazarine sashes to be tied with the sky, sky sashes to be tied with the mazarine.'

The most important ceremony in which the individual member was involved was his initiation into the lodge. This was always

[1] Rules of the Nottingham Ancient Imperial Order of Oddfellows, 1835 ed., forms to be used on various occasions (C).

surrounded by an atmosphere of mystery and awe for it marked
his entry on a new and fuller conception of life, a life of Oddfellowship and as a member of a lodge of other Oddfellows. 'The
lodge is always considered as sacred ground; and no sooner do
those, who in any other place might meet together as enemies,
enter into its precincts, than their bad feelings seem to vanish, as if
by magic, and in their stead, the desire to promote the well-being
and happiness of all reigns predominant.' [1]

The actual form of ceremony for initiation into a lodge of the
Manchester Unity changed during this period and some description of the two forms was given by S. T. Davies in a lecture
delivered to members of the Loyal Guithavon lodge. In the early
nineteenth century 'The candidate for membership on being led
into the lodge-room was carefully blinded, and after passing the
outside and inside guardians he felt a peculiar and mysterious awe
steal over his senses, in consequence of the solemn and death-like
silence that prevailed at the time. Anon, the perverted sense of
hearing became fearfully awakened by the rattling of huge iron
chains, and the un-meaning sounds of men's voices. At this stage
of the inauguration (that is provided he was not tossed and
tumbled among the brushwood, or soused over the head in a
large tub) the bandage is removed from his eyes, and the first
object that his visual organs discovered was the point of a naked
sword close to his seat of love. As soon as he could draw his attention from the worthy warden and his blade, ten to one but his
eyes would rest upon a large transparency of the Old Mortality,
whose ghastly grin would be sufficient to freeze the warm blood
in his veins; while every part of the room was filled with symbols
both of holy and profane things, the meaning of which few could
explain . . . The making ceremony over, each member pledged
the newly initiated brother in a flowing glass, for which he had the
honour of paying.' Davies went on to explain that much of this
had now been abandoned (1850s) in favour of a ceremony 'with
but very little superfluity'—the details of which were secret—
followed by an address 'embodying all the principles of religion

[1] Laws for the government of the Independent Order of Oddfellows, Manchester Unity, Preface to 1855 ed.

ALREWAS: 580, Earl of Litchfield; — Lester, Crown Inn, Litchfield Road.

RUGELEY : 169, Anglesea; — Brandrick, White Horse Inn, Bow-street.

POTTERY AND NEWCASTLE DISTRICT.

District Quarterly Committees.— On March 21, *June* 20, *Sept.,* 26, *all at seven o'clock in the evening ; and* *Christmas Day at two in the aft

BURSLEM: 93, St. John; — Wetherby, Swan Inn; every fourth Monday. 8.

FENTON: 56, Alfred; — Scriven, Roebuck Inn; every fourth Monday. 7.

GOLDEN HILL: 911, Nelson; Obadiah Booth, Nelson Arms Inn; every other Monday. 2.

HANLEY: 101, St. Peter's Victory ; — Hall, George and Dragon, New-street; every fourth Monday. 7.

KEELE : 707, Good Samaritan ; Joseph Cooper, Black Lion; every fourth Saturday. 33.

LANE-END: 334, Magnet; — Bradbury, Union Hotel, Market Place ; every other Saturday. 1.

NEWCASTLE-UNDER-LYNE : 74, St. George; — Shufflebottom, George and Dragon, Iron Market; every fourth Monday. 9.

SCOTTHAY: 374, Farmer's Glory; — Fearnclough, Cross Keys; every fourth Saturday. 35.

SHELTON: 1035, St. Andrews ; Ralph Bowyer, Star Inn, Marsh-steeet ; every other Monday. 2.

STOKE-UPON-TRENT : 136, Lilly of the Valley; — Ferncough, King's Arms; every fourth Monday. 8.

TUNSTALL : 69, St. Martin; — Owen, Sneyd's Arms Hotel ; every fourth Monday. 6.

Facsimile page from a list of the Lodges, 1836.

PLAN REFERRED TO FOR THE YEAR 1836.

No.	WHEN HELD.	JAN.	FEB.	MARCH.	APRIL.	MAY	JUNE.	JULY.	AUGUST.	SEPTEM.	OCTOBER.	NOVEM.	DECEM.
1	Every other Monday	11 25	8 22	7 21	4 18	2 16 30	13 27	11 25	8 22	5 19	3 17 31	14 28	12 26
2	Do.	4 18	1 15 29	14 28	11 25	9 23	6 20	4 18	1 15 29	12 26	10 24	7 21	5 19
3	Every third Monday	4 25	15	7 28	18	9 30	20	11	1 22	12	3 24	14	5 26
4	Do.	11	1 22	14	4	16	6 27	18	8 29	19	10 31	21	12
5	Do.	18	8 29	21	11	2 23	13	4 25	15	5 26	17	7 28	19
6	Every fourth Monday	11	15	14	11	9	6	4	1	5 19	17	14	12
7	Do.	18	15	7	4	9	6	4	8	5 19	17	14	19
8	Do.	25	22	21	11	16	13	11	8	26	3	21	19
9	Do.	4	29	28	18	16	13	11	8	12	31	28	26
10	First Monday in each Month	4	1	7	4	2	6	4	1	5	3	7	5
11	Monday before Full Moon	4	29	28	4	25	27	25	22	19	17	21	20
12	Every other Tuesday	12 26	9 23	8 22	5 19	3 17 31	14 28	12 26	9 23	6 20	4 18	15 29	13 27
13	Do.	5 19	2 16	1 15 29	12 26	10 24	7 21	5 19	2 16 30	13 27	11 25	8 22	6 20
14	Every third Tuesday	5 26	16	8 29	19	10 31	21	12	2 23	13	4 25	15	6 27
15	Do.	12	2 23	15	5	17	7 28	19	9 30	20	11	22	13
16	Do.	19	9	22	12	3 24	14	5 26	16	6 27	18	8 29	20
17	Every fourth Tuesday	12	9	1	5	3	14	5	16	6 20	18	15	13
18	Do.	19	16	8 15	5	10	28	26	23	20	18	22	20
19	Do.	19	16	22	12	17	14	12	9	27	4	29	27
20	Do.	5	26	29	19	26	21	19	16	13	11	6	6
21	Every other Wednesday	13 27	10 21	9	6	4 18	15 29	13 27	10 24	7	5 19	2 16 30	14 28
22	Do.	20	3 17	2 16 30	13 27	11 25	8 22	6 20	3 17 31	14 28	12 26	9 23	7 21
23	Every other Thursday	7 21	4 18	16 30	14 28	12 26	9 23	8 22	4 18	1 15 29	13 27	10 24	15 22
24	Do.	14 28	11 25	10 24	7	5 19	2 16 30	14 28	11 25	8 22	6 20	3 17	1 15 29
25	First Thursday in each Month	7	4	3	7	6	3	7	4	1	6	3	1
26	Every other Friday	1 15 29	12 26	11 25	22	6 20	17	1 15 29	12 26	23	21	18	2 16 30
27	Do.	8 22	19	4 18	1 15	13 20	10 24	15 22	5 19	2 16 30	28	11 25	3 17
28	Every other Saturday	2 16 30	13 27	12 26	23	7 21	18	2 16 30	13 27	10 24	8	5 19	3 17 31

Facsimile page from a Table of Lodge Nights.

and virtue, the effect of which, upon many, has never been effaced'.[1]

A comparable modification took place in the initiation ceremony of the Ancient Order of Foresters during this period. The ceremony of the old Royal Foresters was used until 1835, when this took its place: 'The Chief Ranger addressed the candidate thus, holding two cudgels or quarter-staves in his hand:—"Stranger, We never admit of any becoming members of our ancient and honourable institution but those who are possessed of a bold, valiant and enterprising spirit; and, therefore, before you can be admitted we must have some proof of your courage and ability. You may depend upon being used with the strictest honour."

' "Here are two such weapons as we generally make use of: take them, and give the other to any one of my worthy brothers in the room as your antagonist, and he will show you the use of them."

' "Worthy Sub-Chief Ranger, Senior and Junior Woodwards, you will attend the combat, see the courage of the candidate fairly tried, according to ancient custom, and report the same to me." '

After the combat the Chief Ranger explained its significance to the initiate: how as Adam had to fight with the wild and strange beasts of the forest, so faithful Foresters had to contend with the world, the flesh and the devil.[2] The combat was struck out of the ceremony by the High Court Meeting of 1843. Whatever the society, the initiation ceremony remained very important, even although it became less exotic in later years.[3]

The Grand United Order of Oddfellows published in 1833 a special song which was sung at the initiation ceremonies of that

---

[1] S. T. Davies, *Oddfellowship; Its History, Constitution, Principles and Finances*, 1858.

[2] J. B. Stead, *Historical Sketch of the A.O.F.*, 1891, pp. xiii and xiv.

[3] Similar initiation ceremonies in the trade unions may have been copied from the orders. S. and B. Webb, *History of Trade Unionism*, p. 18, wrote: 'The fantastic ritual peculiar to the Trade Unionism of 1829–34, was . . . taken from the ceremonies of the Friendly Society of Oddfellows.' On p. 113, they quoted a letter claiming that the initiation ceremony of the Leeds Clothiers' Union at that time was derived 'from the ceremonial of one division of the Oddfellows . . . who were flannel weavers at Rochdale, in Lancashire; and all that could well be turned from the rules and lectures of one society into the regulation of the other was so turned . . .'

order. It was called 'The Making Song' and was sung to the tune
of 'God Save The King'.[1]

> Brother, attentive stand,
> While our Most Noble Grand,
>   Gives you the charge;
> The bonds of Society,
> Friendship and Unity,
> Honour and Secrecy
>   Do us unite.
>
> Brother, you've nought to fear,
> Momus's court is here,
>   Love, mirth and joy;
> Harmony here abounds,
> Order our evening crowns,
> Whilst every voice resounds,
>   Long may we be!

Initiations took place during the normal monthly meetings of
the lodge and formed part of what must have been quite an im-
pressive meeting. The first part of the evening was devoted to
business matters, dealing with contributions, the claims of the sick,
elections to various offices or making arrangements for feast day.
After this a lecture seems often to have been read on some aspect
of Oddfellowship and the password necessary to gain admittance
to the lodge-room for the next meeting would be given out.
Sometimes a member who was progressing in the Order would
take another 'degree'. After 1845 there were five successive degrees
in the Manchester Unity and set lectures were read to those taking
these degrees on Charity, Truth, Knowledge, Science and Pro-
gression. Before 1845 there were four degrees designated white,
blue, scarlet and gold. In the first part of the century the ceremony
of admittance to the 'gold' degree included this dialogue:

Noble Grand: 'Whom do you represent?'
Supplicant: 'The son of Onias, the High Priest, who repaired the
House of God and fortified the Temple.'

[1] Harmonia or Song Book for G.U.O.O.F., 1833, p. 31.

Noble Grand: 'In what light will you appear in the lodge?'

Supplicant: 'As the morning star or the moon at full, I shall cheer and refresh the minds of my brethren like the Sun on the Temple of the Most High or the rainbow in the heavens.'[1]

At the end of this business, the meeting would turn its attention to lighter matters and those 'scandals' so much complained of by well-to-do critics would appear. The drinking was usually accompanied by singing and recitations. In 1823 the Annual Moveable Committee of the Manchester Unity resolved that the Harmonia or Song Book be revised, corrected and reprinted 'and that it be generally understood such songs, recitations, toasts, sentiments etc be of a moral, chaste and instructive nature'. Here is the first verse of a song written round the motto of the Order—'Friendship, Love and Truth'—which appeared in the Song Book of 1866.[2]

> When 'Friendship, Love and Truth' abound
> Among a band of brothers,
> The Cup of joy goes gaily round,
> Each shares the bliss of others.
> Sweet roses grace the thorny way
> Along this vale of sorrow;
> The flowers that shed their leaves today
> Shall bloom again tomorrow.

> *Chorus:* How grand in age, how fair in youth,
> Are holy 'Friendship, Love and Truth'.

Interspersed with these songs were suitable toasts. The *Oddfellows' Magazine* for April, 1860, suggested a number that were thought suitable. These expressed a number of widely differing and contradictory sentiments. One toast was 'Farewell to noise and nonsense in all our social gatherings' which contrasted strangely with 'Wine to enliven the heart, and Friendship to uncork the bottle'.[3]

Apart from the initiation ceremony, the only other ceremony

[1] G. J. Holyoake, *Sixty Years of an Agitator's Life*, 1906, pp. 205 ff.

[2] This song along with a number of others has been reprinted in R. W. Moffrey, *A Century of Oddfellowship*, 1910, Appendix IV.

[3] *Oddfellows' Magazine*, 1860, New Series, II, pp. 383-4.

K

which the ordinary Oddfellow could be assured would be held to honour him was the funeral rites of the Order. The local societies had made a point of enforcing attendance at the funerals of deceased members and the local lodges of the Oddfellows practised the same custom. There was also a funeral service to be read at the grave of the deceased after the officiating minister had completed his service. The general laws of the Order governing these matters stated that 'No regalia be allowed at funerals except black sashes, hatbands, white or black gloves and aprons bound with black. And that lodges and districts shall have the power to make such laws as they may think proper for the attendance of members who may reside within the distance of five miles of the lodge house at funerals and anniversaries.

'That it be optional with districts whether they read the funeral service at the grave of the deceased or not . . .'[1] While the general laws were permissive by the middle of the century and did not compel local lodges to enforce attendance, most lodges do seem to have made use of this permission to insert requirements with this effect in their own rules.

Emblems, costume, regalia, ceremonies, passwords and special forms of handshake were used by all the main orders to encourage the enthusiasm and to strengthen the loyalty of their members—especially was this so at a time when a considerable part of the membership was not literate. The secret orders were able to offer the mysteries of membership of a large brotherhood as well as the social attractions of monthly meetings and an annual feast which was as much as the local societies could offer. Probably the attraction of belonging to such a brotherhood or movement played its part in attracting working men to the orders and away from their rivals. The greater financial stability of the bigger orders was, no doubt, a powerful attraction, but it was certainly not the only one. If the outstanding development in English friendly societies between 1815 and 1875 was the growth of the affiliated orders, the form of social companionship offered by them was not insignificant in bringing this about.

[1] Laws for the government of the Independent Order of Oddfellows, Manchester Unity, 1853 ed., Rules 71-2.

Outside of the orders and the local societies, social activities did not play an important part. The failure of the societies run by honorary members to attract large numbers of working men may well have been partly due to the absence or attenuated character of any social activities, while the ordinary large societies had a special appeal for those who disliked 'the nonsense and mixed company of club nights'.

CHAPTER SIX

OTHER ACTIVITIES OF FRIENDLY SOCIETIES

THE work of friendly societies in the fields of medical attendance and of education could not be described as major activities. Yet they are significant because of their effects on the lives of individual members, and, in the case of the former, because of its effect upon the later development of general medical practice in this country. Moreover they also provide good illustrations of the easy adaptability of the friendly societies in meeting the varied social needs of their members.

MEDICAL ATTENDANCE

The principal material benefits offered by friendly societies of all types were sickness and funeral payments, but alongside these there grew up the custom of providing medical attendance in addition in most of the societies. The phrase medical attendance usually meant little more than provision for taking advice from a 'surgeon', 'apothecary' or 'medical officer' as he was variously termed, and by 1875 it often included the supply of such medicines as he might recommend. It did not normally include the provision of facilities at the society's expense for surgical operations or any other form of specialist treatment.

In 1815 it seems to have been customary for most societies to make no regular arrangements of any sort for medical attendance. The typical societies, the local town or village clubs, set forth in their rules the sickness and death payments which they offered but did not mention any free medical attendance among the advantages which membership conferred. The well-nigh universal custom in the latter part of the nineteenth century of requiring a doctor's certificate as proof of incapacity to work before paying sick benefit to their members did not prevail in the average society in 1815. The usual method of ascertaining whether or not a member was sick was that followed by the Friendly Society of Joiners in Newcastle. When any member notified the secretary that he was sick, the stewards were to visit him 'within twenty-four hours' if he lived within a mile and a half of where the society held its meetings. They were to continue visiting him at least once each week during his illness and to report each time to the secretary. Proof of sickness on the part of country members —defined as those living more than one and a half miles from the society's meeting place—was to take the form of a certificate 'signed by the parson or two churchwardens of his parish, or his employer and two respectable householders, declaring where and how he came by his disorder';[1] there was no mention of any certificate signed by a medical attendant and if such a certificate had been sent in by a member the rules made no provision for it being accepted as evidence of sickness against which the allowance could be paid.

The Amicable Society at Patrington required the steward to visit any member 'rendered incapable of working' within twelve hours to find out whether he were a 'proper object' and entitled to sick pay. Any member residing outside of Patrington might send a certificate from the minister and churchwardens or, if he were attended by an apothecary, a certificate from the apothecary would be accepted.[2] The Friendly Brothers of Westminster arranged for their stewards to visit the sick up to a distance of three miles; beyond that a certificate was required from the minister, churchwardens or apothecary.[3] In the local societies the primary duty of determining whether a member was sick enough to qualify for benefit lay not with a doctor but with the stewards, ordinary members of the society, who were to visit the sick man and make up their own minds. In the case of the comparatively few members living at a distance, the certificate of the local minister always seems to have been acceptable evidence; some

[1] Rules and Regulations to be observed by the Friendly Society of Joiners, Newcastle, 1821, Rule XII.

[2] Articles of the Amicable Society at Patrington, 1822, Article VII.

[3] Rules and Orders of the Friendly Brothers, held at the Duke's Head, Westminster, 1810, Rule VII.

societies were also willing to accept a certificate from apothecaries, householders and employers.

The practice of the friendly societies at the beginning of the century was based upon the usual habits of their members for many working men were sick and recovered without ever resorting to an apothecary. The later custom of requiring medical certificates to prove inability to work may well have been connected with the spread of the custom of resorting to a medical practitioner in times of sickness.

By 1875 the position here had changed greatly. The principal societies of the time, the orders, by now normally provided medical attendance as one of the ordinary benefits available to a sick member. The Manchester Unity in the General Rules for the whole Order stated among the objects for which it existed 'providing proper medicine and medical attendance for members'.[1] The cost of medical attendance was to be a charge on the management funds of individual lodges[2] and medical attendance was to be allowed to members of other lodges who lived beyond the limits of the surgeon of their own lodge.[3] Thus by 1871 a comprehensive system of medical attendance had been organised among the Oddfellows of the Manchester Unity which ensured medical attendance for the individual member wherever he might be.

The Ancient Order of Foresters had developed an equally comprehensive system of medical attendance by this time; the individual courts had their own medical officers, and in order to ensure that even those members who lived at some distance from their courts should, if possible, have medical attendance when required, the General Laws stated that 'should a member reside at a distance from his court, and desire the assistance of a medical officer of a court in his neighbourhood, he shall be allowed such a privilege, upon being accepted by such medical officer, and by paying the same contributions into the court as may be paid by the members thereof, during which time he shall

[1] Rules of the I.O.O.F.M.U., 1871 ed., Rule 1.
[2] Ibid., Rule 61.
[3] Ibid., Rule 64.

not be compelled to contribute to the medical officer of his own court'.[1]

The patronised or county societies usually had a medical officer by the 1870s and included his advice among their benefits. There could not be any comprehensive system either in the patronised or in any other type of society as well organised or as widespread as that of the affiliated orders simply because they were not national in scope, and while benefit payments and contributions might be sent from a distance, it was impossible for a society's medical officer to travel the country visiting members living at a considerable distance from the headquarters of their society.

A large ordinary society such as the Hearts of Oak was faced with a special difficulty in trying to organise a system of medical aid. There was no real centre around which its members lived, and it would hardly have been practicable to appoint a medical staff in London with the duty of travelling to visit the sick. Some members of the Hearts of Oak combined together in the Chatham and Gillingham districts and organised their own medical relief association for which they paid thirteen pence a quarter, a shilling to the doctor and a penny for management. This arrangement became more widespread so that by 1871 the members had formed such associations in seventy-three different places.[2] Yet these associations were of necessity only local self-help and no complete provision for the whole society could be organised.

By 1875 the earliest local medical aid associations had been formed. One of these was the Bradford Oddfellows Manchester Unity Medical Aid Association. This was formed as a result of complaints concerning the attendance to members by the part-time medical officers of the various lodges. The association employed a surgeon full-time and forbade him to take any other practice; the association provided him with a house and with all the medicines that he needed. Lodges joining paid three shillings for each member; an individual member whose lodge did not join could do so for three shillings and sixpence each year. For

---

[1] General Laws of the Ancient Order of Foresters, 1865 ed., Law 78.
[2] Young, p. 88.

a further seven shillings annually, the association undertook to provide for the family of a member.[1] In 1884 there were said to be 42 of these medical aid associations in the country containing 164,000 members.[2] During the last quarter of the nineteenth century the growth of these associations was rapid; they were valuable in that they gave medical attendance to the whole family, although many were not large or prosperous enough to be able to employ a doctor full-time and often only contracted with a local practitioner to look after their members.

The change which led to the introduction of medical attendance as a benefit offered by most friendly societies came about only gradually. At an early date the patronised societies required their members to produce the certificate of a surgeon before paying them sickness benefit. In 1826 the Burford Friendly Institution, which was 'under the management of twelve trustees . . . chosen by the Honorary Members' and which met in a school-room, stated in its rules that a member who fell sick 'must forthwith transmit to the Secretary the certificate of a surgeon, of his sickness or infirmity, and his allowance will commence from the date of his certificate'.[3] The society did not provide medical attendance at this stage, it merely demanded the certificate as a guarantee of genuine ill-health. In 1825 E. B. Portman put forward a set of rules for the future Dorset County Society and explained that 'every member assuring any allowance in sickness, and residing within five miles of the office of the agent, upon whose book the assurer's name is entered, shall, in addition to such allowance, be entitled at all times to require and receive from the surgeon, at the expense of the Institution, medical attendance, advice and medicine'.[4] Here again, sick pay was conditional on the certificate of the surgeon. The introduction of medical attendance to the benefits offered by the patronised societies was due to a number of causes. These societies wished to protect their funds against 'shamming' by only paying benefit against a medical

[1] Stanley, p. 206.   [2] *Friendly Societies' Journal*, May, 1884.
[3] Burford Friendly Institution, Rules and Regulations, 1826, Rule 23.
[4] E. B. Portman, *Rules and Regulations for a Friendly Society in the County of Dorset*, 1825, p. 4.

certificate and it was difficult to insist on this unless medical attendance were made available. Medical relief for the poor was chargeable to the rates, and as the sponsors of these societies were moved by a desire to diminish the poor rate, this was another way of accomplishing this aim. Thirdly, it is possible that the founders of such societies were themselves more accustomed to send for the doctor in times of illness than most working men were; for them there was a much closer connection between medical attendance and sickness than there was for the working men who formed and managed the local clubs.

The member of a local society which did not provide a doctor, and who had to resort to one for some reason, if he could not afford the fee would have to fall back on the poor law. The restrictions placed upon medical relief by the Commissioners after the Poor Law Amendment Act of 1834 may have played some part in increasing the number of societies providing medical aid. In one of their circulars the Commissioners discussed the question of whether a member of a friendly society ought to receive an order for the medical officer of the union. 'In the administration of medical relief in this class of cases . . . the Commissioners recommend to the Guardians that they should in general give relief by way of loan, and enforce strict attention to the recovery of the loan by instalments, however small, after the party has returned to his labour. This they will find to be an effectual course to prevent the full and liberal relief which they may naturally be disposed to give on the occasion of sickness, being invaded at the expense of the ratepayers, to the prejudice of the medical profession in general, and above all to the injury of the sick clubs and societies.' [1]

By the 1840s medical attendance was provided by many lodges of Oddfellows. A letter from John Gaskell of Stockport, who was medical officer to a number of Oddfellows' lodges in the town, appeared in the *Oddfellows' Magazine* in 1841 suggesting that there should be some arrangement whereby members who were away from their own lodge could be treated by the surgeon of the

[1] Official Circular No. 3 of the Poor Law Commissioners, 4 April, 1840, p. 31.

lodge nearest to where they were living—on the lines of the scheme which did, in fact, exist by 1875.[1] Another letter suggesting such an arrangement appeared in the *Oddfellows' Chronicle* in 1846 from the surgeon of the Good Intent lodge, Northampton, who complained that the want of some such system involved lodge medical officers in hardship, for of twenty travelling or visiting Oddfellows that he had treated in the past twelve months, in only one case had the man actually paid him.[2] That these suggestions for making medical aid available to members at the nearest lodge were made shows that in the experience of these writers lodges usually had a medical officer.

The appointment of medical officers was not required by the general rules of the Order at this time, nor were medical certificates always required before sick pay was issued. One writer in the *Oddfellows' Chronicle* complained that the Order could get no overall picture of the sickness from which its members suffered since lodge sick visitors had not sufficient knowledge to judge a member's illness in cases where there was no professional evidence. 'Our general laws do not provide that sick members, when supported by the general contribution funds of their lodges, shall be under medical or surgical treatment.'[3] Thus while medical treatment provided by the lodges was usual in the Manchester Unity by the middle of the nineteenth century, it was not yet universally enjoined by the general laws.

It was among the small local societies that a system of medical relief was least developed. The rules of the Independent Friendly Society held at the Jug and Glass Inn, Whitwell, showed that in 1859 the society had no medical officer; resident members in Whitwell were to be visited by the Society's wardens within twelve hours of becoming sick, and from those living at a distance a certificate was required 'attested by a surgeon or by his employer'.[4] In the rules of the Friendly Society of Dinnington of 1866, no medical attendance was included among the benefits of

---

[1] *Oddfellows' Magazine*, VI, 1841, p. 252.
[2] *Oddfellows' Chronicle*, 15 October, 1846.   [3] Ibid., May, 1847.
[4] Rules of the Independent Friendly Society of Whitwell, 1859, Rules XVII and XIX.

membership and sickness was to be determined by visits by the master of stewards 'at least once every week'.[1]

But these small local societies which did not provide medical aid were a fast decreasing proportion of the friendly society movement by the close of this period. Medical attendance had by then come to be accepted as one of the normal benefits which the membership of a friendly society conferred. The widespread recognition which friendly society medical practice had won was shown by its inclusion in the act of 1858 to regulate the qualifications of practitioners in medicine and surgery. 'After the first day of January, 1859, no person shall hold any appointment as a physician, surgeon or other medical officer . . . to any friendly or other society for affording mutual relief in sickness, infirmity or old age, or as a medical officer of health, unless he be registered under this Act.'[2]

Most friendly societies employed their 'surgeons' or 'medical officers'—as they seem to have been indifferently termed—on a contract basis. The medical men usually undertook to attend any member in sickness and to supply medicines in exchange for a payment of so much per member per year for all of the society. A typical arrangement was that made by the Foresters' Court No. 2,988 in Northampton. Rule 20 stated that 'A surgeon or surgeons shall be elected who shall continue in office during the pleasure of the Court. It shall be his duty to examine all candidates; attend the sick members residing within three miles of the court-house, and provide them with proper and sufficient medicine during their affliction. . . . The surgeon shall receive for each financial member, residing within the distance of three miles from the courthouse, 1s. 6d. per half-year for his services, which shall be considered full remuneration for the surgeon's trouble and care, which shall be paid from the management fund of the Court. . . .'[3]

The surgeon was conceived of as the servant and employee of the members of the society; the method of appointment—

---

[1] Rules and Orders of a Friendly Society at the Falcon, Dinnington, 1866, Rule XVI.

[2] 21 & 22 Vict., c. 90, section xxxvi.

[3] Rules of Court No. 2,988, 'Centre of England', 1871, Rule 20.

by all of the members gathered in their court or lodge—emphasised this. A medical officer who failed to give satisfaction would also fail to be re-elected. This system was often criticised by the doctors who felt that election depended upon the wrong things. 'The election, being scarcely ever unanimous, leaves a dissatisfied minority, which any accidental circumstance readily converts into a majority. Another surgeon is then named, and if the proposal is backed by a lower offer of pay—e.g. if the candidate is willing to farm the club at 2s. per head when the old surgeon required 2s. 6d.—the change is almost sure to be made! Complaints among members of insufficient and careless attendance, under such wretched arrangements, are inevitable.' [1]

The actual rate of remuneration also led to friction between the societies and the medical profession. One of the earliest clashes took place between the Manchester Unity and the medical profession in Glasgow in 1844. Twenty-seven surgeons there had accepted contract practice for lodges at 2s. 6d. per head; a meeting of the medical men of the city was called and a dispute broke out between the twenty-seven who held contracts and the rest of the profession who did not. Those practitioners who worked for the societies were regarded as 'blacklegs' by their brethren in the city for accepting such mediocre and un-professional rates of pay.[2] The *Oddfellows' Chronicle* put the Society's case in this dispute. 'One of the most important benefits connected with Oddfellowship is the advantage of securing medical attendance to every member during sickness, for the moderate annual sum of 2s. to 2s. 6d. on the principle of mutual cooperation. For this sum, paid by every member, the services of the most respectable of the medical profession are freely obtained. A mere trifle taken separately, in the aggregate is found to be reasonable compensation. Throughout the entire Unity, indeed, the most skilful medical officers are secured, and there is often considerable rivalry at the annual election of the medical attendant of the lodge. The system is found to work in every respect most admirably, and we have never heard of any well-grounded complaints.' [3]

---

[1] H. W. Rumsey, *Essays in State Medicine*, 1856, p. 158.
[2] *Oddfellows' Chronicle*, 15 May, 1845.   [3] Ibid., 27 December, 1844.

In 1844 the Select Committee on Medical Poor Relief was told that the usual rate of pay was 2s. to 3s. per head and was further told that medical men had to take such terms 'for bread, and in the hope that it may lead to something better'.[1] It is clear either that the doctors were willing to work for such remuneration or else that they were so badly off that they were not in a position to refuse, for there was no outstanding rise in the rate of pay in the next thirty years. According to the British Medical Journal doctors were still accepting appointment at 3s. and 4s. as late as 1900, but 2s. or 2s. 6d. were no longer mentioned.[2]

The main conflict was with the larger societies and orders, but the more local societies also appear to have been able to get medical attendance at equally low rates. It was not a case of the large affiliated orders using their size to force down the rates of remuneration. In 1848 the Dorset Friendly Society came into conflict with some local practitioners for offering 2s. 6d for each member, 2s. for a wife, 1s. for the first three and 9d. for each additional child under the age of sixteen.[3]

About twenty years later the medical profession tried to organise a withdrawal of labour in the course of a struggle with the societies of Birmingham. A local committee of doctors was formed and demanded 5s. per head per annum. The struggle centred around the Cannon Street Male Adult Provident Institution, a large ordinary friendly society, which refused to increase its figure of 2s.6d. per annum; all but two of the Society's medical officers resigned. The Lancet and the British Medical Journal urged all practitioners to stand firm on this issue and an attempt was made to spread the movement for a 5s. minimum payment to the whole country. Wolverhampton practitioners decided not to work for less than 5s. per head and support came from Southampton, Whitby and South Yorkshire.[4] Yet where resident doctors boycotted a club, strangers were usually willing to enter

[1] Evidence of H. W. Rumsey before the Select Committee on Medical Poor Relief, 5 July, 1844, qq. 9078–81.

[2] British Medical Journal, 1900, II, p. 1039.

[3] Provincial Medical and Surgical Journal, 26 January, 1848.

[4] Accounts of the movement appeared in the Lancet and in the British Medical Journal in 1868.

the district and to take up their appointments, in spite of the calls for unity and loyalty in the *Lancet*.[1]

The system of friendly society contract practice may, in fact, have attracted the less well-qualified type of practitioner who could not make a living from fees alone and the young man anxious to make himself known in a district. Thus although the penalty for not pleasing the members would often be that a society would get another medical officer, the treatment and attendance which club members received may well not have been of the highest quality. This at any rate was the opinion of some who were neither doctors nor members of the societies. An Assistant Commissioner to the Poor Law Board told the Select Committee on Medical Relief of 1854 that 'the club patients do not get anything approaching the attendance which the paupers get from the medical officers of the unions'.[2] A guardian from Dewsbury told the same Committee that he had heard many complaints from members of friendly societies of neglect on the part of their medical men.[3] Dr. Rumsey explained this feeling on the part of members of the societies as a result of 'the consciousness that their medical contractor was underpaid which naturally rendered them suspicious as to the proper fulfilment of the contract'.[4] The medical profession, as represented by the British Medical Association, complained about contract practice for many years and the *British Medical Journal* printed complaints concerning it for year after year in the latter part of the nineteenth century.

Yet in spite of the criticisms made by doctors and others of friendly society contract practice, this system did enable many men to have some medical attendance who would otherwise have lacked it or have been compelled to conform with the poor law requirements before obtaining medical relief. Whatever its critics might have said, it was this system, developed by the friendly societies, which formed the pattern on which the National Health Insurance scheme was based after 1911 and this, in its

---

[1] *Lancet*, 6 March and 8 April, 1869.

[2] Evidence of R. Weale before the Select Committee on Medical Poor Relief, 30 May, 1854, q. 369.

[3] Evidence of J. Ellison before the same Committee, 16 June, 1854, q. 2606.

[4] H. W. Rumsey, *Essays on State Medicine*, 1856, p. 159.

turn, was expanded into the general practice branch of the health service in 1948. The medical man today still receives an annual sum per head for those on his panel and undertakes to provide them with medical attendance, even although the annual composition is now paid by the state instead of the friendly society. Historically the main importance of friendly society contract practice may well lie in the basis it formed for the much wider scheme now in operation.

EDUCATION

It cannot be claimed that the friendly societies played any part of comparable importance in spreading education as they did in bringing the developing medical facilities within the reach of a large section of the population; yet although education was not of such immediate apparent concern to the friendly societies as medicine, the educational ferment of the middle years of the nineteenth century in the nation as a whole had its effect on the largest friendly society of the time, the Manchester Unity.

The 1840s were a period of great educational activity and strife. Kay-Shuttleworth produced a scheme which was accepted by the Committee for Education of the Privy Council for a state training college and model school. The scheme was rejected by the advocates of the voluntary principle on the issue of the religious instruction which would be given in such an institution. Kay-Shuttleworth then founded a training college privately at Battersea; his example proved to be decisive and training colleges run by the rival sects were rapidly established throughout the country. 'The system was consolidated by the Minute of 1846—apprenticeship to a master, a course in a training college, the certificate, additional pay for the trained teacher and the unkept promise of a pension at the end.' [1]

The Minute also established the new grant system of £1 from the Treasury for every £2 raised locally for the schools. The new scheme was bitterly attacked by the dissenters who claimed that since the Church of England was the richest of the denominations,

[1] G. M. Young, *Early Victorian England*, 1934, II, p. 466.

it would receive the largest share of the grant under this new system. The Oddfellows of the Birmingham District petitioned Lord John Russell's government supporting the new grants. They claimed 'That the means of educating the present juvenile population is exceedingly limited, and quite inadequate to the wants and necessities of the great masses of the people. That your memorialists believe that nineteen-twentieths of the juvenile and adult crime of this country is caused by improvidence, intemperance and poverty; and that such improvidence, intemperance and poverty are as a rule brought about exclusively by the gross state of ignorance in which the people have been allowed to remain. That your memorialists have viewed with astonishment and regret the opposition that has been got up to the contemplated grant for educational purposes by some of the religious sects of the community.' [1]

During the agitation of 1846 and 1847 which accompanied the inauguration of a system which was to form the basis of elementary education until the end of the century, the *Oddfellows' Chronicle* for the months of August, September and October, 1846, was largely concerned with the problem of national education. The Prussian system was described in some detail, particular attention being given to the method of administering the schools and of training teachers in that country. The Prussian example was commended as suitable for imitation here. As for the religious difficulty, the clergy had become incompetent to discharge the duty of public education. 'The circles of Church and State are no longer co-extensive. All citizens have a right to be taught. The Church can no longer teach all. Facts prove that a large proportion cannot procure knowledge for themselves. Who, then, is to discharge this primary debt of society to its members? Europe answers, "THE STATE".' The official journal of the Manchester Unity—the *Oddfellows' Magazine*—urged in January, 1847, that the new educational system should include not only schools but also libraries which should be paid for out of the rates to avoid the need for charging fees.

The educational ferment of the 1840s was not confined to

[1] *Oddfellows' Chronicle*, May, 1847.

education for children; this decade also witnessed much activity in adult education. Mechanics Institutes had first appeared twenty years earlier, but a considerable number were still being established. These institutions provided classes in a variety of subjects and at varying standards of difficulty in the evenings. Often they acquired their own building and opened a library and newspaper room in addition to running formal classes. 'A feature of the late 'forties, however, both in Lancashire and Yorkshire, was an outburst of missionary activity which penetrated to the country-side.' [1] The institutes were also improving their organisation and in 1848, after some difficulties, the 'Lancashire and Cheshire Union of Mechanics Institutes' was constituted with Thomas Hogg as its paid secretary and lecturer.[2] An article in *Eliza Cook's Journal* described how mutual improvement societies and classes were springing up in many places and went on, 'In addition to the numerous Mutual Improvement Societies established by young men in their immediate localities, many others have recently been established by lodges in connection with Odd Fellows' Societies. And when we consider the extensive organisation of Oddfellow-ship throughout Great Britain . . . it will be obvious how powerful an instrumentality for good would be such institutions.' [3]

The Oddfellows' institutes were occasionally the subject of articles in the *Magazine*. The Provincial District Grand Master of the Birmingham district wrote of the institute there 'We are going on most gloriously in this district with our library and schools, and we have every reason to believe that, in a short time, we shall have the most valuable and useful literary institution in the town. From the catalogue you will perceive that we have about six hundred and twenty volumes, and that many of them are of a very valuable and expensive kind. We have also classes on Sunday mornings, Tuesday, Wednesday and Thursday evenings. . . .' In 1845 a new building was erected to house the institute. The ground floor consisted of a hall capable of holding

---

[1] M. Tylecote, *The Mechanics Institutes of Lancashire and Yorkshire before 1851*, 1957, p. 67.
[2] Ibid., p. 85.
[3] *Eliza Cook's Journal*, 19 May, 1849, p. 33.

five hundred, 'well ventilated and lighted with gas'. Lectures on topics in philosophy and mechanics were to be held for the benefit of members in this hall. On the next floor the library was housed in a room fitted to take about 1,500 volumes. There was also accommodation for a house steward and committee rooms. It had cost the Birmingham district of the Manchester Unity a little over £1,000 to build.[1] These institutes did not always confine their membership to Oddfellows. The institute founded by the Poor Man's Friend lodge at Rochdale had by 1848 widened its entry to permit those who were not Oddfellows to become subscribers.[2]

A recent historian of the Mechanics Institutes has described them as serving 'a limited class of persons . . . the lower middle class and the "superior order of the working class" (defined by Samuel Smiles as those who were receiving from twenty to thirty shillings a week in wages)'.[3] The Manchester Unity itself seems to have had at this time a smaller proportion of the poorly-paid and a larger leavening of self-made men among its members than most of the societies, moreover the latter tended to occupy the leading positions in the Order. The reflection of the Mechanics Institutes movement within the Oddfellows is, therefore, hardly surprising.

In lodges which were not connected with an Oddfellows' institute the current enthusiasm for adult education sometimes took the form of a definite scheme of lectures planned for 'intellectual and moral elevation'. 'The plan for introducing instructive lectures on literary and scientific subjects is evidently calculated to be most highly beneficial. . . . The members have imbibed something of the taste for literature and science and with this taste have acquired more of the capability for intellectual

---

[1] *Oddfellows' Magazine*, VIII, 1845, p. 170.

[2] *Oddfellows' Chronicle*, April, 1848. A prospectus of the Oddfellows' Literary Institution at Rochdale was printed in this issue of the *Chronicle*. This gives a picture of the nature and extent of the activities undertaken by such institutions and it is reproduced in full in Appendix E. Most of the Oddfellows' institutes were naturally in the North in such towns as Bradford, Manchester and Preston where the Order's main strength lay.

[3] Tylecote, op. cit., p. 258.

enjoyment, and are now beginning to seek and to demand increased opportunities for mental culture.' [1]

It is of some interest to examine the arrangements actually made in one of the lodges for such lectures. On 17 February, 1840, the Clarence lodge, Lewes, resolved that 'It is highly desirable to blend instruction with amusement, so as to enhance the moral and intellectual character of the brethren'; a committee was set up to organise a programme of essays and readings. There was to be a reading on every alternate lodge night and the contents of the readings and essays were to be recorded in a book set aside for this purpose. An introductory address was given to the lodge by Provincial District Grand Master George Cooke, who suggested the study—among other things—of astronomy, geology, geography, natural history, science, music and the arts.[2]

One of the attributes of any large social organisation in an age when literacy is becoming more widespread is usually a journal. The affiliated orders produced a literature which might be regarded as a contribution and an encouragement to education among their members. The *Oddfellows' Magazine* appeared first in 1824 and continued until 1847 when there was a break in publication of ten years, starting again in 1857. From 1844 to 1848 the unofficial *Oddfellows' Chronicle* was published on the Isle of Man and had a national circulation. The *Foresters' Miscellany* was first issued by the Ancient Order of Foresters in 1836 and continued through this period in some form. The *Rechabite Magazine and Temperance Recorder* first appeared in February,

---

[1] *Oddfellows' Magazine*, VI, 1840, p. 270.

[2] Ibid., p. 205.

'Some further idea of the topics which came under review can be gained from the list of subjects on which papers were read to the City of London lodge during the winter of 1862–3:

"On Social Economy."

"How far do benefit societies conduce to the prosperity of a nation?"

"On the Life of Lord Macaulay."

"On Old English Music, with illustrations."

"On the importance of the culture and development of the mental faculties, and the expediency of the Manchester Unity encouraging the intellectual improvement of its members." '

—*Oddfellows' Magazine*, New Series, IV, 1863, p. 133.

1840, and established itself as the magazine for friendly society teetotallers. It continued under slightly varying titles and with some breaks in publication throughout the nineteenth century.

Although magazines published by friendly societies were naturally regarded primarily as vehicles for the dissemination of information concerning the society and its activities, an important subsidiary aim was that of spreading culture and enlightenment generally to the members. A good deal of space was devoted to these cultural topics. Articles appeared in the *Foresters' Miscellany* on 'The Elevation of the People', 'History in Names', 'Modern Civilisation', 'The Press', and 'Physical Education'. The *Oddfellows' Magazine* devoted more space to this type of article, along with short stories and poetry, than to purely friendly society matters. The eight quarterly numbers covering 1857 and 1858 contained forty-nine poetic compositions, a number of short stories including one by Leigh Hunt and articles on Beaumarchais, Italian History, Der Freischutz, Rabelais and William Cowper. The *Magazine* for these years was in no way exceptional; the amount of poetry and the number of very solid articles for which some Oddfellows must have had a taste is astonishing. The *Rechabite Magazine and Temperance Recorder* was, perhaps, an exception to the enthusiasm for general adult education shown by these journals; even its short stories pointed the moral and its articles were on such subjects as 'Remarkable Deaths of Drunkards' or 'Teetotalism in Cockermouth'. The poetic contributions were equally barbed; 'The Curse of the Nation' or the 'Temperance Star' were typical.

The current enthusiasm for education which spread in England in the nineteenth century was shared by the larger friendly societies. It showed itself in the form of Oddfellows' institutes, lectures, magazine articles and petitions; in all these ways the societies reflected the widening diffusion of interest in popular education.

CHAPTER SEVEN

FRIENDLY SOCIETIES AND THE STATE

IN any study of the development of friendly societies the attitude of the state and of the governing classes generally must
play an important part, for those who controlled the state had it
in their power to create conditions which would help or hinder
the societies. It is most convenient to treat the development of the
state's attitude and of the societies' relations with the state in three
main sections: firstly, the attitude towards friendly societies of
those classes whose opinions usually prevailed in matters of
governmental legislation and administration; secondly, the legislation itself; and, thirdly, the establishment of the office of
Registrar and the growth of that office into a department of
government.

THE ATTITUDE OF THE 'INFLUENTIAL CLASSES' [1]

The instructions which Her Majesty's Friendly Societies' Commissioners issued to their Assistants in 1871 charged them to
obtain evidence not only from the societies and their members,
but also from 'magistrates, stipendiary and other, county court
judges, the clergy of the Church of England, dissenting ministers,
guardians of the poor, relieving officers, medical practitioners,
actuaries, and other public functionaries, or private persons, who
may be conversant with the subjects of inquiry, or any branch
of them'.[2] It was the opinions of men such as these which greatly
influenced the attitude of the state towards friendly societies
throughout this period. The gentry and clergy were only doing

---

[1] Term used by E. Lynch Daniell, Assistant Commissioner, in his Report on
Ireland, 1874, p. 1.
[2] Instructions to Assistant Commissioners, 1871—among the unpublished
papers of J. M. Ludlow. The nature of 'influential classes' itself changed during
this period. The inclusion of actuaries and medical practitioners, for instance,
would have been unlikely in such a list fifty years earlier.

their duty towards the working man when they gave freely of their advice as to how the societies should be organised and run —that was the prevailing feeling in 1815 and it still prevailed in 1875, although by the latter date the growth of the affiliated orders meant that the societies and their members were also considered to be in a position to advise.

The attitude of these classes did not remain constant. In 1815 and until about 1830 there was considerable fear that friendly societies were revolutionary in some way, and even those who did not fear that benefit clubs were themselves agents of revolution feared that they might be used as cloaks behind which revolutionaries might do their work. There are many letters preserved among the Home Office papers which show this fear. A memorial from five engineering employers of London dated 27 May, 1813, complained of the conduct of their journeymen, 'Your memorialists were anxious to believe that the existing laws of the realm would have been adequate to repress these evils, but they are sorry to declare after long and painful experience that these laws are artfully and efficaciously evaded and defeated by and under the mask of Benefit Societies, institutions which have created, cherished and given effect to the most dangerous combinations among the several journeymen of our district. . . . This state of things cannot long exist, and if there is not shortly some legislative regulation adopted, your memorialists are deeply impressed with the most serious apprehensions that absolute ruin will overtake the master manufacturers of the empire, and the journeymen will assume an overbearing, oppressive and mischievous character that will be alike dangerous to the prosperity and tranquillity of the country. Your memorialists are fully persuaded that the recent mischievous associations, disgraceful riots and ruinous burnings in the neighbourhoods of Nottingham and Manchester have had much of their origin in compacts of this nature, and as long as bodies of journeymen are allowed to constitute themselves into societies under any denomination of benefit while the present laws of management of such societies exist, your memorialists have no hope of having the evils redressed which they have lamentably experienced.' The reception which this

'Memorial respecting Combinations and Benefit Societies' received at the Home Office may be judged by a note added there. 'This appears to me to be worth supporting. . . . Benefit Societies [unless better regulated] will be the ruin of the country.' [1]

Four years later, in 1817, the Town Clerk of Kidderminster wrote to Viscount Sidmouth stating that the strikes in his town were over and that he hoped it would not be necessary to use the soldiers any more. He added a paragraph which illustrated how ostensibly genuine friendly societies gave support to striking workers. 'There are many sick clubs in this town and nearly the whole of the men are members of them, and the funds are placed in the hands of the manufacturers and others at interest. As soon as the men struck, most of this money was called in for the purpose of maintaining the weavers out of employ, and it is feared a deal of it is spent. I am fearful as they have found such funds useful to them, that they may materially increase them and use them at some future combination. . . . As the law stands now, these clubs, otherwise of great use, may become injurious.' [2] The attitude of the Home Office in 1818 was succinctly expressed by this sentence taken from a letter sent by the Under-Secretary, Henry Hobhouse, on 21 August, 1818, '. . . You cannot please me better than by turning your attention to the friendly societies, by which I have no doubt the system which is the bane of your country is in a great degree supported.' [3]

There is little doubt that friendly societies were regarded as a means of overcoming the legal disadvantages under which working men laboured as a result of the Combination Acts.[4] Even those who saw the value of the societies as agencies of genuine sick relief often warned against their potential political danger. In a pamphlet in 1801 Eden, while supporting the general principle of friendly societies, found it necessary to warn that 'Association is the prevalent malady of our times. In all cases its real object should be ascertained, and its progress vigilantly watched, by

[1] H.O. 42/133. This and the following Home Office Papers are reprinted in A. Aspinall, *Early English Trade Unions*.
[2] H.O. 42/172.   [3] H.O. 73/3/261.
[4] A. Aspinall, *Early English Trade Unions*, p. xxiv.

those who are entrusted with the government of the country.'[1]
In 1806 Colquhoun in a general account of a scheme for dealing
with the poor included a chapter on friendly societies which was
by no means hostile in tone, yet, after a description of their size
and extent, he felt obliged to add that a time might come 'when
numerous societies of ill-informed individuals, open to seduction,
and heated by political frenzy, artfully worked up, and holding
164,424 public meetings, under a benevolent and legal pretence,
at 9,672 different alehouses, may alarm and afflict the peaceful subject: and here a question arises; how far it may be practicable to
organise these excellent institutions, so as on the one hand to
render them productive of benefits infinitely more extensive to
the parties interested, and on the other to divest them of their
tendency to moral and political evil'.[2] In 1819 Thomas Courtenay,
in seeking permission to introduce his Friendly and Parochial
Benefit Societies bill into the Commons, admitted that it was
commonly believed that friendly societies were used for subversive purposes, but he pleaded that his bill (which was designed to
improve their financial stability) would at least make matters no
worse than they already were in this respect.[3]

This fear that friendly societies were subversive, or at least
capable of being used for subversive ends, was said by Stanley
in his Report to have persisted until the Reform Bill of 1832;
'there is no doubt that what with corresponding societies, radical
unions and other associations of workingmen, it was a hard thing
for any group of such persons to associate themselves without
being accused of being Jacobins and Levellers'.[4] Certainly by the
1870s any fear of the societies among the better-off had subsided,
yet there were still some people in influential positions who
harboured suspicions as late as the middle of the nineteenth
century. In 1848 a Committee of the House of Lords which had
been appointed to inquire into the measures that would be necessary to enable the Manchester Unity to register, found that in

---

[1] F. M. Eden, *Observations on Friendly Societies*, 1801, p. 24.
[2] P. Colquhoun, *A Treatise on Indigence*, 1806, p. 117.
[3] Parliamentary Debates, XXXIX, 25 March, 1819.
[4] Stanley, p. 3.

general it was a useful institution but added that 'it is clear that an affiliated body with such resources at its command must become highly dangerous if it should ever be turned from its legitimate objects', also that 'certain customs have been adopted by the lodges of the Society, which, without contributing to its utility, are open to very serious objections; viz. the employment of secret signs, the circulation of lectures, and the introduction of orations after the burial service'.[1]

Along with suspicion in the years before the Reform Bill, there mingled what might be called an attitude of paternalism, that the working man must be looked after and told what to do since he was incapable of managing his own affairs. This usually took the form of recommendations to compel working men to join 'properly supervised' societies so as to reduce the poor rate—or even to abolish it altogether—and coupled with this there was the notion that in some way the societies ought to be taken over by the poor law authorities or that they should come under the control of those who were 'more responsible'.

Various schemes on these lines had been put forward in the eighteenth century. Thomas Gilbert in 1782 had proposed that parochial friendly societies should be aided from the poor rate so as to encourage the poor to join them. In 1787 he proposed that the contributions of the unemployed to their sick clubs should be paid out of the rate so as to maintain them in full membership.[2] In 1796 Pitt brought forward the 'Heads of a Bill for the Better Support and Maintenance of the Poor'. This provided for compulsory parochial clubs which were to collect subscriptions from the fit and pay benefits to the sick and aged, the benefits to be supplemented if necessary from the poor rate.[3] This bill was abandoned before it passed through the Commons. In 1806 Colquhoun published proposals for a scheme for a 'National Deposit Bank for Parochial Societies' which should be established under government patronage for assuring allowances to members

[1] Report of the Select Committee of the House of Lords on the Bill to permit affiliated Societies to register, 1848.
[2] Walford, *Insurance Cyclopaedia*, 1870–8, IV, pp. 385–6.
[3] Printed in Eden, *The State of the Poor*, 1797, III, p. cccxiii.

of parochial benefit societies in accordance with their rate of subscription. While compulsion on individuals to join the parochial
society was not recommended as such, six copies of the scheme
were to be sent to the minister and churchwardens in each parish
who were to summon the overseers, arrange with them for a
meeting of all the parishioners 'to whom the scheme, with all its
advantages, shall be fully disclosed', and attempt to enrol them.[1]
Colquhoun estimated that 3,500,000 would be eligible to join
such societies and that the organisation would have a total income
of £7,000,000 per annum. He claimed that 'perhaps through no
other medium will it be possible to establish a hedge or barrier
against the misfortunes of indigence'.[2]

This paternalistic feeling appears to have reached its height in
the period between the last years of the Napoleonic Wars and the
1830s. In 1814 Jerome de Salis, Count of the Holy Roman
Empire, published his *Proposal for Improving the System of Friendly
Societies*.[3] He proposed that there should be a Poor Assurance
Office in each parish run by the overseer of the poor. All working
men were to contribute, the gentry could join as honorary
members and help to raise the initial capital for the society
by their donations. Where it was still necessary, the poor rate
might be used to supplement income initially, but the object of
the whole exercise was to enable the poor rate to be abolished
'in process of time'. de Salis expressed a point of view whose
influence was growing and which may be seen in other works,
official reports and in the foundation of patronised societies at this
time.

The theme of developing 'managed' societies and reducing
the poor rate can be found in the Report of the Commons' Committee on the Poor Law in 1817. The Committee believed that
'these societies, judiciously managed, have in some parishes tended
greatly to the melioration of the condition of the People' and
'that it will be expedient to enable the Parishes to establish
District Parochial Benefit Societies, under the joint management

[1] Colquhoun, *A Treatise on Indigence*, pp. 123–4.
[2] Ibid., p. 120.
[3] J. de Salis, *A Proposal for Improving the System of Friendly Societies*, 1814.

of the contributors and nominees of the Parish'.[1] In the same year the Vicar of Harrow wrote: 'It is the great benefit of Friendly Societies that they teach a man to avert his eye from the workhouse; to look to the blessing of God on his own endeavours; to get his bread by the sweat of his brow. . . .' [2] In 1819 Thomas Courtenay, in the course of his speech in the Commons on the Friendly and Parochial Benefit Societies bill, said that many persons thought the provision through such societies for the needs of the poor so desirable 'that its operation ought not to be left to the voluntary acts of individuals, but that the poor should be compelled to resort to it'.[3]

Thus the position had been reached where many of the influential classes were anxious that working men should be obliged to join government-supervised friendly societies because it would be good for them in a moral sense and to relieve the poor rate of the greater part of its burden. One reason why compulsion was never enforced was the difficulty of deciding the financial basis for any scheme as early as the 1820s; the failure of the Committees of 1825 and 1827 to find reliable tables has been noticed above.[4] By the time such tables were available, the desire to enforce membership of publicly managed societies had gone; in 1834 the passing of the Poor Law Amendment Act changed the situation; moreover, many of those whose political influence increased after 1832 worshipped efficiency in the business of government as in the business of commerce and showed little concern for the welfare of others in the paternalistic sense.

In the absence of compulsion, the 1820s were a period when magistrates and clergy endeavoured by voluntary efforts to found societies under their own control ('properly managed') and in this way to accomplish a moral purpose and to diminish the poor rate. Perhaps the best-known—because it was the most publicised —society of this type at the time was the Southwell Friendly Institution founded on 23 April, 1823, as a result of the efforts of

[1] Report of the Select Committee of the House of Commons on the Poor Laws, 1817, p. 12.
[2] J. W. Cunningham, *A Few Observations on Friendly Societies*, 1817, p. 22.
[3] Parliamentary Debates, XXXIX, 25 March, 1819.
[4] Supra, ch. IV.

Thomas Becher who was both prebendary of Southwell and chairman of the Quarter Sessions at Newark.[1] These county type of societies, founded and run by honorary members often on the initiative of the local magistrates, were intended 'as a means of improving the condition of those classes which are in part dependent on the rates, and with the hope of eventually superseding the poor law by their means'.[2]

From the 1830s a new attitude grew up towards friendly societies just as there were changes in some other aspects of the political outlook at the time; the feeling that all would be well if the societies were left alone by the government was spreading and the new approach to the poor law problem in 1834 meant that the possibilities of using officially sponsored societies in conjunction with the poor relief system received less notice. The main point that came to be stressed was the need to encourage independence, to get the societies and their members to stand on their own feet—the necessary corollaries of this attitude being a denial of the value of state interference or aid and the assertion that financial stability could not be imposed upon friendly societies by legislative means but only by persuasion, by getting the individual members to realise where their true interests lay and to act accordingly.

These points had become generally accepted well before the end of this period, and in the debate on the second reading of the Friendly Societies bill of 1875 in the Commons, spokesmen for and against the measure still found it necessary to claim that the encouragement of the independence of the individual was the mainspring for their arguments either for acceptance or rejection. A government speaker replying to Lowe for the Liberal opposition said that the right hon. gentleman had urged the desirability of leaving the working classes to manage their own affairs and this was exactly what the bill proposed to do. Lowe, in leading the attack, had already asserted that the working classes were able

[1] J. T. Becher, *Observations on the Report on the Laws respecting Friendly Societies*, 1826, p. 13. Concerning Southwell Friendly Institution, see also *The Constitution of Friendly Societies* by the same author, 1824, and his evidence before the Commons Committee of 1825.

[2] Stanley, p. 8.

to manage their own affairs and that it was a pity that they were not to be left alone to do so.[1] In the climate of opinion neither side dared to confess that there was any virtue in state interference, both sought to pose as the more effective champion of independence.

As early as 1831 the Society for the Improvement of the Working Population in the County of Glamorgan in a pamphlet on Friendly Societies appealed to this notion of the independence of the individual as the main advantage which such societies could offer. The ideal labourer was the one who could say, 'Poor as I am, I am obliged to no man for a farthing, and therefore I consider myself as independent as any gentleman or farmer in the parish.'[2]

Looking back on the period from the beginning of the reign of Victoria to the time at which he wrote in 1890, C. S. Roundell thought that 'the record of the progress of Friendly Societies is a record of the sturdy self-help, the self-dependence, the independence of Englishmen, of which as a nation we may well be proud'.[3] This was a fairly typical comment by one of the 'influential classes' on the success achieved in spreading the idea of self-reliance and independence among working men. In the 1880s Dr. Baernreither, an Austrian deputy, published his book on *English Associations of Working Men*[4] and spent more than a year in England gathering materials for this. He moved mostly among the 'influential classes' and the views he put forward in his book reflected their acceptance of the importance of self-reliance and independence.[5]

The principal enemy of independence was thought to be state aid or interference in the field of friendly society activity. The superiority of English over foreign working men was constantly stressed in this respect. Roundell claimed that what the state was

[1] Parliamentary Debates, Third Series, 222, 25 February, 1875.
[2] Cowbridge Tracts, No. 5, *On the Advantages of Friendly Societies*, 1831, p. 2.
[3] C. S. Roundell, *The Progress of the Working Classes during the reign of the Queen*, 1890, p. 22.
[4] J. M. Baernreither, *English Associations of Working Men*, London, 1889. First published at Tübingen, 1886.
[5] Ibid. (trans.), especially ch. 4, section 3.

doing for the Germans, English working men were doing far better for themselves, and to illustrate this point he set these two statements side by side. The first was taken from a speech by the Kaiser in 1890 to his Council of State. 'By my decree of the 4th inst you were informed that it is my desire to hear the views of the Council of State regarding those measures which are necessary for the better regulation of the condition of the working classes. . . .

'I rely upon the tried loyalty and devotion of the State Council in the labours which now lie before it. I do not lose sight of the fact that all the desired improvements in this domain cannot be attained by State measures alone. The labours of love, of church, of school, have also a wide field for fruitful action, by which the ordinances of the law must be supported and aided; but if, with God's help, you succeed in satisfying the just interests of the labouring population by the proposals you make, your work may be sure of my Kingly thanks, and of the gratitude of the nation.'

The second statement was taken from a speech by the Postmaster-General on 14 December, 1880. 'It cannot, I venture to say, be too constantly borne in mind that self-help and self-reliance are the only sure guarantees for social, national, and, may I add, moral progress. Legislation which encourages the people rather to rest upon State-help than to rely upon themselves, however well-intentioned, will prove incalculably mischievous in the end; and to every measure which is brought forward with the object of improving the condition of the people, this simple test should be applied—will it tend to encourage them to rely upon self-help?' [1]

This whole question of the extent to which state aid might be desirable was discussed by the Royal Commissioners in their Report. After setting out the theoretical case for and against state regulation, they came to the conclusion that the troubles of friendly societies could be divided into two main groups, '(1) those which arise from the want of proper information, and which generally affect the principles on which the society is

[1] Roundell, *The Progress of the Working Classes during the Reign of the Queen*, 1890, p. 22.

founded; and (2) those which arise from improper management, which may be the result either of ignorance, or of negligence, or of fraud. As regards the first class of evils, we believe that it is in the power of the government to do a great deal to correct it without inconvenience to the public, and without any undue interference with the liberty of the promoters of societies. As regards the second class, there is more difficulty. . . .' [1] The point which the Commissioners made here—that the duty of the state was not detailed supervision but the collection and distribution of actuarial data—had been made by Edwin Chadwick in an article in the *Westminster Review* as early as 1828.[2] Chadwick argued that one of the most important duties of a government was to provide the community with the means to defend itself, at least expense, against the evil consequences which flowed from sickness and death. This the government should do by collecting records of deaths and sickness and the circumstances surrounding such occurrences and by drawing up tables for insurance purposes based on this information. The government alone was in a position to secure the necessary information. The wealthier classes had 'ardent desires to render disinterested service to the labouring population within their immediate neighbourhoods. The misdirection of these sympathies, and their operation in inconsiderate charities and the profuse expenditure of the poor's rates, have formed the most potent means of retarding the improvement of the labouring population; and it seems to us that the wealthy have yet to learn what are the means by which they may render the best services; which means, we conceive, will be found to be in acting with the labouring classes rather than for them: in enabling them to act for themselves, by provident institutions, securely based on sound knowledge of the nature of that which we have treated.' These ideas were especially noticeable in the attitude of the Poor Law Commissioners towards the societies after 1834.

[1] R.C.F.S., 4th Report, 1874, para. 58.
[2] E. Chadwick, 'An Essay on the Means of Insurance against the Casualties of Sickness, Decrepitude and Mortality', *Westminster Review* (No. XVIII), April, 1828.

The advantageous terms on which registered societies were able to invest in government securities was seen by some as an unjustifiable subsidy from public funds. Those who were of this opinion were the foremost opponents of state aid and in 1873 Gladstone seems to have been among their number. In a private memorandum which the chairman of the Royal Commission circulated to his colleagues on 1 December, 1873, he stated that he had had a note from Gladstone in which he hoped that the Commission would draw attention to the charge which friendly societies imposed upon the Treasury. Northcote added, 'We must, of course, say something on that point, though I hope we shall agree in justifying the charge. I will endeavour to draw a paragraph.' [1]

It was generally felt that the state should go no further in helping societies to become solvent than the preparation and publication of suitable tables; to compel the societies actually to use such tables would have been an unjustifiable interference and it might have involved the state in some moral liability if a society thus acting on the orders of the government experienced a spell of sickness among its members which did not coincide with the national averages and in consequence found itself bankrupt. The Royal Commission discussed and rejected a suggestion to fix by law a minimum contribution which friendly societies should be required to demand for particular benefits.[2] That a main cause of the widespread insolvency of societies was the inadequacy of rates of premium for the benefits promised was admitted; the remedy was felt to lie in the collection and publication of data and the power of persuasion and publicity to cause the more backward societies to adopt safer tables.

Such publicity and pressure had in fact been exercised for many years before 1874 and there was never any lack of advice recommending the increase of subscriptions and the adoption of 'reliable' tables. When efforts to enforce sound tables were abandoned after the act of 1834, the advocates of 'soundness-

---

[1] 'A Memorandum on the present state of our work' by Sir S. Northcote, 1 December, 1873—among the unpublished papers of J. M. Ludlow.

[2] R.C.F.S., 4th Report, 1874, para. 57.

through-persuasion' redoubled their efforts and a whole literature on the actuarial aspect of friendly society management was published.

The more extreme opponents of state aid or interference were even prepared to find positive virtue in insolvency. In the debate in the House of Commons on the bill of 1875, Sir Charles Dilke found no objection to the idea of the state making a small annual outlay to collect and spread information concerning the soundness of various sets of tables so that the best of the working classes and small tradesmen might make use of such information, but 'to force this upon them by government interference is to make them at once dislike it, and in reality to defeat your own ends. . . . When difficulties arise they will shift the responsibility from off their own shoulders, and caste the entire blame on the government and its officials. If you leave them to find out the value of actuarial skill for themselves, they will value it in a higher degree, and be less likely to resign the advantages which once they will have conquered. By what means have caution and prudence in the investment of savings been, so far as they have been, instilled into the minds of the richer classes? By experience, taught and brought home to them through the losses of the less intelligent.' [1]

Alongside the feelings of suspicion and the attempted paternalism before about 1830 and the emphasis on self-reliance after that time, there persisted throughout the whole period to 1875 a tendency on the part of clergy, magistrates and publicists generally to pass judgements on the purely moral effects of the friendly society movement. Such judgements had their effect on the attitude of the state to the societies since they could either help to create a sympathetic or an unsympathetic view of them among those who made and administered the law.

The earlier magazines of the Manchester Unity of Oddfellows contain a number of refutations of allegations brought against that 'secret' society as well as more general statements defending the Order's conception of its function. One of these magazines gave an account of a disputation which took place before the public between the Past Provincial Grand Master of the Potteries

[1] Parliamentary Debates, Third Series, 222, 25 February, 1875.

M

district and a Methodist minister on the subject of Oddfellowship.[1] The minister summed up his arguments in a final speech in which he explained that members of such societies were required to take 'horrid oaths', that he had proof that God condemned such societies since He had sent His judgement on four men who were Oddfellows 'by cutting them off in their sins' and that no man had a right to enter secret societies since there could be no secrets where a man was a Christian. This disputation took place in 1834; in the next year the Vicar of Leeds refused a request to preach to the Oddfellows of that district on the occasion of their annual procession, stating that 'he did not preach sermons for Oddfellows, or anything of the kind'.[2]

Clerical disapproval was shown again in 1841 when the Archdeacon of Durham in his Visitation Charge to his clergy wrote: 'And here I desire for a moment to draw your attention to the practice sought to be established by the society of Oddfellows, that of offering public prayers and making orations at the graves of their comrades. This is to supersede the church service, even that beautiful funeral office which stands first among human compositions; and to introduce in its place a novelty savouring in its character more of Deism than of Christian faith, for we find no mention of the Saviour; no, that holy name at which we bow, "at the name of Jesus every knee shall bow", is wholly omitted. It is enough to name this pretension in order to indicate your course; but it is my duty to give it you as well as the church-wardens in charge, to prevent, as far as in you lies, by friendly reasoning, remonstrance and even stronger measures, the contempt of our holy office, and the desecration of our holy places, which such an act involves; and when overborne by force or clamour, to appeal to the ecclesiastical courts for protection.'[3]

These protests, Anglican and Nonconformist, seem to have arisen out of a certain clerical feeling of jealousy towards the Oddfellows as a secret order with beliefs and rites of its own which might rival those of the churches in the eyes of their members. The clergy who took this view were scarcely likely to

---

[1] *Oddfellows' Magazine*, III, 1834, pp. 1–8.
[2] Ibid., IV, 1837, p. 47.   [3] Ibid., VII, 1843, p. 230.

permit the 'good works' of the societies in a material sense to mollify the harshness of their judgements or to soften their denunciations. Other clergy based their opposition to the orders on a feeling that they were in some way atheistic. When legislation was before the House of Lords to permit the affiliated orders to register for the first time in 1850, the Bishop of Oxford raised objection to the legalisation of the Manchester Unity on the ground that their lectures had been written by an atheist, George Holyoake. He concluded that the lectures must, therefore, have been atheistic.[1]

At the same time there were many clergy who felt that even the secret societies were useful and should be encouraged. The minister of Queen Street Chapel, Leeds, was presumably among these for he offered to preach to the Oddfellows when the Vicar refused his services in 1835.[2] The feeling of something akin to jealousy among some of the clergy did not extend beyond the secret (or affiliated) orders; local clubs might need to be admonished or encouraged on moral grounds but they made no spiritual pretensions which were likely to provoke clerical wrath. The clergy were, in fact, foremost among those who encouraged the formation of the county societies and were sometimes honorary members of village clubs. Some of these men sought to establish societies which would serve as vehicles of moral training as well as insurance concerns. Cunningham, Vicar of Harrow, was typical of many clergy when he denounced the alleged vices of many existing societies vigorously but also put forward plans for the formation of more moral organisations: 'let the clergyman of every parish in the empire, in conjunction with the leading authorities in his parish, establish a friendly society, of which this is the corner stone, THAT NO ONE OF ITS MEETINGS BE HELD AT A PUBLIC HOUSE'.[3]

Drinking and dissipation were universally deplored among the influential classes, clergy and others. The Society for the Improvement of the Working Population in the County of Glamorgan

---

[1] G. Holyoake, *Sixty Years of an Agitator's Life*, 1906, Part II, p. 202.
[2] *Oddfellows' Magazine*, IV, 1837, p. 48.
[3] J. W. Cunningham, *A Few Observations on Friendly Societies*, 1817, p. 27.

told the 'Farming and Labouring Population' that 'The funds of the society being wasted in riotious living, and at the same time the amount of payments to sick and infirm members being greater than the receipts would allow, the box of the society soon became empty'.[1] As late as 1874 the Royal Commission included a condemnation of drinking on club nights in its Report and printed in paragraph 668 an extract from the *Manchester Examiner* telling how one Thomas Steinthorp at a club meeting 'had drunk so freely of whisky that he died on his way home'. This was said to have happened in 1871. The labouring classes were not very well off, thus, apart from all questions of temperance, it was wrong that through their friendly societies they should spend any of their substance on drink, feasts, aprons, banners 'and other trumpery'; such was the prevailing view among the more prosperous during this period. The Registrar did his best to enforce the legal prohibition of these activities among the registered societies, yet these customs continued—and so did the condemnations.

Throughout the period the 'influential classes' appear to have understood the attitude of the members themselves to their societies only very partially—if at all in many cases. This failure to understand naturally made their advice not only less welcome but also much less effective than it might otherwise have been. In the early days when a mixture of the paternalist and anticombination spirits prevailed, the state made its first legislative foray. According to Eden's inquiries, in many places 'the good intentions' of Parliament were 'misunderstood'. The registration by the local magistrates was often regarded as the preliminary to 'inquisitorial police' and even the confiscation of funds; consequently in many places he found that the societies had dissolved themselves and shared out their funds before the government could seize them. In Yarmouth there were about twenty societies at the time the act of 1793 was passed but by 1795 only three remained; 'unfortunately they conceived that it was intended to place their funds under the control of the magistrates'.[2] In the

---

[1] Cowbridge Tracts, No. 5, 1831, p. 4.
[2] Eden, *Observations on Friendly Societies*, 1801, p. 5.

industrial districts when the Combination acts were in force there was a great reluctance to accept the supervision that registration was thought to imply.

Whether the 'influential classes' were advocating a form of paternal assistance, repression of combinations or the importance of independence, their arguments were all too often invalidated by an absence of understanding of the true situation. The Society for the Improvement of the Working Population in the County of Glamorgan in its Tract on Friendly Societies in 1831 claimed that as a result of the act of 1829 'those who wish to feast must feast at their own expense' since 'not even a shilling can be taken from the common fund to be applied to the expenses of feasting'.[1] Just how accurately this statement represented the true condition of affairs in 1831 is shown in an earlier chapter.[2]

Thirty years later *The Times* could comment: 'There is no greater puzzle in this country than its friendly societies. They are at variance with the sound principles of morality and prudence; they belie the boasted honour and good sense of the Englishman; they prove him incapable of self-government; not a word can be said in their defence.' [3] Ignorance here was tinged with an attitude of condescension, and advice given in a condescending manner came to be increasingly resented, especially in the main orders.

The reaction of the friendly societies to the lectures that were read them can be judged to some extent by the articles which appeared in their own magazines reflecting their attitude to self-appointed advisers. In April, 1857, Charles Hardwick, Deputy Grand Master of the Oddfellows, wrote: 'Many but partially-lettered operatives know sufficient, from practical experience, to smile at the blundering attempts at instruction essayed by parties who are not only incapacitated for the task from sheer want of knowledge of the subject, and of the temper and condition of the people, but who are sometimes so ill-bred as to leave their manners at home, and adopt a supercilious and impertinent tone when they condescend to address the people.' [4] One year later the

[1] Cowbridge Tracts, No. 5, 1831, p. 5.
[2] Supra, ch. 5.   [3] *The Times*, 7 October, 1860.
[4] *Oddfellows' Magazine*, New Series, I, 1859, p. 70.

Oddfellows' Magazine again printed an article defending the societies by pointing out the shortcomings of those who presumed to give advice. 'These men of common sense and sound feeling . . . too often gain their experience from the overseer's office and the jail, and afterwards expend a prodigious amount of philanthropic eloquence on the depravity of the "people", concerning the best portion of which they know just about as much as they do of the internal economy of the household of the King of Timbuctoo.'[1]

The effect of this advice on the societies might best be judged in the story of their development and none of the theories so popular among the 'influential classes' concerning the duties and conduct of the societies had much more than a very limited direct effect. The condescending and, perhaps, patriarchal magistrates and clergy who founded the county type of societies did serve some of the poorer rural labourers of the South, but this type of society had no following in the industrial districts. The Report of the Assistant Commissioner for Wales, Monmouthshire and Herefordshire stated that the influential gentlemen and clergymen 'prompted by feelings of benevolence alone' were 'patronising and endorsing right and left these ricketty schemes, with apparently no more sense of the responsibility they were incurring than if the proposed society had been one for supplying soup to the poor under exceptional pressure, or flannel petticoats during a sharp winter'.[2] The lack of attention to the advice and opinions of such gentlemen on the part of the main working men's orders was probably advisable from the point of view of the material welfare of their members. The picture which emerges is of the larger societies and especially the orders developing steadily in their own way, paying little attention to the cries of influential bystanders.

In an indirect manner, however, the attitude of the 'influential classes' was more important for it virtually decided the nature of the legislation passed by Parliament and the government's administration of those laws. All societies were affected by the attitude of the ruling circles in as much as they reacted to the laws passed concerning them.

[1] *Oddfellows' Magazine*, New Series, II, 1860, p. 70.
[2] Report of E. Lynch Daniell, Assistant Commissioner, 1874, p. 1.

FRIENDLY SOCIETY LEGISLATION

From the first friendly society act in 1793 to the act of 1875 Parliament passed nineteen acts whose main purpose was to regulate the societies in some way; during the same period five parliamentary committees inquired into some aspect of their activities in addition to the Royal Commission appointed in 1870. The principles lying behind this governmental activity fell broadly into two main groups. Until about 1830 the idea of encouraging the friendly societies to develop under the supervision of the local justices with a view to relieving the demands of the poor rate can be seen in the legislation enacted. Proper supervision by the magistrates would eliminate any temptation to indulge in or to support illegal combinations or to help trade unions. In 1825 and 1827 parliamentary committees showed some concern for the financial stability of the societies, for if they were to be effective in keeping the poor off the rates, they would have to be financially sound.

From the 1830s the legislation reflected the feeling that the government should stand back, that there should be some other solution of the problem of a high poor rate than magisterially supervised societies and that such government administration as there was could be carried out by a central agency rather more efficiently than some local justices appeared to administer the law.

The main principles which guided legislation until 1830 can be seen in the act of 1793 which also established a pattern which all the other main acts were to follow during the nineteenth century in that it offered certain benefits in return for voluntary registration. This act, for the Encouragement and Relief of Friendly Societies,[1] was introduced into the Commons by George Rose who believed that the societies should be encouraged as they offered the poor an alternative to living on the rates in time of sickness. It governed the position until 1819 with such minor modifications as were contained in the acts of 1795[2] and 1809.[3] The measure enacted 'that it should be lawful for any number of

[1] 33 Geo. III, c. 54.
[2] 35 Geo. III, c. 111.   [3] 49 Geo. III, c. 125.

persons in Great Britain to form themselves into and to establish one or more society or societies of good fellowship, for the purpose of raising from time to time, by subscriptions . . . a stock or fund for the mutual relief and maintenance of all and every the members thereof in old age, sickness and infirmity, or for the relief of the widow and children of deceased members . . .' The second clause required all rules and regulations of societies to be taken before quarter sessions where the justices might confirm those which were in accordance with the provisions of the act while no alteration of the rules might take effect until it had the approval of the justices.

The hope that the societies, supervised by the magistrates, would lead to the reduction of the poor rate was expressed in the preamble which declared that the formation of such societies 'is likely to be attended with very beneficial effects, by promoting the happiness of individuals, and at the same time diminishing the publick burthens'. Section 17 established that any member of a society who could produce a certificate of membership was not to be removable under the laws for the settlement of the poor unless he actually became chargeable to the poor rate. Among the other benefits which were made available to such registered societies was security for its funds which arose from their ability to sue and to be sued; thus they could protect themselves against dishonest officers. Priority of claim for any of the monies of the society on the estate of a deceased or bankrupt officer and exemption from certain stamp duties were also granted by this act. These privileges were added to by the Savings Bank act of 1817[1] which gave registered societies the right to deposit their funds in savings banks at the very favourable rate of interest of 3d. per cent per day which prevailed at that time.

The distress which followed the war served to emphasise that whatever other achievements might be credited to the act of 1793, it had not lightened 'the heavy burthens upon the parishes' of the poor rate of which its preamble complained. Moreover the instability of the finances of many local societies which had registered under the act was pronounced. In 1818 a bill was introduced

[1] 57 Geo. III, c. 130.

into the Commons to secure the establishment of parochial friendly societies; this passed through the committee stage but was not taken any further as a consequence of the dissolution of Parliament in that year.[1] In 1819 an act was passed 'for the further protection and encouragement of Friendly Societies'.[2] The preamble to this act began 'whereas the habitual reliance of poor persons upon parochial relief, rather than upon their own industry, tends to the moral deterioration of the people, and to the accumulation of heavy burthens upon parishes; and it is desirable, with a view as well to the reduction of the assessments made for the relief of the poor, as to the improvement of the habits of the people, that encouragement should be afforded to persons desirous of making provision for themselves or their families out of the fruits of their own industry . . .' Thus the aim of the act of 1793 remained unchanged: the poor rate was to be reduced and, if possible, the morals of the poor were to be improved; but the method of achieving this aim was to be more closely supervised than under the previous act for the magistrates were not merely to be asked to approve the rules of a society but also its tables. The justices were instructed to confirm the tables only after they had been approved by two persons known to be 'professional actuaries or persons skilled in calculation'. It was sometimes suggested that societies became insolvent because there were too many of them, therefore the justices were now to consider whether the formation of any new society would be useful, regard being had to the existence of other societies in the district. The act conferred the privilege of investing funds directly with the National Debt Commissioners.

These financial safeguards and privileges along with closer supervision would, it was hoped, make friendly societies both more stable and, by this means, more popular among those likely to come to the parish for relief. In fact, the requirements laid down proved to be too elaborate and consequently impractical. The requirement that the consent of two experts and of the justices be given to tables was ineffective since the raw material for assessing

[1] Appendix to the Registrar's Report, 1860.
[2] 59 Geo. III, c. 128.

their validity in terms of facts and figures of working-class sickness and mortality were not available. The formation of a new
society in a district, far from making existing societies smaller
through defections to it, might well bring in men who had hitherto been attracted to no society.

The failure of this legislation to achieve its desired aim of reducing the numbers who resorted to poor relief by attracting an increased number of working men into financially stable societies
led to the appointment of a Committee of the House of Commons
to investigate the question of the laws respecting friendly societies
generally. The Report[1] of this Committee began with an historical
review of the position since 1793; it proceeded then to deal with
the various complaints against the societies and accepted that some
had served as a disguise under which funds had been raised to support strikes and combinations,[2] but it felt that the supervision of
the magistrates under the act of 1819 would deal adequately with
this problem. The question which was discussed at length in the
Report was that of financial solvency in the societies. The Committee's conclusion was that the provision in the act of 1819 requiring the certificate of two men skilled in calculation and of the
magistrates before a table of contributions and benefits could be
adopted was a sound one and had been productive of much good.
But the picture was marred by certain difficulties; some benches
had accepted the certificates of 'men skilled in calculation' whose
opinions on the probability of sickness were not to be depended
upon and there were too many societies with fewer than two
hundred members, which was believed to be the smallest 'safe'
number. The Committee also felt that societies investing with the
National Debt Commissioners should have their tables approved
by their actuary and that they should make regular returns to the
Commissioners.

A further Select Committee in 1827 concerned itself almost
entirely with the consideration of life and mortality tables.[3] The

[1] Report from the Select Committee of the House of Commons on the Laws
respecting Friendly Societies, 1825.
[2] Ibid., p. 23.
[3] Report from the Select Committee of the House of Commons on the Laws
respecting Friendly Societies, 1827.

wisest conclusion of this Report was that 'the materials for decision are even yet incomplete'. This second Committee recommended that returns from societies should be sent to the clerk of the peace and not to the National Debt Office.

The Reports of these two Committees formed the background to the act of 1829 and by this date it was becoming clear that some of the elaborate requirements of the act of 1819 were not of practical value. The new act[1] repealed all the earlier statutes and consolidated many of their provisions. The principal change introduced concerned the mode of registration. The rules of a society had in future to be confirmed by the barrister appointed by the National Debt Commissioners to certify the rules of savings banks before being submitted to quarter sessions; the certificate given by the clerk of the peace remained the legal evidence of a society's registration. Other important changes required registered societies to publish an annual balance sheet which was to be available to members and to make a quinquennial return of sickness and mortality to the clerk of the peace for transmission to the central government. Thus the first links with the central government were established by this act—although they were only indirect. The requirement of a certificate for the tables from a person 'skilled in calculation' was now dropped, but the justices were still required to satisfy themselves in a general way that the tables of payments and benefits 'may be adopted with safety to all parties concerned'.

The act of 1829 is important in any review of the legislation concerning friendly societies down to 1875 because it was the last act before the change in heart on the part of the governing groups became apparent in the attitude of Parliament to the societies. The old idea that the societies should be encouraged so as to lessen the poor rate and to impove the morals of working men and that the local gentry—through the bench—should keep an eye on the societies to keep them out of mischief, both financial and social, all of this can still be seen in 1829. But now, for the first time, the central government began to take a part in the administration of registered societies, although it was only an indirect function and

[1] 10 Geo. IV, c. 56.

the returns had to be sent in the first place to the clerks of the peace. Later legislation bears the mark of the advent to power of men who believed in more efficient organisation dependent on the central government rather than on the enthusiasm of the local J.P.s. A central registrar was soon to be appointed and the growth of efficient administration was part of the growth of the organs of central government at the time. This may be viewed against the background of a great increase in the political importance of men who believed in efficiency in their businesses and of the demands of the Philosophic Radicals for a like efficiency in the reorganisation of the poor law and of local government. Indeed, it has been asserted that Chadwick took the new centralised administrative machinery provided for the friendly societies in 1834 as his model for the new poor law organisation.[1]

The Friendly Societies act of 1834[2] began by repealing earlier provisions requiring tables of contributions and of benefits to be submitted to the justices and leaving the question to be determined by the societies themselves. This was a significant move away from the paternalist concept. The next clause repealed the earlier requirement that the rules should be submitted to quarter sessions and be confirmed by the justices before being binding. In future two copies of the proposed rules were to be sent by the secretary of a club direct to the barrister appointed to certify the rules of savings banks; provided that the rules did not in any way contravene the law, he was to certify them, returning one copy to the society and sending the other to the clerk of the peace for the county to be filed with the Rolls of the Sessions. The justices were now 'required, without motion, to allow the same'. These rules were to be binding on a society from the date when they were confirmed by the barrister, not from the date when they were eventually filed by the clerk of the peace. The returns of sickness and mortality specified in the act of 1829 were in future to be sent to the barrister confirming the rules and no longer to the clerk of the peace. One more important change was made by the act and that was an addition to the purposes for which friendly societies

[1] S. E. Finer, *The Life and Times of Edwin Chadwick*, 1952, p. 90.
[2] 4 & 5 Wm. IV, c. 40.

might be formed; to a list of specified aims was added the phrase 'or for any other purpose which is not illegal'—a very wide definition. This act marked the change from local to central administration and gave the registered societies a good deal more freedom than they had enjoyed hitherto. The movement away from close control by the magistrates may well have been the beginnings of the effect of the spread of ideas of 'laissez-faire' in this aspect of public life. Central registration certainly proved to be more systematic and less haphazard than local.

A comparison of the requirements which the founders of a society had to meet in 1820 (under the act of 1819) with those which the sponsors of a society had to meet in 1840 (under the act of 1834) illustrates the difference in the attitude of the government over the period of twenty years.

1820	1840
The magistrates, before authorising the registration of a society, were to satisfy themselves that it was really desirable and that there did not already exist some other society in the same district adequately fulfilling the same need. If such another society existed, it was considered inexpedient to register a second.	No restriction or requirement.
Rules of a proposed society were to be submitted to the justices in quarter sessions; they would approve or not as they considered 'fit and proper'.[1]	Two copies of the rules were to be submitted to the government barrister who was to certify them as long as they were 'in conformity with law'.[2]
The tables of payments and contributions were to be submitted to the justices who were not to confirm them 'until it shall have been made to appear to such justices, that the said tables . . . are such as have been approved by two persons at the least, known to be professional actuaries or persons skilled in calculation'.[3]	No requirement respecting tables.

[1] 59 Geo. III, c. 128, section ii.
[3] 59 Geo. III, c. 128, section ii.

[2] 4 & 5 Wm. IV, c. 40, section iv.

1820	1840
Permitted aims of the society had to fall within the following definition: 'A Friendly Society or Institution, whereby it is intended to provide by contribution, on the principle of mutual insurance, for the maintenance or assistance of the contributors thereto, their wives or children, in sickness, infancy, advanced age, widowhood or any other natural state or contingency, whereof the occurrence is susceptible of calculation by way of average . . .' [1]	Permitted aims of the society were extended by the addition of the clause 'or for any other purpose which is not illegal'.[2]
No requirement in respect of returns of sickness and mortality.	'The returns of the rate of sickness and mortality . . . shall be transmitted to the barrister or advocate by whom the rules of the society may have been certified.' [3]

The tendencies to leave the societies alone, to refuse state aid (or interference), to encourage independence and to bring members to realise and to act in their own interests so far as the financial stability of the society was concerned—all of these tendencies governed the pattern of friendly society legislation from 1834 until the end of this period. In 1840 an act[4] was passed which limited the exemption from stamp duties and the right to invest in savings banks or with the National Debt Commissioners to those societies whose individual assurance policies did not exceed £200. This restriction was aimed at those mutual life offices which had registered under the act of 1834 to obtain these financial concessions.

In 1846 the title of Registrar was given to the barrister who certified the rules of societies by the act of that year.[5] This act abolished the last vestiges of local registration; in future an official to be known as the Registrar of Friendly Societies was to certify rules and to file copies of them instead of forwarding such copies to the clerk of the peace. The barrister holding this appointment was to receive a net salary of £1,000 per annum in place of the fees which he had charged applicants for registration hitherto. The

[1] 59 Geo. III, c. 128, section ii.   [2] 4 & 5 Wm. IV, c. 40, section ii.
[3] Ibid., section vi.   [4] 3 & 4 Vict., c. 73.   [5] 9 & 10 Vict., c. 27.

Registrar was to collect the quinquennial returns of sickness and mortality and power was given him to settle disputes, but as no authority was conferred on him to compel witnesses to attend inquiries, this power could hardly be exercised. The list of purposes for which friendly societies might be formed was made more explicit since 'it is expedient that such purposes be better defined', yet a blanket clause remained covering 'any other purpose which shall be certified to be legal'. Among the purposes stated explicitly were insurance against fire, flood and shipwreck; the limit of £200 for any one person's insurance was maintained.

The affiliated orders seem to have been in the minds of the sponsors of the act when they included section ix, for this declared that the Corresponding Societies act and the Seditious Meetings act should not apply to any society duly established under the statutes in force relating to friendly societies. This did remove one major obstacle to the registration of the 'secret' orders, but there remained others which prevented them from registering and thus securing legal protection for their funds. Because of the great increase in their membership, these affiliated orders were receiving more attention than hitherto, and in 1848 a Select Committee of the House of Lords considered a bill which would have made it possible for them to register. The Committee recognised the utility of the orders and recommended that they should be permitted to register provided that they abandoned their secret signs, lectures, funeral orations and the like.[1] The main obstacles to registration which remained and which Parliament would have had to remove were, firstly, the requirement that every lodge should register separately—in the case of the Manchester Unity the fees would have amounted to £4,200 at the rate of £1 per registration for its 4,200 lodges—secondly, the fact that the procedure for dealing with disputes in the orders was not acceptable to the law and, thirdly, that the annual moveable meetings of the Oddfellows and the Foresters could not be considered as general meetings called in the county where the society was established as the law demanded.

[1] Report of the Select Committee of the House of Lords on the Provident Societies Fraud Prevention Bill, 1848.

The outcome of the recommendations of the Lords' Committee and of a second Committee from the Commons was the act of 1850.[1] The most important provision of this act was that which made it possible for a society 'or branch thereof' to register, thus permitting societies of the affiliated order type to protect their funds and property at law. The societies were now required to make returns annually to the Registrar showing their 'funds and effects' and the penalty for failing to provide these was to forfeit the right to sue at law. The Registrar was to lay before Parliament abstracts of these annual and quinquennial returns. The first of these was issued in 1852 and was followed by a Report and set of tables (Finlaison's) from the National Debt Office.

The act offered two grades of registration, establishing 'certified' and 'registered' societies. The certified societies were to be those whose tables were certified by the actuary to the National Debt Commissioners; societies whose rules alone were submitted were to be known as registered friendly societies. Any society which granted an annuity had to comply with the requirements of a certified society.[2] This position did not survive the next friendly society act, for in 1855 the distinction between certified and registered societies was dropped although an actuarial certificate in accordance with the terms set out before was still required if a society offered 'a certain annuity or a certain superannuation'.[3]

The act of 1855[4] was to remain virtually unchanged for twenty years—longer than any other between the years 1815 and 1875. The purposes for which friendly societies might be formed were once again re-defined; this time the limitation of risks to those of which 'the probability may be calculated by way of average' was dropped while the blanket clause became 'any purpose which shall be authorised by one of Her Majesty's Principal Secretaries of State'. All fees for registration, which had been reduced to half a crown in 1850, were now abolished. The jurisdiction of the Registrar in matters of dispute was also abolished and the right of appeal to the county courts in such cases was enacted, although this was not to interfere with the right of a society to settle its disputes in

[1] 13 & 14 Vict., c. 115.   [2] Ibid., section vii.
[3] 18 & 19 Vict., c. 63, section xxvi.   [4] 18 & 19 Vict., c. 63.

LAWS

FOR THE

GOVERNMENT OF THE INDEPENDENT ORDER

OF

ODD-FELLOWS,

MANCHESTER UNITY,

FRIENDLY SOCIETY.

ADOPTED BY THE A.M.C., JUNE 14, 1851.

REGISTERED UNDER FRIENDLY SOCIETIES ACT, 13 AND 14 VIC., CAP. 115.

MANCHESTER :

PUBLISHED AND SOLD BY THE G.M., AND BOARD OF DIRECTORS, 22, DALE STREET.

1851.

The first registered rules, 1851: facsimile title page.

GENERAL LAWS.

NAME, CONSTITUTION, AND OBJECTS OF THE SOCIETY.

I. — This Society shall be called the INDEPENDENT ORDER OF ODD FELLOWS, MANCHESTER UNITY FRIENDLY SOCIETY ; and shall consist of a Committee, called the Annual Moveable Committee, or A.M.C., composed of deputies appointed by Districts as herein provided for. A Board of Directors, Three Officers of the Order, called the Grand Master, or G. M., the Deputy Grand Master, or D.G.M., the Corresponding Secretary, or C.S., and branches, called Districts and Lodges.

II. — The objects of the Society are the following, namely :—To raise a fund by entrance fees, subscriptions of the members, fines, donations, and by interest on capital ; for insuring a sum of money to be paid on death of a member to the widow or children, or executors, administrators, or assigns of such member, or for defraying the expenses of the burial of a member ; and also for insuring a sum of money to be paid to a member on the death of his wife : provided always that no sum of money which may have been insured and become payable on the death of a member or his wife shall be paid, unless the party applying for the same shall produce and deliver a certificate, signed by a Physician, Surgeon, Apothecary, or Coroner, except in cases where, from the nature of the circumstances, it is impossible to procure such certificate, as provided for by the 13th & 14th Vict. cap. 115, s. 3 ; for the relief of members in sickness and old age ; for granting temporary assistance to the widows and children of deceased members ; for providing members with assistance when travelling in search of employment ; and for assisting members in distressed circumstances, in accordance with 12th, 13th, and 42nd Law.

APPLICATION OF FUNDS.

III.—That all monies received on account of entrance fees, subscriptions, fines, donations, and interest, on capital, shall be applied in carrying out the objects of the society, and in paying the expenses of management according to the rules thereof.

INVESTMENT OF FUNDS.

IV.—That so much of the funds of the society as may not be wanted for immediate use, or to meet the usual accruing liabilities, shall, with the consent of the society, to be had and testified in such manner as the rules direct, be invested pursuant to the 13th and 14th Vict. cap. 115, s. 12.

ESTABLISHMENT OF BRANCHES.

V.—That the Annual Moveable Committee of the Society, shall have power to establish branches called districts. The Board of Directors shall have power to establish branches called lodges, as herein provided for. Every branch of this society shall be bound by these rules, but may make such other rules as such branch may think fit ; provided such additional rules made by lodges, are not inconsistent with the rules of the district, and the general rules of the society; and provided also, that the rules made by districts are not inconsistent with the general rules of the society ; and such other

The first registered rules 1851: facsimile page.

accordance with its own rules where they made provision for such a settlement—an important point for the affiliated orders. Societies which did not wish to register could gain recognition as legal bodies and the consequent right to sue by merely depositing a copy of their rules with the Registrar. The Registrar was instructed by section 45 of the act to lay before Parliament a report of his proceedings every year in addition to the abstracts of returns which had been required previously.

Two short acts were passed in 1858 and 1860 which amended slightly the act of 1855. The first of these[1] gave a right of appeal to the magistrates in certain cases of dispute and empowered societies to change their names with the consent of the Registrar. The second[2] permitted the Registrar to dissolve a society and divide the funds on the written request of five-eighths of the members where a society appeared to be in an insolvent condition. It also repaired an omission of the 1855 act in that it enacted a penalty for the officers of any society who failed to make a return.

No further legislative change was made until after the inquiry and Report of the Royal Commission which sat from 1870 until 1874, and which made the most comprehensive survey of the position of friendly societies in England that had ever been carried out. The appointment of the Commission arose out of the series of events which followed the death of Tidd Pratt, Registrar of Friendly Societies, in January, 1870. The government of the day decided not to appoint a successor but to abolish the office and to transfer such of its functions as were to be left to the Board of Trade. The proposal stirred various interests and the bill for the abolition of the office was dropped while a Commission sat, the warrant for which was first issued on 29 October, 1870.[3]

This warrant listed the main topics for inquiry as follows:

(1) The operation of existing legislation.

(2) The organisation and condition of the societies established under this legislation.

(3) The office and duties of the Registrar of Friendly Societies.

Sir Stafford Northcote was appointed chairman of the Royal

[1] 21 & 22 Vict., c. 101.   [2] 23 & 24 Vict., c. 58.
[3] Printed at the front of the 4th Report of the R.C.F.S., 1874.

N

Commission; the other members were Hicks-Beach, Waterlow, Bonham-Carter, Richards, Roundell, Bircham, and Pattison. The Commission began its work immediately after the Royal Warrant was issued in 1870. In a confidential letter to the other members dated 24 December, 1870, the chairman suggested that they needed to apply 'not only to the government for Assistant Commissioners, but to Parliament for powers to arm them with'.[1] Owing to the opposition of some societies to the powers proposed, a bill granting them was withdrawn after the first reading; but the Assistant Commissioners were, nevertheless, appointed by the government.[2] The work of these Assistant Commissioners, especially that of Sir George Young and of E. L. Stanley, proved invaluable to the Commissioners, who made many of their recommendations their own.

Apart from hearing witnesses, the Assistant Commissioners gathered much information by sending out questionnaires. Specially printed forms were used for various sections of the community from whom information was sought. Ordinary friendly societies, affiliated societies and their branches, burial societies, the clergy, magistrates, county court judges, boards of guardians and coroners, all of these received appropriate questionnaires which they were requested to fill up and return. In his letter instructing the Assistant Commissioners in their duties, Sir Stafford Northcote stated that he hoped they would be able to terminate their labours by the end of November, 1872,[3] but in fact the quantity of evidence prevented them from finishing before the following year.

Towards the end of 1873 the Commission began to draw up papers on various aspects of their inquiry which were destined to figure as chapters in the final Report of 1874. By the time the Report was drawn up, the main Commission, sitting in London, had itself heard evidence from 277 witnesses, much of it lengthy. The Commissioners and their Assistants between them had

---

[1] A copy of this letter is among the unpublished papers of J. M. Ludlow.

[2] Parliamentary Debates, 15 August, 1871, Third Series, vol. 208.

[3] Instructions to Assistant Commissioners from the Chairman, 1871—letter among the unpublished papers of J. M. Ludlow.

gathered far more information about friendly societies than had ever been brought together at any time.

The recommendations of the Commission greatly influenced the shape of future legislation. The main points were that the office of Registrar should be continued and he should have local deputies in England and Wales and Assistant Registrars in Scotland and in Ireland; actuarial staff should be appointed to the Registrar's department; tables of contributions and benefits should be issued, but should not be made compulsory; every registered society should be valued every five years; each society should be efficiently audited annually; annual and quinquennial returns should be collected regularly with penalties for those societies which failed to make a return on time; the Registrar should be empowered to arbitrate in disputes and should have more effective power to prosecute when necessary; the Registrar should have power to dissolve a society or to vary its tables of contributions or benefits on application by a number of members of a society; the insurance of the lives of infants under three should be prohibited.

The principal aim behind all these recommendations was to make the societies which registered more reliable as insurers and to achieve this by more efficient management of their financial affairs on the part of the societies themselves. The Registrar and his colleagues were conceived of as encouraging the sound and advising on ways of improving the weaker insurers rather than as dictating to the societies—this was all in keeping with the prevalent opinion of the time.

After the appearance of the Report and before it could be given legislative expression, there was a general election. The consequence of this was that the chairman of the Royal Commission, Sir Stafford Northcote, became Chancellor of the Exchequer and took charge of the Friendly Societies bill of 1875 in the House of Commons. The act of 1875[1] was the most lengthy and comprehensive measure concerning the societies enacted up to that time. The opening statement of permitted aims which societies registered under the act might have was extended to include fire

[1] 38 & 39 Vict., c. 60.

insurance on the tools of trade belonging to a member and to include the establishment of working men's clubs, also it kept a blanket clause permitting any purpose which the Treasury might authorise. The other principal features of the act were as follows:

(1) There was to be a Chief Registrar and an Assistant Registrar in England and Wales along with Assistant Registrars for Scotland and Ireland. The idea of having deputy registrars for different districts in England, put forward in the Report, was not accepted (section 10).

(2) The functions of the central office followed largely the recommendations of the Commission, registration, collection of returns, construction and circulation of tables were the main duties (section 10).

(3) Registered societies were to submit to an audit of their accounts annually, either by a public auditor or by one of their own choice: they were to forward annual returns of receipts and expenditure to the central office; quinquennial returns of sickness and mortality were also to be made as were quinquennial valuations of assets and liabilities. Failure to carry out these provisions became a punishable offence (section 14).

(4) Disputes within a society were to be settled in accordance with the society's rules or appeal might be made to the Registrars who were empowered to require the attendance of witnesses and the production of documents relating to the matter at issue (section 21).

(5) Insurance on the lives of children under ten years of age was limited to a total of £10 or, for a child under five, to £6 (section 28).

As a consequence of this act, if a man had sponsored the registration of a society in 1856 and the registration of another society in 1876, the main differences in the regulations governing such registration which he would have noticed were these:

1856 (under the act of 1855)	1876 (under the act of 1875)
Minors under the age of 21 years could be accepted as members although they could not hold office.	No member of an adult society was permitted to join before attaining his 16th birthday.
No restriction.	Life insurance on those below ten years of age was severely limited.
Each branch of an order needed to register as a separate society.	Affiliated orders could register as such.
Investment in land not permitted (other than for a building to hold meetings).	Power to acquire any amount of land and to build if the rules permitted.
Dividing societies could not register.	Dividing societies could register.
Registrar certified that the rules of the society were in accordance with law.	No formal certificate, only an acknowledgement of registration, was sent out by the Registrar.
Rules which failed to fulfil the requirements for registration might be 'deposited'; this gave societies the right of action for fraud or misappropriation of funds.	No deposit of rules permitted.

Direct contact between the government and the societies centred very largely around the question of registration throughout the period and the various acts passed had the effect of varying the conditions under which societies might register and, it was hoped, of changing the organisations themselves in some way. The advantages which the state offered to those societies which conformed to the pattern it prescribed remained essentially similar throughout. The main change was some reduction in the favourable rate of interest offered on friendly society investments in the National Debt and this was the outcome of the growth of a public opinion which opposed the payment of subsidies in any form, overt or concealed, by the Treasury.

The principal advantage which the registration conferred on societies was their recognition at law as bodies which had an existence and which could, therefore, sue and be sued through their appropriate officers as agreed by the society.[1] In this way societies were able to protect their funds against dishonest officials. The inability of the affiliated orders to register and thus to protect their funds was not merely potentially dangerous, as the Odd-fellows of the Manchester Unity found to their cost in 1848 when the Corresponding Secretary of the Order pocketed some thous-ands of pounds and was discharged at Liverpool Assizes on tech-nical grounds, the Order as such not being recognised at law.[2] It was this privilege of recognition and consequent protection by the law which formed the strongest attraction drawing societies towards registration. 'The most important advantages conferred by registration are the capacity to sue and be sued in representative names, and the protection conferred against defaulting officials. That these are the considerations which influence a large number of societies in registering seems to be indicated by the circum-stance that in Scotland, where the existence of a public prosecutor to a great extent protects them against fraud, and the common law affords greater facilities for legal proceedings in the case of unregistered societies, the proportion of such societies is vastly greater than in England—so much so that they embrace 84 per cent of the number and 64 per cent of the membership of Scottish friendly societies.' [3]

The act of 1793 granted members of friendly societies a second important privilege, and that was security against being removed under the poor law until they actually became chargeable to a parish in which they had no legal settlement. In 1795 an act[4] was passed providing that no one should be removable until they became chargeable, thus this soon ceased to be a privilege. The first friendly society act also granted exemption from certain stamp duties payable on bonds or securities given by trustees or officials of the societies; this exemption was continued in later acts.

In 1819 the privileges were extended to include permission to

[1] This provision first appeared in 33 Geo. III, c. 54.
[2] Moffrey, A Century of Oddfellowship, 1910, pp. 60 ff.
[3] Transactions of the National Association for the Promotion of Social Science, 1874, p. 795 (paper entitled 'Legislation on Friendly Societies' by C. Cameron).
[4] 35 Geo. III, c. 101.

invest the funds of societies in savings banks and to provide specially advantageous facilities for investing sums of not less than £50 with the Commissioners of the National Debt.[1] This provision was re-enacted in 1829 when the rate of interest to be paid by the Commissioners on such investments was fixed at three pence per cent per day. The special privileges of investment were continued by subsequent acts until the Royal Commission examined the position after 1870.

In the Report of the Royal Commission the privileges of registered societies at that time were summarised in these terms:

'They can hold property in the names of trustees;

'Can sue and be sued in representative names;

'Can proceed against their officers in any case of fraud or misconduct;

'May make provision for the settlement of disputes among their members by arbitration;

'Can invest their funds with the Commissioners for the Reduction of the National Debt;

'Are exempt, within certain limits, from Stamp Duties;

'And can be dissolved on cheap and easy terms when occasion arises.'[2]

The act of 1875 continued these privileges but modified them in some particulars. The rate of interest which the National Debt Commissioners were required to pay was reduced to two pence per cent per day since to pay more was felt to be to subsidise the societies.[3] The field of permitted investment was widened beyond investment in the National Debt or similar securities.

The privileges offered were never strong enough to attract a proportion of societies within the state's scheme of registration. The Royal Commission admitted that these were so numerous 'that their existence must have a most important bearing upon the value of the law itself'.[4] These societies were not in any sense unlawful because they had failed to acquire a statutory status. The

---

[1] 59 Geo. III, c. 128, sections x and xi.
[2] R.C.F.S., 4th Report, 1874, para. 10.
[3] 38 & 39 Vict., c. 60, section xvii.
[4] R.C.F.S., 4th Report, 1874, para. 642.

Select Committee of 1825 reported 'Your Committee apprehend, that although the act of 1793 appears to begin by rendering lawful the institution of friendly societies, there neither was at that time, nor is now, any law or statute which deprives the King's subjects of the right of associating themselves for mutual support'. Such societies were held to be partnerships or clubs and, in the latter, the governing committee could not bind the credit of its members. In criminal proceedings the member of such a society could not be prosecuted for embezzling its funds since he was himself a partner. In 1868 Russell Gurney's act[1] gave some protection to the funds of unregistered friendly societies for it enacted that 'if any person, being a member of any co-partnership etc. . . . shall steal or embezzle any such money etc. . . . of or belonging to the co-partnership . . . every such person shall be liable to be dealt with . . . as if such person had not been or was not a member of such co-partnership or one of the beneficial owners'.[2] But whatever the legal disabilities suffered by unregistered societies, the fact remains that there were many who preferred such disabilities to the enjoyment of the privileges which their registration and conformity to the state's requirements would have conferred.

THE OFFICE OF REGISTRAR OF FRIENDLY SOCIETIES

In any consideration of the relationship of the state to friendly societies in this period, the emergence of a new government department cannot be ignored. It grew as a result of the need for some machinery through which the legislation might be effectively administered. Until 1829 the agents of the state in its dealings with the societies were the justices of the peace, but, as noticed above, the act of that year required that the approval of the barrister appointed to certify the rules of savings banks should be obtained for the rules of friendly societies.[3]

The barrister in question was John Tidd Pratt and the emergence of this office of government owed many of its features to his personality. He continued to preside over the office until his death in

---

[1] 31 & 32 Vict., c. 116.   [2] Ibid., section i.
[3] 10 Geo. IV, c. 56, section iv.

January, 1870. His father was a surgeon. Tidd Pratt himself was called to the bar in 1824 and four years later was appointed as 'Barrister to certify the Rules of Savings Banks' by the National Debt Commissioners. In 1834 by the act of that year, Tidd Pratt's certificate alone was sufficient for the registration of a friendly society and mortality and sickness returns were to be sent directly to him.[1] He became the holder of a salaried office and no longer dependent on fees in 1846 when it was enacted that 'the Barrister or Advocate appointed to certify the rules of friendly societies in England, Scotland and Ireland respectively shall be appointed by the Commissioners for the Reduction of the National Debt and shall hold his office during the pleasure of the said Commissioners, and that the Registrar of Friendly Societies in England shall be paid by salary instead of fees'.[2] Provision was also made in the same measure for payment from the Consolidated Fund if necessary of office expenses, salaries of clerks, stationery, etc. By 1846 the department had come fully into existence in a physical sense.

From 1846 until his death, Tidd Pratt was not satisfied merely to fulfil the obligations placed upon him by law—the comparatively innocuous functions of certifying rules and collecting returns. He spent his time crusading for societies to become sounder in a financial sense and more reliable as agents of insurance. With this aim in view, he published both privately and officially books on such subjects as *Suggestions for the Establishment of Friendly Societies*, *The Law Relating to Friendly Societies* and *Instructions for the Establishment of Friendly Societies*. The annual reports which the act of 1855 required that he should present to Parliament often had lengthy appendices which were filled with advice that Tidd Pratt felt he should give.

In his first Report he wrote, 'the Registrar is not able to offer any observations of much interest in reference to the societies with which his official duties are connected'.[3] The Report itself was a mere five pages, but there were 130 pages of appendices, the greater part consisting of three lengthy articles containing well-meant advice and entitled: 'Instructions on Book-keeping for

[1] 4 & 5 Wm. IV, c. 40, sections iv, v and vi.
[2] 9 & 10 Vict., c. 27, section x.   [3] Registrar's Report, 1856, p. 3.

Friendly Societies'; 'Instructions prepared by John Tidd Pratt Esq., Registrar of Friendly Societies in England, for the framing of Rules for Friendly Societies'; 'Suggestions by John Tidd Pratt Esq., Registrar of Friendly Societies in England, for the Establishment of Friendly Societies'.

The second annual report was twenty pages in length but again the appendices were much longer and consisted for the most part of articles on the position of friendly societies in various European countries including France, Belgium, Austria, Bavaria and Spain. These accounts cannot have been of much use to English societies and it is not easy to see why Tidd Pratt published some of them. The article on Poland, for instance, stated simply that 'There is no friendly society in this country yet, but application has been made to the Registrar for information on the subject on behalf of a Polish nobleman, for the purpose of turning it to a practical use ultimately, and therefore their introduction into this country may be regarded as not improbable'.[1]

These activities, which were not actually enjoined by the law, called forth a certain amount of criticism of the Registrar. The evidence heard by the Royal Commission showed that those societies which had received Tidd Pratt's advice were not always clear when he was telling them what the law required of them and when he was simply giving his opinion as to which would be the best course for them to adopt. In their Report the Commissioners remarked that 'The organisation of the registration system is due to him, and his zeal in the fulfilment of his duties and the deep interest which he took in the subject of our enquiries, need only be referred to'.[2] The scope of Tidd Pratt's activities was such that he became virtually the embodiment of the state so far as the societies were concerned.

In these circumstances it was not surprising that the death of the only holder of this office should bring into question the future of the office itself. The Liberal government introduced a bill to abolish the office and to enable friendly societies to operate within the laws governing joint stock companies. The societies would

[1] Registrar's Report, 1857, p. 62.
[2] R.C.F.S., 4th Report, 1874, para. 21.

simply have registered with the Board of Trade, and disputes, the winding up of societies and the division of funds would have been dealt with by the county courts. This bill roused much opposition and, as stated above, led to the appointment of the Royal Commission which inquired into the whole purpose and effect of registration. Some of the questions to which the Commission sought answers on this topic were set out by Sir Stafford Northcote in a letter to the Assistant Commissioners in these terms, 'As respects the office and duties of Registrar, your branch of inquiry will mainly consist in ascertaining how these are viewed by the members of the societies themselves, or those who have been connected with them, e.g. whether they look upon the office as useful or the reverse, whether they would wish for its suppression, its enlargement, or its transfer to some other branch of the government; whether its duties are deemed too extensive or too narrow, whether the discharge of them has given satisfaction, or whether it has created the desire for an appeal to some higher authority.' [1]

In the light of the evidence collected the Commissioners felt that registration was worth while and that there should continue to be a special department 'collecting and diffusing information and of superintending generally the working of the various institutions. Such an office may be of great use in preparing statistics, and in framing tables which may assist promoters to place their societies on a proper financial basis. It may collect and note results; may publish, in annual reports or otherwise, particulars relating to the working of the system; may see to the fulfilment of the conditions on which Parliament has granted legislative privileges; and may act as a kind of intermediary between the societies and the various departments of government with which they may be brought into relation.' [2]

The recommendations as to how this special department should be organised and how it should work which were put forward in the Report of the Royal Commission seem to have been almost entirely the work of the secretary to the Commission, J. M.

[1] Instructions to Assistant Commissioners from the Chairman, August, 1871— letter among the unpublished papers of J. M. Ludlow.
[2] R.C.F.S., 4th Report, 1874, para. 59.

Ludlow. There still exists a paper which Ludlow drew up at the end of 1873 or the beginning of 1874, much of which is repeated almost verbatim in the final Report.[1]

In discussing the possible courses of action, Ludlow surveyed what had already been attempted. 'Three systems have been tried, two have been discarded as failures, viz 1st, independent local registration; 2nd, central registration with local control. The third system, now in operation, is that of central registration only.' The benefit of this system was its uniformity; its disadvantages were said to be:

(1) Its failure to persuade about one-third of all societies to register.

(2) It was only able to obtain annual returns from some 56 per cent of those registered.

(3) Such returns as were made were often incomplete.

This system had, therefore, failed so far as efficient enforcement was concerned. 'How is one man in London to keep nearly 22,000 bodies of men in all parts of England, in the most remote villages, in the most crowded cities, bodies composed to an enormous extent of the ignorant and prejudiced, to a large extent of the ignorant and self-willed, to some extent it is to be feared of the dishonest and malevolent, up to any conceivable standard, however low it may be fixed?'

It was against this background that the Commission recommended that there should be local machinery for purposes of enforcement under central control. The proposal that local 'Deputy Registrars' should collect returns, hold copies of the rules of societies within their districts and generally act as local enforcement officers acting on behalf of the Chief Registrar at the central office was Ludlow's answer to the problem which he posed as a result of his analysis of the existing situation. Both the analysis and the remedy were accepted by the Commission.

The act of 1875 did not incorporate all of these recommendations and no deputies were appointed in England, but the office of

[1] Paper entitled 'Suggestions by the Secretary' is among the unpublished papers of J. M. Ludlow and the section of the final Report of the Commission which was based upon it is to be found in paras. 870 ff.

Chief Registrar was established with Assistant Registrars for England, Scotland and Ireland. A general reorganisation of the Registrar's department was undertaken to enable it to meet the requirements of the new act. In December, 1875, the establishment of the Registry Office of Friendly Societies was determined by the Treasury as:

(1) England:
    1 Chief Registrar
    1 Assistant Registrar
    1 Chief Clerk
    2 Clerks
    4 Copying Clerks
    2 Writers
    1 Messenger

(2) Scotland and Ireland:
    2 Assistant Registrars with an allowance for clerical assistance

In July, 1876, the establishment was increased to include an actuary, an additional clerk and two temporary writers, a total of sixteen.[1]

When Tidd Pratt had first been appointed to certify the rules of societies he had been expected to make what he could from fees and to pay from his income the clerical and other expenses involved. By the time of his death the department had come to consist of three Registrars, for England (salary £1,000 per annum) and for Ireland and Scotland (salaries £150 per annum). The Registrar for England had in his office a chief clerk, three clerks, one messenger and two supplementary clerks, giving a total establishment of ten.[2] It was of this establishment that the Chief Registrar's Report for 1875 remarked as having 'long been insufficient for the due performance of its functions under previously existing legislation'.[3] The net effect of the act of 1875 on the office of the Registrar was to strengthen the central department both in its establishment and in its powers—for in future the

---

[1] Chief Registrar's Report for 1875, p. 9.
[2] R.C.F.S., 4th Report, 1874, para. 21.
[3] Chief Registrar's Report for 1875, p. 9.

Assistant Registrars in Scotland and Ireland were subordinated to the Chief Registrar in London. The failure to develop a network of local offices was, perhaps, the consequence of the government and Parliament being less anxious than the Royal Commission to give wide and effective powers to the Registry.

This same tendency to limit the powers of the department can be seen in the conditions attached to the exercise of some of its functions. The only power of initiation the act gave the Registrars was that of deciding the forms of the returns.[1] They needed to obtain the approval of the Treasury before circulating statistics or model accounts, dispensing with quinquennial returns, appointing inspectors, calling special meetings of societies or hearing disputes. Moreover the appointment of inspectors, calling of special meetings and dissolving by award could only be undertaken where some fixed proportion of members had made an application to the Registrar. Before any dispute could be decided, the consent of both parties to the dispute had to be obtained, and where the society's rules forbade such arbitration, even this consent was insufficient. Thus although the office of barrister to confirm the rules of friendly societies grew into the Registry Office of Friendly Societies during a period of about forty years, yet its legal powers —as contrasted with its influence—remained narrowly circumscribed.

In these circumstances the future role of the office depended to a great extent on the new Chief Registrar, who was, in fact, J. M. Ludlow. He remained Chief Registrar from the creation of the position until 1891 when he retired at the age of seventy. Like Tidd Pratt, he was a barrister. He had always shown a keen interest in social questions, and both as Secretary to the Royal Commission and in his new office he had an outstanding opportunity of bringing his influence to bear directly on the social policy of the state. A friend of Maurice and of Kingsley, he was deeply religious and his social and political views were an expression of his Christianity. To judge from his collection of pamphlets and papers, he concerned himself with the co-operative, adult education and trade union movements from about the middle of the

[1] 38 & 39 Vict., c. 60, section xiv.

century, some twenty years before he became actively interested in friendly societies. It was largely due to the personality of the first Chief Registrar that, in spite of the narrow legal limits within which his office was confined, its influence was so widespread in the last part of the nineteenth century.

CHAPTER EIGHT

FRIENDLY SOCIETIES AND THE POOR LAW

MUCH of the legislation of this period which was directly concerned with friendly societies was the result rather than the cause of their growth and development, but the action of the state with regard to the provision made for the poor did have some effect on the rate at which societies grew. The interaction of the friendly society movement and the Poor Law was generally recognised by contemporaries. In the instructions to Assistant Commissioners, the chairman of the Royal Commission wrote of 'the very important bearing of the Friendly Societies' Acts, and of Friendly Societies generally, upon the self-maintenance of the people, and the administration of the Poor Laws, both in rural and town districts. Whether any, and what relations can be established between Friendly Societies and the Poor Law system is a question which has been much discussed, and remains yet unsolved.' [1]

It has already been noticed that the possibility of using nationally supported friendly societies to reduce the burden of the poor rates received much less attention after the reformed Poor Law had been introduced in 1834. The increasingly important affiliated orders offered uncompromising opposition to any form of direct link between the official provision for paupers and the facilities which they offered to their members. Charles Hardwick, who was for some time Grand Master of the Manchester Unity, expressed this point of view when he wrote that 'the true origin and rapid growth among the sound-hearted British populace of sick clubs and other friendly societies' was 'the honourable substitute for the parish relief of the semi-slave by act of Parliament'. [2] Or again, 'The true object and mission of friendly societies, when properly considered and as regarded by the working man himself, is to afford

[1] Instructions to Assistant Commissioners from the Chairman of the Royal Commission, August, 1871, among the unpublished papers of J. M. Ludlow.

[2] Hardwick, *A Manual for Friendly Societies*, 1859, p. 32.

a competent support and complete independence during periods of sickness, incapacity, and disease, however protracted; and it is to accomplish this object that not only the earliest but the most recently and best organised societies make special provision. Their object is not to form a stepping stone, to aid the industrious and prudent to pass from the active and manly independence of their days of vigorous labour to the degraded pauperism of the work-house.'[1]

The only actual link which had existed before 1834 between the friendly societies and the Poor Law authorities took the form of individual contributions to the societies being paid out of the poor rate. The overseers of the poor seem to have felt that in the case of the sick or aged the rates would gain rather than lose if a pauper who had been a member had his rights of membership preserved so that the benefit which might be due could be claimed by the parish. The Reports from Assistant Commissioners in 1834 gave a number of examples of this practice. In Skipton it was found to be customary for the town to assist aged people in paying their contributions to friendly societies, and the expense involved was said to amount to about £7 per annum.[2] In Gisburn the parish was reported to pay regularly the contributions of two members of the local society, a sum of ten shillings each year.[3] In Dewsbury the practice of paying the subscriptions of poor members from the poor rate was being discontinued.[4] In Oldham distress among the weavers was said to be due to the spread of the power looms, but they were considered to be 'an orderly and industrious class' and 'their contributions to friendly societies are frequently paid by the township'.[5] How widespread this practice was it is difficult to estimate. After 1834 such payments were forbidden; this ban produced no outburst of indignation throughout the country so it may well be that the instances reported by the Assistant Commissioners were fairly isolated.

Even if there was no direct link between the societies as a whole

[1] Ibid., p. 63.
[2] Appendix to the Report from the Royal Comm. on the Poor Laws, 1834, p. 743A.
[3] Ibid., p. 747A.   [4] Ibid., p. 811A.
[5] Ibid., p. 918A.

o

and the Poor Law before 1834, the societies themselves, by the way in which they conducted their affairs, seem to have had some effect upon the act of that year. The Commissioners in their Report argued that the principle of 'less eligibility' and the need for the workhouse test were both demonstrated by the manner in which working men ordered their friendly societies.

The principle of 'less eligibility' was found by the Commissioners to lie behind the low rates of sick pay which friendly societies offered to their members. Tidd Pratt was asked, 'In these institutions is the condition of a member receiving relief, or living without work, ever allowed to be as eligible on the whole, as the condition of a member living by his work?' He answered, 'In most cases the allowances made by the societies are so adjusted as to make it the interest of every member not to receive relief from the society so long as he can earn his usual wages. The average allowance which they make is about one-third of what a member can earn. Thus, if the average earnings of the members of a benefit society were £1 4s. a week, the allowance in case of sickness would be, on an average for the whole time of the sickness, about 8s. a week. During the last session Mr. Slaney brought in a bill for the purpose of sanctioning the formation of societies for the relief of members when out of employment. At his instance I made inquiries amongst some of the most intelligent and respectable of the labouring classes as to what should be the extent of allowance to those who were out of work. I suggested to the parties that one half of the usual wages might be a proper allowance. The unanimous reply of the operatives with whom I conversed on the subject was, that an allowance of one third would be ample, and that more than that would only induce the members to continue on the society rather than endeavour to find work.' [1]

Further evidence was given by the same witness and was quoted in their Report by the Commissioners to show how undesirable friendly societies felt any system of partial relief to be, whether it was in aid of wages or because of the size of family.[2] They argued from this that there should be no partial relief from the poor rate.

[1] Report from the Royal Comm. on the Poor Laws, 1834, p. 130.
[2] Ibid., p. 153.

Vigilance at all times was said to mark the administration of benefits by the societies. 'This vigilance in the administration of outdoor relief to the sick, a vigilance to which we have never found any parallel in the administration of the Poor's rates, would a fortiori, be requisite in the case of the administration of out-door relief to the able-bodied. But this is obviously impossible. No salaried officer could have the zeal or the knowledge of an inspector of a friendly society, who is always of the same class, and usually of the same trade as the claimant. And if it were possible, we believe that it would not be effectual. The labouring classes themselves find these daily visits and strict regulations inadequate substitutes for the means of supervision and prevention which well regulated workhouses afford, and which those classes, if their circumstances permitted, would doubtless adopt.'[1] The Commissioners appear to have completely misconstrued the aims of societies. It is difficult to conceive of any society lasting a day which offered its members the privilege of paying when fit to be sent to the workhouse when sick. Yet, whether the conduct of the societies was misunderstood or not, they provided—or seemed to provide—the Commissioners with another argument in favour of the abolition of outdoor relief.

In the Reports sent in by the Assistant Commissioners from particular districts the idea was apparent that by being strict in the administration of poor relief, the authorities would be helping the friendly societies to flourish; working men would become more eager to provide for themselves, thus they would seek to form and to join societies for that purpose. In his Report on the administration of the Poor Law in the South-East, Ashurst Majendie wrote, 'Wherever the Poor Laws are best administered, there the contributions of labourers to savings banks and benefit societies are the most numerous. In those districts where the most lavish payments are made from the rates, these establishments are neglected, and are considered in the labourer's language "a good fence for the parish".'[2] Another Assistant Commissioner, Henry Bishop,

---

[1] Ibid., pp. 153–4.
[2] Appendix to the Report of the Royal Comm. on the Poor Laws, 1834, p. 166A.

found that at Uley in Gloucestershire a workhouse test had been enforced since 1830 and that in the workhouse such discipline was practised as to make it an unpleasant place for all who could possibly keep out. All this, he claimed, had had a very beneficial effect since 'the pauperism existing previously to 1830 had so completely destroyed all providence, that the friendly societies of the place had completely sunk under it'.[1]

Whether the evidence of the condition and practices of the friendly societies played a major part in leading the Commissioners to the conclusions which they stated may, perhaps, be doubted, but the societies certainly provided them with arguments to support the case which they put forward for a complete overhaul and strengthening of the Poor Law in the direction of making relief much more difficult to obtain.

After the passing of the Poor Law Amendment Act the members of the Commission who were charged with the task of enforcing the new measure acted in what they considered to be a manner which would help friendly societies generally.

The most important practical issue to be decided was the extent to which benefits received from a man's friendly society should be taken into account by the guardians in assessing the amount of poor relief to which he might be entitled. Some boards of guardians were prepared to argue that the prudent man who had joined a friendly society ought to be treated more leniently than an improvident man in times of personal difficulty. Instead of taking the whole of his income from benefits into account the guardians often only included half of the amount of the benefit payment when assessing how much parish aid should be offered.

This particular problem became sufficiently pressing by 1840 for the Poor Law Commissioners to issue a Minute on the subject in their official circular.[2] The Minute of 1840 was thereafter regarded as the standard statement of the correct administrative practice and remained in force for the rest of this period. The

---

[1] Appendix to the Report of the Royal Comm. on the Poor Laws, 1834, p. 886A.

[2] Official Circular No. 3 of the Poor Law Commissioners, 4 April, 1840, pp. 30 ff.

Minute took the form of an answer to the question, 'In what cases
and to what extent a man who, as a member of a friendly society,
is entitled to certain advantages in respect of it, ought to receive
parochial relief?' It began by claiming that the members of the
societies themselves were strongly opposed to the whole notion
of partial relief and argued that the payment of such relief simply
made it more difficult for the societies to prevent fraud owing to
the possibility of 'an undue reliance on the divided and extended
sources of relief'. After considerable discussion designed to show
the undesirability of such relief, the Commissioners gave this
ruling:

'With regard to the money allowance granted by the friendly
society, the Guardians cannot but take into account this allowance
in estimating the resources of the applicant and his family; and if
they acted in consistency with universally admitted principles of
poor-law administration, the Guardians would not grant further
aid than would be sufficient, together with this allowance, to
relieve the destitution of the applicant and his family to the same
extent as they would relieve the destitution of any other applicant
and his family not being a subscriber to a friendly society.

'The Commissioners, however, believe that in practice, the
Guardians have treated the friendly society allowance as in some
degree more immediately destined for the restoration of the health
and strength of the subscriber, and have, therefore, granted a
larger allowance to the family than would have been given if no
such consideration had presented itself. The Commissioners have
not deemed it advisable for the present to interfere with this mode
of proceeding; but they entertain no doubt that it will, at no distant period, be found to be more in accordance with the interest
of the labouring classes to carry out the principles adverted to at
the commencement of these observations, and not to permit the
contributors of friendly societies to receive relief at the same time
from the funds of the contributors and the poor rates. . . .'

'The Commissioners finally remark that they think it desirable
that the Guardians should furnish once a quarter to every friendly
society in the union a list of the persons receiving relief.'

The policy of the Commissioners might be summarised as

working towards the elimination of preferential treatment for members of societies in the granting of relief; medical relief to be granted only by way of loan; and lists of paupers to be circulated to societies so as to prevent a man from drawing sick pay from his society and poor relief at the same time without the full extent of his income becoming known. The argument on which all this was based was that these measures would serve best the interests of the working man and his friendly society, fortunately it also coincided with economy in the expenditure of the rates.

Some societies did not always see the situation in the same light as the Commissioners and did not feel that official policy was helpful. In 1843 the clerk of the Bourn (Lincs) union wrote to the Commissioners complaining that several societies had decided to refuse to pay their usual allowances to sick members where such a payment would disqualify them from parish relief when the guardians reckoned it among their assets. The Commissioners in their reply admitted that there was no immediate solution which they could recommend to the guardians at Bourn, but they did suggest that if members of societies were offered only workhouse relief 'in all cases admitting of removal to the workhouse' this 'would, in many instances, prevent the evil consequences apprehended by the guardians'.[1]

The attitude of the state towards the societies was that they would flourish better if left alone and if contact with or aid from the public authorities was kept to a minimum; this was demonstrated by the advice given by the Commissioners to boards of guardians in the years following 1834. The clerk of Hardingstone union in 1843 wrote to the Commissioners concerning one Edward Underwood who was a pauper and whose contributions to a friendly society had been paid by the union for five months so as to preserve his claim to sickness benefit. In the fifth month he fell ill and drew eight shillings per week from his society, although he remained in the workhouse he refused to hand the money to the guardians. The local board wanted to know if they could collect the money without it passing through the pauper's hands. The

[1] Official Circular No. 26 of the Poor Law Commissioners, 30 June, 1843, p. 97.

Commissioners replied condemning the board for ever having paid Edward Underwood's subscriptions and told the guardians that they could not claim direct payments of the benefits arising out of it. The letter added, 'Nor is it desirable that such institutions (friendly societies) should be supported out of the poor rates. The value of these institutions consists in the character of independence and self-support which ought necessarily to belong to them.' [1]

In 1849 the clerk to the guardians of Brecknock union wrote saying that a benefit society had refused to pay the board the funeral money in respect of a pauper who had been a member of the society; the clerk wanted to know whether the sum might be recovered at law. The Commissioners replied that in such a case the friendly society had no liability as the law stood to pay the sum due to the union which had paid the expenses of the funeral.[2]

The strengthening of the friendly society movement was thus claimed to be one of the aims of the Poor Law Amendment Act and of the policy which guided its administration. Soon after the act was passed, the Commissioners began to claim that this desired effect was, in fact, being achieved. The act was said to have led to the immediate formation of many new societies.[3] In their first Annual Report, the Commissioners cited the evidence of Tidd Pratt to support their assertions on this point. He had submitted a statement which was repeated in this Report which said 'that the increase in the number of friendly societies since the passing of the Poor Law Amendment Act has been very considerable as compared with the year previous thereto. From the month of August 1833 to August 1834, the number certified by me was 360; but from August 1834 to the present time I have certified nearly 750, being an increase of 390, or more than double the number certified in the previous year. Independently of which, I am happy to say that these societies appear to be founded on calculations

[1] Official Circular No. 27 of the Poor Law Commissioners, 26 August, 1843, p. 116.

[2] Official Circular No. 39 (New Series) of the Poor Law Commissioners, July, 1850, p. 100.

[3] First Annual Report of the Poor Law Commissioners, 1835, p. 31.

more likely to enable them to fulfil their engagements with the members than those which were heretofore in existence; . . .' [1]

Similar claims continued to be made officially and similar evidence was cited from time to time by the Commissioners. In their fourth Annual Report they claimed that the increasing number of friendly societies bore testimony to the 'stronger will' on the part of the labouring classes to provide for future wants and unexpected contingencies. The evidence furnished by Tidd Pratt extended over more years this time. 'The Benefit Society Act passed in 1829, and the number enrolled from July 1829 to August 1830; I put the period of August on account of the Poor Law Amendment Act coming into operation in the month of August; in the first year there were 510, and in the second 560, and in the third 1180. The reason of the great increase was a new act of Parliament coming in which gave a rather larger extension than the previous act; in 1833, 470; in 1834, 350; since that, under the Poor Law Amendment Act, the next year was 700; the next 670; the next 739, and from August last to the present time, about 552.' [2] Lest it were objected that there might be some other reason for the increase in the number of registrations apart from the Poor Law Amendment Act, Tidd Pratt explained that his conclusions were based on conversations and correspondence with the founders of the societies, and concluded 'in addition to which it has been stated to me in letters that now is the time that parties must look to themselves, as they could not receive outdoor relief under the new law'.[3]

Evidence of an increase in the support given to friendly societies was sometimes provided by Assistant Commissioners in their reports. In 1842 the Assistant Commissioner for Kent and Sussex wrote that he did not know that a better testimony could be born to the beneficial operation of the amended Poor Law than the 'vaste increase' which it has occasioned in those valuable institutions, friendly societies, 'proofs of which I have given you in former reports, of which the following is an example:—In the Midhurst union in 1835, which was just previous to the operation

[1] First Annual Report of the Poor Law Commissioners, 1835, p. 32.
[2] Fourth Annual Report of the Poor Law Commissioners, 1838, p. 247.
[3] Ibid., p. 58.

of the new system, all the benefit societies within its limits numbered 849 members, while in 1838, the latest period for which I have a return, the numbers amounted to 1,320.'[1]

The Commissioners certainly believed that the new act and its administration had led to an increase in the number of societies and in their membership. The Secretary to the Commissioners, Chadwick, republished his 'Essay on the Means of Insurance' from the *Westminster Review* of 1828 in 1836 and explained in the Preface that the essay was now being reprinted in consequence of the increase of benefit societies and sick clubs 'created by the operation of the Poor Law Amendment Act'.[2]

The statistics available—both for registration and for the foundation of lodges and courts by the Oddfellows and Foresters —do show a rapid increase in the size of the friendly society movement in the years following 1834, but it is not easy to assess the extent to which the Poor Law Amendment Act was responsible for this. Of the 3,074 English lodges of the Manchester Unity of Oddfellows which were still active in 1875, 1,470 were founded between 1835 and 1845.[3] This decade saw the foundation of far more lodges than any other in the nineteenth century. The most notable increases were in the counties of Lancashire, Yorkshire, Staffordshire, Cheshire, Derbyshire and Warwick.

The claims made by the Commissioners can be tested in a limited way by examining in some detail the situation between 1834 and 1841 in the county with the largest number of newly founded lodges, Lancashire. In their Report of 1838, the Commissioners described the difficulties which had been encountered in this county which had delayed the operation of the new act. In spite of the difficulties, unions were formed and by 1838 the act was being applied in Chorlton, Leigh, Blackburn, Haslingden, Salford, Wigan, Preston, Prescot, Ormskirk and Warrington.[4] According to the eighth Annual Report, the whole of Lancashire with the exception of Ashton-under-Lyne, Oldham and Rochdale

[1] Eighth Annual Report of the Poor Law Commissioners, 1842, Appendix B, No. 8, p. 247.
[2] E. Chadwick, *Essay on the Means of Insurance*, 1836, from the Preface.
[3] Supra, p. 34.
[4] Fourth Annual Report of the Poor Law Commissioners, 1838, pp. 28, 29, 30.

'is now placed under the operation of the Poor Law Amendment Act'.[1]

The date of the earliest foundation in each district makes it clear that it was not that the idea of 'Oddfellowship' had just arrived for the first time and caught on at once after 1834. The figure for the Manchester district shows a much smaller increase

TABLE 15

The number of lodges founded in the seven years preceding and the seven years following the Poor Law Amendment Act in six Oddfellows' districts of Lancashire

District	No. founded during: (a) 1828-34	No. founded during: (b) 1835-41	Total in 1875	Earliest foundation
Liverpool . .	4	21	27	1818
Manchester . .	3	2	11	1814
Preston . . .	3	17	20	1815
Blackburn . .	3	17	24	1819
Bury	4	10	19	1814
Wigan . . .	3	5	13	1819

Figures from the List of Lodges of the I.O.O.F.M.U. for 1875-6.

in these years than any other given here. This may be due to the so-called Manchester district of the Oddfellows not including the whole of the Manchester conurbation even at that time; also in Manchester itself there was an unusually high proportion of very early foundations (pre-1830). A similar sudden increase to those shown in most of these districts is apparent in the rest of Lancashire and in the West Riding of Yorkshire.

The most probable explanation of this increase is that it owed much to the Poor Law Amendment Act. To put the act into force in a district there were various distinct steps to be taken—registration, formation of the union, application of the new regulations— all of which meant that local discussion went on for some time before the new system actually came to be applied. Local discussion and even agitation must have been particularly lively in areas where the opposition to the new measure was keen, and even the Commissioners had to admit special difficulties in these areas. In the atmosphere of rumour and speculation as to what was going to happen, it seems quite natural that more would try to

[1] Eighth Annual Report of the Poor Law Commissioners, 1842, para. 90.

make some provision for themselves in time of sickness or distress regardless of what a changed and more severely circumscribed Poor Law might have to offer. This may well be the explanation of the increase in other areas also. As one of the poor stated, 'We must look out for ourselves, and provide for a day of sickness and old age, now that there is no parish to look to.' [1] This may not have been true in a legal sense, but it was a widespread belief.

The probability that it was the Poor Law Amendment Act which led to the rapid increase in friendly societies after 1834 is strengthened when the conditions of trade and employment are considered. Gayer, Rostow and Schwartz, in their study of fluctuations in the economy, show that the years between 1836 and 1842 saw no burst of prosperity which might have led to a considerable increase in the size of the friendly societies.[2] Such industrial districts as the West Riding and Lancashire suffered quite severely from the depression of trade from the opening of 1837 and the Poor Law Commissioners had to discontinue their previous policy of encouraging the emigration of southern labourers to the northern manufacturing districts. This depression lasted with varying degrees of severity until 1842.[3]

The attitude of the Poor Law administration to the friendly societies did not change materially during the years from 1834 to 1875; there was never any formal connection between the societies and the Poor Law. The existence of the friendly societies must have saved some part of the burden which would otherwise have fallen on the poor rate, but it is impossible to estimate what that saving amounted to. E. W. Bradbrook, who succeeded Ludlow as Chief Registrar, wrote in 1898 that 'since the great reform of the Poor Law that took place in 1834, it has been applied with more or less strictness to its proper purpose of the relief of destitution. That reform has undoubtedly led to the formation of

[1] Second Annual Report of the Poor Law Commissioners, 1836, Appendix B, p. 337.

[2] Gayer, Rostow and Schwartz, *The Growth and Fluctuation of the British Economy, 1790–1850*, 1953, vol. I, pp. 275–6, 300–3. The usual relationship between industrial prosperity and the growth of friendly societies may be seen in Appendix F, below.

[3] Ibid.

friendly societies, but it is another thing to say that it has saved so much in poor rates.' [1]

The Royal Commission on Friendly Societies found that the situation established after 1834 was in no need of reform in the 1870s. The complete separation of friendly societies from the Poor Law was again justified by arguments similar to those put forward earlier. The 'best managed' friendly societies would object to any such connection which would only 'pauperise the flower of the working classes' and would 'strengthen the conviction, already too prevalent in the ordinary labourer's mind, that the outdoor relief, known by him under the suggestive name of "sick pay", is his by right'.[2]

The idea that members of friendly societies should in some way be treated more leniently by the guardians was examined and rejected; 'the tendency of holding out such favours to members of friendly societies is to encourage men to insure for less than their real needs with a friendly society, and to count on Poor Law relief to make up the sum required for their support'.[3]

The Poor Law Commissioners in the years following 1834 felt that the workhouse was the best way of driving men into friendly societies, and the Royal Commission offered a similar opinion in its Report: '. . . if outdoor relief (for the aged) could no longer be reckoned on with comparative certainty, a great stimulus would be given to exertions towards making some provision for old age . . . the workhouse test would invest providence with new and hitherto unknown attractions.' [4]

[1] E. W. Bradbrook, *Provident Societies and Industrial Welfare, 1898*, p. 46.
[2] R.C.F.S., 4th Report, 1874, para. 831.
[3] Ibid., para. 828.
[4] Ibid., para. 833.

CHAPTER NINE

1875 AND AFTER

IN one sense the passing of the friendly society legislation of 1875 may be taken to mark the entry of the societies—or at least of the affiliated orders—to something approaching the promised land. The procedure of registration was now adapted to suit the convenience of societies with branches; the societies themselves made far more rapid progress towards becoming sound insurers in the decade or so following 1875 than they had ever done before; numerically they continued to expand rapidly. Small wonder that J. M. Baernreither, writing in the 1880s, found much to praise in recent developments in friendly societies; in many ways his *English Associations of Working Men* reflected the views of the official classes with whom he mixed in this country. Yet the very nature of the societies themselves was changing. The insurance function came more and more to dominate the larger societies and the practice of good fellowship and conviviality became less important while the local democracy of the individual lodge found its powers circumscribed by limits imposed by the Order in the interests of sound finance. These fundamental changes in the societies were the result of changes in the national life and outlook during the last twenty or thirty years of the nineteenth century. The rapid growth of commercial insurance among the working classes, the spread of professional entertainment and the change in economic and political ideas were foremost among the causes of change in friendly societies after 1875.

The Friendly Societies act of 1875 established the system of relationship between friendly societies and the state which remained substantially unchanged until the introduction of the national health scheme in 1911. It did not change the direction of the societies' development, but was similar to most friendly society legislation of this period in that it tended to follow and to give legal recognition to what was already taking place. The state sought better management and sounder insurance from the societies and tried to encourage this through voluntary registration with the Registrar of Friendly Societies. It tried to insist upon periodical valuations and it was hoped that the financially unsound would be shamed into following the path of reform which the Manchester Unity had already begun to take. The Ancient Order of Foresters had adopted graduated scales of contributions at their High Court Meeting of 1872, but these were not enforced in reluctant courts until 1885 after valuations had revealed their importance. The Grand United Order of Oddfellows with about 80,000 members adopted graduated scales in 1889, while the National Independent Order of Oddfellows required all those joining that Order after 1 January, 1889, to pay contributions on a graded scale.[1] According to J. Frome Wilkinson writing in 1886, 'We shall be well within the mark if we state that the vast majority of the orders have adopted reforms more or less radical owing to the condition of their finances as revealed by the requirements of the valuation clause of the Friendly Societies' Act.'[2]

A general improvement in the business methods and management of many societies became apparent. The Chief Registrar wrote that '. . . a distinct improvement is felt from year to year in the work of the officers of societies generally; rules and amendments come up in better shape, and the requirements of the acts are more intelligently carried out. This is, perhaps, especially noticeable in some of the smaller orders, who now evidently select for their general secretaries men of much greater ability than formerly.'[3]

The growth of the affiliated orders continued at a high rate. On 31 December, 1875, the Ancient Order of Foresters had 491,000 members, ten years later the figure had reached 667,000. The Manchester Unity of Oddfellows increased from 508,000 on 1 January, 1876, to 605,000 on 1 January, 1886.[4] Between 1876 and 1890, 2,674 new registrations were effected by local societies

---

[1] Chief Registrar's Report for 1890, pp. 88 and 95.

[2] J. Frome Wilkinson, *The Friendly Society Movement*, 1886, p. 101.

[3] Chief Registrar's Report for 1885, p. 5.

[4] Figures from the annual Directories of the A.O.F. and Lists of Lodges of the I.O.O.F.M.U. and show the total membership of the respective orders.

while 7,056 branches of larger societies registered for the first time—reflecting to some extent the rapid growth of the orders in these years.[1]

The restrictions which the more business-like arrangements for insurance necessitated on the degree of local democratic control which the local lodge or court might exercise did not evoke any cry of lamentation among commentators representing the views of the 'official' class. Yet it was this control of contributions from the centre which caused much trouble in the orders as it came to be introduced. There had been trouble in the Manchester Unity much earlier on this issue and some lodges were still resisting the efforts of the Unity government after 1875. The Ancient Order of Foresters found it easier to get delegates to agree to graduated scales when in conference at their High Court Meeting than to persuade the individual courts to accept the High Court's ruling in this matter. The ultimate weapon which an Order could use in enforcing its control over a reluctant lodge or court was expulsion, but clearly this was impracticable if too many local branches were willing to run the risk of incurring such a penalty. The first step was often to insist upon a graduated scale for all members joining after a certain date since the acceptance of such a rule by the existing membership would at least not involve them in any personal financial loss. An example of this can be seen in a new rule registered by the National Independent Order of Odd-fellows in 1890 which they had adopted a year previously requiring all districts to 'adopt a graduated scale as the basis upon which all contributions shall be paid for the benefits of all members admitted after 1 January, 1889'.[2]

Before 1875 the branches of affiliated orders had to register as independent societies, under this act they might re-register as branches of an Order provided that their application was counter-signed by the general secretary of the national organisation. Naturally the orders encouraged their lodges and courts to do this and 10,304 did so between 1876 and 1890.[3] This again tended to strengthen the position of the central government of the orders

---

[1] Chief Registrar's Report for 1890, p. 42.
[2] Ibid., p. 95.   [3] Ibid., p. 42.

and to weaken the position of the branches. The control by the centre continued to increase and in the course of a lecture given in 1912 to the Institute of Actuaries, Alfred Watson, speaking of the Manchester Unity, justified the steady weakening of the power of the lodges claiming that 'it must be recognised that if an affiliated order is to have effective control over its lodges, it must have power of a punitive order'.[1] Whatever the justification for such a transfer of power, there can be no doubt that it was bound to weaken the local lodge; the local democracy lost control of an important part of its activities and this was a major step on the way to the local lodge becoming an agency, collecting and paying out on the instructions of a superior body.[2]

Another consequence of standardised contributions and benefits was the limitation on the expenditure of lodge funds on conviviality. Lodge night beer and the annual feast had to be paid for by the members separately, it became virtually impossible to pay from the normal contributions a sufficiently large 'room rent' to cover the cost of liquor on club nights. Thus the increasing emphasis on graduated tables and better management ultimately achieved the suppression of a custom against which Tidd Pratt had disclaimed vainly for many years. When E. L. Stanley had met local secretaries of societies at Manchester in 1872, he pointed out to them that 'To form a club for the purpose of meeting convivially to drink beer was not one of the purposes mentioned in the Act' and he urged them to pass a resolution condemning the practice, 'but the meeting did not appear to consider that it would be advisable for this step to be taken . . . there was a strong feeling

---

[1] W. Beveridge, *Voluntary Action*, 1948, p. 38.

[2] The independence of local lodges had been further weakened as a result of the verdict in the case of *Schofield* v. *Vause* in 1886. The Caledonian lodge of the Manchester Unity at Bolton had declined to register as a branch of the Unity under the act of 1875 and when pressed it tried to secede from the Order. The trustees of the Order began an action in Chancery to prevent the lodge from registering as a separate society while the demands of the Unity remained unsatisfied. The matter was carried to the Court of Appeal in 1886, and that Court decided that when a member joined a lodge he also became a member of the Unity of which that lodge formed a part and the tie between the two could only be severed in accordance with such rules as the Unity might lay down.
—Moffrey, *A Century of Oddfellowship*, p. 107.

that . . . if the beer was not provided very few members would attend at the meetings of the friendly societies'.[1] As the custom of providing liquor was gradually abolished so did many friendly society meetings become less convivial and the societies grew rather into mutual insurance societies; the main business of club night became the collection of contributions.

These changes in the nature of friendly societies, which were making themselves manifest in the last quarter of the nineteenth century, reflected changes in the social and economic life of the period. The purchasing power of the classes who joined the friendly societies was coming to be recognised as increasingly important by business men engaged in selling a variety of wares from clothing to insurance and entertainment. This can be seen most easily, perhaps, in the emergence of the department store. These sprang from usually humble beginnings as the general standard of living rose in the last part of the nineteenth century and as individual entrepreneurs saw the profits to be made from catering for the masses. 'By the end of the nineteenth century, as a result of their (the department stores') influence, large scale retailing for the masses had become more important than retailing for the classes.' [2] By 1885 Lewis's had the largest store in Liverpool with branches in Manchester, Sheffield and Birmingham. In 1872 William Whiteley began to call himself the 'Universal Provider'. It was becoming a commercial proposition to provide for both the working man's insurance and his relaxation, thus the friendly societies gradually came to be in competition with outsiders in respect of both of their main forms of activity.

The industrial assurance business expanded very rapidly after 1875. Between 1878 and 1887 the annual income from premiums in this field increased from £1,488,829 to £4,181,852. The profitability of this business may be seen from the amount expended upon management, 51 per cent of the premium income in 1878 and 44 per cent in 1887.[3] The most remarkable progress during these years was made by the Prudential whose income had risen to £3,058,500 in 1887. At the end of 1886 the Prudential had

[1] Stanley, pp. 94-5.   [2] A. Briggs, *Friends of the People*, 1956, p. 2.
[3] D. Morrah, *A History of Industrial Life Assurance*, 1955, p. 53.

P

7,111,828 industrial assurance policies in force. So successful was the Prudential that 'its remarkable achievements attracted attention beyond the ocean; it was after studying the methods of the Prudential that the Metropolitan Life Office of New York offered employment in the United States to competent and experienced agents and superintendents working in England'. Some eight hundred apparently crossed the Atlantic to set up and operate a system there similar to that which the Prudential operated in England.[1]

When the Royal Commission reported in 1874 it had little to say about deposit societies for the largest of them, the National Deposit, had fewer than a thousand members while Holloway societies were not mentioned at all. Both of these forms of society grew rapidly after 1875 and neither was much concerned with the social activities of the traditional type of friendly society but concentrated upon the financial function. Their rise in the last quarter of the century within the legal framework of the friendly societies' acts was another illustration of the divorce of even mutual insurance from conviviality and of the increasing specialisation of the time.

The Surrey Deposit Society was founded in 1868, in 1872 it changed its name to the National Deposit Friendly Society. Each member's contribution in such a society was divided so that a part went to a savings account while part went to the society's sick fund. In sickness part of the benefit due was drawn from the member's own account, thus each member had a personal interest in avoiding claims and the sickness experience of the National Deposit has always been very low. The advantage claimed for this system was that a member could use his friendly society as a savings bank. At the time of the Royal Commission the National Deposit had 906 members; in 1886, 5,576 and in 1899 it had 45,804 members.[2]

In 1874 George Holloway founded the Working Men's Conservative Friendly Society at Stroud. The contributions were larger than they need have been to support the benefits offered

---

[1] D. Morrah, *A History of Industrial Life Assurance*, 1955, pp. 53–4.
[2] Beveridge, *Voluntary Action*, p. 31.

and at the end of each year the surplus on the common fund was
allocated to individual savings accounts held for each member,
the division each received being proportionate to the number of
shares he held in the society. The two largest of these Holloway
societies were to be the Ideal Benefit Society and the Tunbridge
Wells Equitable, both of which had between three and four
thousand members in 1899.

The increasing importance of the insurance aspect of the
societies was also shown by the rapid growth of the largest unit-
ary (or 'large ordinary') society, the Hearts of Oak. This society had no social activities whatever, it was founded in 1841
but its rapid growth began after 1870. In 1872 it had 32,837
members, by 1886 there had been a fourfold increase—to 111,424,
and by 1899 the membership figure stood at 239,075.[1]

The greater emphasis placed on their insurance work and on
the need for graduated scales by the older societies is scarcely to be
wondered at when the work of these various competing agencies
is considered. The act of 1875 with its provisions requiring
valuation and encouraging good management can hardly be
given the sole credit—or blame—for the change in the affiliated
orders in the last part of the nineteenth century.

Not only was the convivial life of the societies overshadowed in
many cases by their insurance work, but it seemed to be less
important in the lives of many members who now increasingly
found alternative forms of diversion. The annual club day with
its feast and possible excursion seemed to matter less after the
passing of the Bank Holidays Act which held out the prospect of
a number of breaks in the usual routine in the course of each year.
The railways, with their offer of cheap excursions to the sea,
were in one sense an alternative to the club committee organising
a feast or an entertainment. The spread of the early finish on
Saturday from the textile trades to other occupations meant
that many men were free on Saturday afternoons by the 1870s.
The diversions of club night were not as essential to men who
could refresh their spirits by going with their friends to a football
match on Saturday afternoons. The competition for the Football
[1] Ibid.

Association Cup was first established in 1871; after this the better-known clubs began to employ full-time players and to attract large numbers of spectators to their matches.

The evidence seems to suggest that a vigorous social life continued in areas where these innovations mattered rather less as in country villages where seaside rail excursions could hardly spread in the absence of a railway station. The present writer's grandfather was secretary for nearly sixty years of an Oddfellows' lodge which continued to hold its annual club day in the village until 1914; this provided the main diversion of the year in village life with its procession, feast, sideshows and sports until the First World War finally broke the barriers which had partially insulated such a village from outside influences.

The final factor to be considered in bringing about a change in the position of friendly societies towards the end of the nineteenth century is the change which took place in the prevailing political and social ideas and which tended to make the friendly society movement appear as a vested interest defending itself against change. It has been suggested that the two decades following 1873 saw a series of economic troubles which resulted in some lack of faith in economic individualism in its most extreme form. Germany and the United States were beginning to rival Britain and even to take her markets, and the belief that social welfare would ultimately be achieved by indirection and by the individual pursuit of gain was no longer guiding legislation in practice even if politicians accepted it still as a theory. This change was recognised by some in the 1870s; Jevons in 1875 wrote that he thought that a considerable change of opinion was taking place in England.[1] 'In exceptions and alternatives to economic individualism in practice and in new statements of philosophy a two-fold idea was gaining wide support: in modern industrial society individuals in isolation, unsupported by the social structure, can achieve neither material welfare nor positive freedom; and it is the function of the State actively to promote a social basis for welfare and freedom.'[2]

---

[1] Quoted by H. Lynd, *England in the Eighteen-Eighties*, 1945, p. 188.
[2] H. Lynd, op. cit., p. 155.

Against this background the introduction of pension schemes for the aged in Germany led to considerable discussion of the problem of provision for old age in England. Both the Oddfellows and the Foresters brought forward schemes whereby members might subscribe for pensions from the age of 65 years. But 'they have failed from want of applicants, though everything has been done to make the insurance an easy one, the member paying into his own branch and the secretary passing on the premiums to the central office'.[1] A Select Committee inquired into a superannuation scheme to be run by the state which was proposed by Canon Blackley. The Committee's Report showed that in spite of their own failure here, the leaders of the orders were strongly opposed to any departure from the prevailing ideas of the mid-nineteenth century. The Committee discussed the attitude of the orders in their Report, and after saying that the representatives of the affiliated orders brought strong objections against the scheme, the Report continues, 'The objections resolved themselves mainly into apprehension, lest operation of compulsory national insurance should interfere in the numerical increase of their own organisations. So keenly apprehensive are the officials of some of these societies of this effect, that Mr. Reuben Watson, Actuary of the Manchester Unity of Oddfellows did not hesitate to reply to Q 909 "If you could devise some scheme which would be for the welfare of all classes in this country, but which would be to the detriment of the friendly societies, you would not object to it on that ground?" Answer, "Well, I think I should object to it. I consider that friendly societies have voluntarily done a very great deal of good in this country, and I think they ought not to be interfered with by the establishment of any system which would be injurious to them." ' [2] The Committee pointed out that a Director of the Manchester Unity had admitted that two years after the introduction of a superannuation scheme into the Unity only four members out of 600,000 had joined.

The idea that the state should 'actively promote a social basis

---

[1] Wilkinson, *The Friendly Society Movement*, p. 188.
[2] Report of the Select Committee of the House of Commons on National Provident Insurance, 1887, pp. vi and vii.

for welfare and freedom' was one that the affiliated friendly
societies could never really bring themselves to accept in the nineteenth century. After years of struggle, they seemed to have acquired a vested interest in the status quo. In spite of the obvious
failure of the Manchester Unity's superannuation scheme, Reuben
Watson could still write in 1888: 'State subsidisation appears likely
to be appealed to in some cases to accomplish that which intelligent men in these dominions seem determined to do for themselves without unnecessary state or other interference or aid.'[1]

The most remarkable development among English friendly
societies between 1815 and 1875 had been the growth of the
affiliated orders. Membership of an order offered a man good
fellowship at all times and succour in time of need. They had
grown up so that working men might join together to meet many
of the hardships of life in an industrial civilisation, and, although
ever professing loyalty to the constitution, had been regarded
with suspicion by the governing classes. It was only in 1875 that
the law had permitted them to register as affiliated orders. Yet in
the twenty-five years that followed this act, the nature of the
societies underwent a change. The financial function came to
predominate over the convivial, the central bureaucracies of the
orders came to dominate the local lodges and the orders sought to
preserve from further change that position in society for which
they had finally won recognition in 1875.

[1] Reuben Watson, *An Essay on Friendly Societies and Sick Clubs*, 1888.

APPENDIX A

Arrangements for Travelling and for Clearances in the Manchester Unity of Oddfellows and in the Ancient Order of Foresters

THE provision made for members who wished to travel in search of work were very similar in both of the main orders. In neither order could a member claim this benefit until he had been a member for at least twelve months. In the Oddfellows he drew a card from his lodge—having proved his need for it—which showed the benefit payable in case of sickness or death should he encounter either of these misfortunes while travelling. The nearest lodge then paid the benefits due and reclaimed the amount from the member's home lodge. The travelling expenses were paid by any lodge at which the member presented his card and the lodges reclaimed the amount they paid out in this way from the central funds. The Unity raised a fund from which travelling claims were met through a levy on each district, based on its membership, and the district claimed contributions from its constituent lodges according to their size. A travelling card was valid for six months, but not more than one card would be issued each year to the same member. In addition to the card, a member had to obtain the current password from the Noble Grand of his lodge before setting out since 'the examining officer (of the relieving lodge) shall refuse the relief to members not in possession of the travelling password'.

Arrangements in the Foresters were similar except that a licence and a number of pre-paid cheques were issued in place of the card. Not more than one cheque was to be presented to the relieving officer of the local court for encashment in a single day. The relief was usually at the rate of 1s. 3d. per day (2s. 6d. on Saturdays).

One provision was made by the Manchester Unity which did not appear in the rules of the Ancient Order of Foresters, for the rules of the former expressly forbade any member to be issued with a travelling card 'who has lost his employment through a strike or turn-out for wages'.

Clearances, or the right to change one's membership from one lodge or court to another without loss of benefits, could be granted in both the Manchester Unity and the Foresters after twelve months' membership. The clearance meant that the member to whom it was granted had settled all his outstanding payments and that he was in a position to enjoy fully the benefits offered by his lodge or court. In the Oddfellows a member who had drawn his clearance had to 'throw it in' at a lodge within four weeks— or whatever was the usual interval between lodge meetings. A lodge was normally obliged to accept such a member, but if he were over forty-five years of age or in poor health it had the option of refusing him membership. The sick pay and funeral benefit remained the liability of the original lodge for twelve months.

The procedure in the Ancient Order of Foresters was slightly different. Sick pay remained the liability of the original court for only six months and funeral pay remained the liability of the original district for a similar period. The Foresters allowed a member two months in which to throw his clearance into another court, but no court was obliged to accept a clearance if it did not wish to do so—in which case the member would have to go back to his original court.

The number of clearances was only recorded by the Oddfellows from 1870 and by the Foresters from 1871.

TABLE 16

The number of clearances 1870–5

Year	M.U.O.F.	A.O.F.
1870	964	—
1871	694	1,074
1872	863	1,069
1873	896	1,043
1874	554	1,008
1875	540	1,095

The number would have been larger were it not that a member of either order could retain membership of his lodge or court after moving away from the district while using a lodge or court in his new district as an agency through which he remitted his subscription and received his benefits.

'The organisation of the affiliated orders therefore lends itself much more than that of the isolated friendly societies to industrial freedom and independence. The working man, who is not satisfied with his lot can leave his place of employment and seek for work elsewhere, and he gets material help while on the search, and finds friends who may give him advice. He may also establish himself in a new home without losing any of the advantages for which he had subscribed.'—From the evidence of the Chief Registrar of Friendly Societies before the Royal Commission on Labour, 1892, Appendix LIII.

NOTE

The information in this appendix is based upon the Laws of the Independent Order of Oddfellows, Manchester Unity, 1855 edition (Laws 221–55); and upon the General Laws of the Ancient Order of Foresters, 1865 edition (Laws 92–8).

The figures for clearances are taken from F. G. P. Neison, *Some Statistics of the Affiliated Orders, 1877.*

APPENDIX B

Officers of the Affiliated Orders

TABLE 17

The Occupations of 69 leading Officers of the Manchester Unity of Oddfellows in this period

Name	District	Occupation
★ Thomas Armitt .	Salford	Earthenware dealer.
D Edward Powell .	Newcastle	'Master'.
D Sidney Mills . .	Oldham	Clog and pattern maker.
Frederick Taylor .	Oldham	Businessman.
★ John Peiser . . .	Manchester	Partner in weaving business.
★ John Ormond . .	Manchester	Licensed victualler.
Thomas Williamson	St. Helens	'Confidential situation' in the Ravenhead Plate Glass Company.
William Ratcliffe .	Tyldesley	Full-time Secretary of the Order.
★ John Lloyd . . .	Stockport	Wholesale brewer.
★ James Mansell . .	Manchester	Owner of a saw-making business.
Alexander Shaw .	Wigan	Doctor.
John Ashurst . .	Manchester	'Well-to-do tradesman'.
D Isaac Lucas . . .	Macclesfield	Unknown but well enough off to pay the lodge's rent himself.
John Davis . . .	Tredegar	Literary pursuits.
★ David Carnegie .	Manchester	Ex-soldier.
Samuel Norton .	Leeds	Shoe-maker.
Robert Naylor .	Manchester	Own business as painter.
Alfred Smith . .	Knaresborough	Surgeon.
★ Edward Davis . .	Manchester	Owner of gas appliance business.
William Bennett .	Selby	Hat manufacturer.
★ John White . .	Manchester	'A respectable position in society' and member of Manchester Town Council.
D William Machan .	Liverpool	Businessman.
D★ George Richmond	Manchester	Owner of printing business.
D William Brown .	Stockport	Broker and accountant.
Samuel Rawson .	Sheffield	Owner of cabinet-making business and government contractor.

Name	District	Occupation
D John MacDougall .	Greenock	H.M. Customs officer.
Samuel Woodhead	Bradford	Grocer and flour dealer.
D William Alexander	Leeds	Saddler (employee).
D George Walker .	Durham	Owner of printing business.
D John Bradley . .	Hyde	Owner of clog-making business.
D* Henry Whaite . .	Manchester	Fine Art dealer.
D Joseph Woodcock .	Glossop	Grocer, draper and corn dealer.
Henry Ratcliffe .	Manchester	Full-time Secretary of the Order.
D William Candelet .	Hyde	Whitesmith.
D* John Dickinson .	Manchester	Owner of book-binding business.
D* Robert Glass . .	Newcastle	Potter.
John Rogerson .	Manchester	Bookseller.
D* James Roe . . .	London	Owner of brushmaking business.
D* John Schofield . .	Ashton-u-Lyne	Partner in 'the most extensive' plumbing business in the town.
D* James Cox . . .	Southampton	Bookseller, owner and editor of the *Southampton Examiner*.
D William Aitken .	Ashton-u-Lyne	Principal of a school.
D* Samuel Daynes .	Norwich	Proprietor of a printing works.
R. C. Davies . .	Merthyr Tydvil	Manager of printing works.
D* Charles Hardwick .	Preston	Literary contributor.
D* Benjamin Street .	Matlock	Licensed Victualler and farmer.
D* Henry Buck . .	Birmingham	Proprietor of building business.
D* John Gale . . .	Liverpool	Proprietor of building business.
D* Thomas Price . .	Merthyr Tydvil	Baptist Minister.
D* Frederick Richmond	Manchester	Worked in an engineering company.
D James Banyard . .	Norfolk	Businessman.
Augustus Greeves .	ex-Nottingham	Became Mayor of Melbourne and member of the legislative assembly.
D* William Hickton .	Stockport	Proprietor of hat business.
James Webb . .	Hyde	Principal of a school.
James Reynolds .	Glamorgan	Auctioneer.
D* Jno Richardson .	Cockermouth	Wholesale brewer.
Bryant Allen . .	Norwich	Proprietor of dyeing works.

Name	District	Occupation
Henry Williams .	Shrewsbury	Businessman.
Thomas Kilner .	Manchester	Manufacturer and Trader.
D Samuel Settle . .	Bolton	Hotel Manager.
D William Smith .	Birmingham	Founder of the *Birmingham Mercury* and of land and building societies.
D★ Vincent Burgess .	London	Hat Manufacturer.
D Thomas Luff . .	Liverpool	Licensed Victualler.
D Edwin Noon . .	Belper	Ale and Porter Merchant.
W. N. Waldram .	Leicester	Partner in and Managing Director of a Brewery.
Henry Glasse . .	Winchester	Clerk to Poor Law Union.
Thomas Collins .	Wellington	Solicitor.
D John Crispin . .	Ipswich	Draper.
William Thompson	Leeds	Manager of a Loan Society.
John Gibson . .	Wigton	Farmer.

All of this information is taken from the relevant numbers of the *Oddfellows' Magazine* (first and new series) between the years 1835 and 1863, with the exception of the occupations of John Lloyd and James Mansell which are from Mark Wardle's biographies of them published in 1832.

There is no reason to suspect that the occupations here listed do not give a fair cross-section of the occupations and social position of the leaders of the Manchester Unity at this time. There are some biographical sketches in the magazines which do not mention the occupation of a man but deal only with his work within the Order, but there seem to have been no omissions because an officer's social standing was felt unworthy of mention. In the later volumes of the *Magazine*, occupations were always stated—that is to say after 1857 when the *Magazine* was resumed after a gap of ten years during which it had ceased publication. The last 31 names in this list are taken from the issues in this New Series and represent the full number of 'portraits' published between 1857 and 1863.

All the officers selected for the honour of having their 'portraits' in the *Magazine* were at least Past Provincial Grand Masters or District Corresponding Secretaries. Of the 69 listed here, 25 had served as Grand Master of the whole Order—or were so to serve—and these have been indicated with an asterisk ★ but socially they were indistinguishable from the P.P.G.M.s; those who had served on the Board of Directors have been indicated by the letter D before their names. (The Board of Directors was only reconstituted to represent the districts after 1844).

TABLE 18

The Occupations of 37 leading Officers of the Ancient Order of Foresters in this period

Name	District	Occupation
John Mallinson . . .	Yorkshire	General Manager of Low Moor Wire and Rolling Mills.
Samuel Shawcross . .	Stockport	Full-time Permanent Secretary.
John France	Glossop	Butcher.
William Long . . .	St. Austell	Owner of Millwright's business.
W. T. Butterwick . .	Bristol	Ship-broker.
Joseph Whitelock . .	Leeds	Tailor (Freeman of Ripon).
Ralph Blackett . . .	Stockport	'Extensive and respectable' Bootmaking business.
Peter Walker . . .	Bolton	Leather Dealer.
Thomas Hodges . .	London	Proprietor of Hairdressing business.
Edwin Mason . . .	Birmingham	Lace Manufacturer.
Francis Fletcher . . .	Shrewsbury	Wine Merchant.
Edwin Russell . . .	Bath	Cabinet Maker.
Henry Buckland . .	London	Tailor.
Edmund Ashworth .	Lancashire	Employed in Engineering firm.
William Sherwood . .	Wolverhampton	L.N.W.R. official.
Ralph Parker . . .	Stoke-on-Trent	Innkeeper.
William Temple . .	Leeds	Cabinet Maker and Furniture Broker.
R. J. Linfoot . . .	London	Tailor.
W. B. Redfern . . .	Stockport	Editor and Newspaper Proprietor.
S. H. Culley . . .	Exeter	General Manager of a Steamship Company.
John Lintott	Brighton	Tailor.
Samuel Oldham . .	Mottram	Druggist and Bookseller.
C. Blackwell . . .	Hull	Proprietor of Brass Foundry.
Enoch Hemingway .	Ashton-u-Lyne	Boot and Shoe Manufacturer.
Henry Swatton . . .	London	Businessman.
Robert Smith . . .	Sunderland	Innkeeper.
Thomas Bradbury . .	London	Foreman Coach Painter.

Name	District	Occupation
George Barnard . .	Chichester	Proprietor of Window Blind business.
Robert Lyne . . .	Derbyshire	Burial Society Collector.
Benjamin Hill . . .	Leicester	Principal of a School.
Henry Wood . . .	Nottingham	Foreman Upholsterer.
Francis Rawling . .	York	Contractor.
John Jenks	Cardiff	Post Office official.
John Vernon . . .	Chester	Manager.
S. P. Greenway . . .	Southampton	Printer.
J. J. Holmes	London	Hairdresser.
Ebenezer Arnold . .	London	Owner of Printing business.

All of these particulars have been taken from various numbers of the *Foresters' Miscellany* for the years 1865–75. This magazine of the Ancient Order of Foresters published its earliest biographical sketches of officers in 1848, but it was only after 1865 that these accounts dealt with a man's life outside of the Order and began to be concerned with his occupation or position in society. After 1865 only three accounts failed to give the occupation of an officer; apart from these three, all of those officers whose biographies appeared between 1865 and 1875 have been included in this table. The annual High Court Meeting voted to decide which officers should be honoured by having some account of their lives published.

APPENDIX C

A Note on the table printed at the foot of page XXXIV of the Fourth Report of the Royal Commission on Friendly Societies, 1874, purporting to show the occupations of members of the Manchester Unity of Oddfellows during the period 1866–70

THIS table was supplied to the Commission by Mr. Ratcliffe, Secretary to the Manchester Unity, and is the only comprehensive analysis of the membership of an affiliated order which the Commission gave or, apparently, was able to obtain. Its value, therefore, would seem to be considerable in this connection, especially when compared with the table given above on p. 74 which analyses the membership of the same Order some twenty years earlier.

Unfortunately such a comparison casts doubts on the validity of the Commission's table. In his Observations on the Rate of Mortality and Sickness of 1850, Ratcliffe printed tables showing the number of years of life observed in twenty-six main occupations followed by Oddfellows during the years 1846–8; the same twenty-six occupations figure in the table he gave the Commission more than twenty years later. A comparison of the two shows that, with one exception, the same proportion of members still followed the same occupations in the period 1866–70 as in 1846–8. In view of the development of the Order in the intervening years, this seems unlikely. A comparison of the actual years of life given for each occupation in the two sets of figures, shows that in twenty of the twenty-six occupations the figures for the second set are exactly double those of the first, in five other cases the figures are almost exactly double save for one digit and the only significant difference appears to be in the case of miners. Apparently there had been no analysis of the occupations of members of this order since the 1840s except in the case of miners whose heavy sickness liability made necessary more frequent review. The figures in question are set out overleaf.

Occupation	Years of life observed:	
	(a) 1846–8	(b) 1866–70
Labourers (rural) . .	53,584	107,168
Labourers (town) . .	42,887	85,774
Miners	30,654	77,161
Carpenters and Joiners .	37,380	74,760
Cordwainers . . .	24,788	49,076
Blacksmiths . . .	23,878	47,756
Tailors	21,139	42,278
Weavers . . .	18,830	37,660
Stonemasons . . .	18,449	36,898
Domestic Servants . .	16,235	32,470
Mill Operatives . .	13,511	27,722
Plumbers and Painters .	11,783	23,766
Spinners (cotton) . .	11,239	22,656
Bricklayers and Plasterers	11,185	22,370
Clerks, etc. . . .	8,488	16,976
Butchers . . .	7,699	15,398
Bakers	6,098	12,196
Printers. . . .	4,893	9,786
Wheelwrights . .	4,610	9,220
Dyers	3,384	8,768
Woolcombers . .	4,259	8,518
Sawyers . . .	4,153	8,306
Hatters	3,658	7,316
Potters . . .	2,560	5,120
Millwrights . . .	2,431	4,862
Coopers . . .	2,201	4,402

The figures in column (b) above were used by the Royal Commission as a guide to the occupations of all the members of the Manchester Unity during the years 1866–70, their value from this point of view is extremely doubtful. It is difficult to suggest an explanation of this curious state of affairs. There may have been a genuine misunderstanding between the Secretary of the I.O.O.F.M.U. and the Commission, or the Secretary may have sought to be more helpful than he was really in a position to be.

APPENDIX D

The Size of the Lodges of the Manchester Unity of Oddfellows and of the Courts of the Ancient Order of Foresters

In both the Manchester Unity of Oddfellows and the Ancient Order of Foresters the lodge or court was the unit for purposes of sickness insurance, and the larger and more varied the membership of the individual lodge or court, the less likely was it to encounter financial difficulties in the administration of sickness benefits.

In both orders there was a steady rise in the membership of individual lodges and courts, although in particular years this trend was sometimes reversed as in the Foresters in 1856 when the number of courts increased at a greater rate than the membership.

The average membership of the lodges of the Manchester Unity increased earlier than that of the courts of the Foresters largely because the period of rapid expansion in the I.O.O.F.M.U. came much earlier. These periods when there was a rapid expansion of influence on a national scale in either Order were marked by the foundation of many new lodges and courts—as in the I.O.O.F.M.U. from 1835 to 1845 or in the A.O.F. from 1855 to 1865. In each case there followed an expansion in the membership of the new branches which helped to consolidate the gains, and which showed itself in the steady rise in the average membership of lodges and courts. The internal crisis in the Oddfellows led to some delay before this process began in earnest in that Order.

The graphs which follow illustrate these changes in both orders and also indicate that while the number of lodges and courts provides a good general guide to the rate of expansion of the membership of an Order, yet there is no constant relationship between the two, and that the number of courts and the number of members may actually move in opposite directions occasionally—as in the A.O.F. in 1855. (These graphs are, of necessity, confined to the years for which reliable and complete statistics are available.)

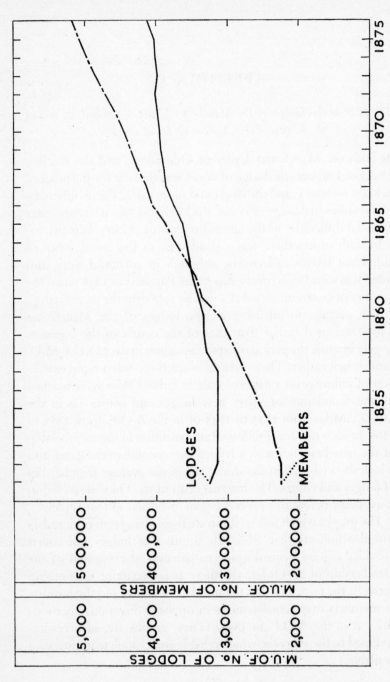

The increase in the number of lodges and the number of members of the M.U.O.F., 1851–76.

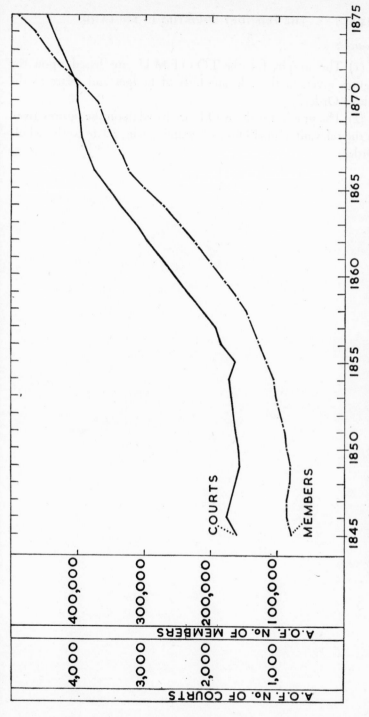

Increase in the number of courts and the number of members of the A.O.F., 1845-1875.

Sources:

(1) The graphs for the I.O.O.F.M.U. are based upon the figures given in the relevant Lists of Lodges and relate to the whole Order.

(2) The graphs for the A.O.F. are based upon the figures given in the relevant annual Directories and, again, relate to the whole Order.

APPENDIX E

Prospectus of Rochdale Oddfellows' Literary Institution[1]

WHAT IS THE ODDFELLOWS' LITERARY INSTITUTION?

AN Institution originally established for the enlightenment of the Oddfellows, and the education of their children by means of a Day-School, but now thrown open to the public. It is a place of instruction for old and young, male or female, which any person may join. All tickets of membership are either quarterly, 1s. 3d., half-yearly, 2s. 6d. or yearly 5s.: but for the convenience of the poor, subscriptions may be paid monthly, whatever kind of ticket is obtained.

Benefits.—All members have the privilege of attending any, or the whole of the classes, taking books out of the library, attending the Saturday evening reading-room, and any other means of improvement or recreation that the directors may hereafter provide, with their annexed conditions.

LIST OF MALE CLASSES

Monday and Thursday evenings, reading and writing. Tuesday evenings, geometry and mensuration.

Wednesday evening, reading, spelling and dictation. Thursday evening, arithmetic, book-keeping and grammar. Friday evening, singing class.

N.B. Parties joining reading classes may find their own books, or, pay 1d. per month to the Institution and books will be found for them. Slates are found for all classes.

LIST OF FEMALE CLASSES

Monday evening, geography, arithmetic and vocal music. Tuesday evening, history, writing, dictation or spelling.

Thursday evening, domestic economy, household accounts,

[1] This Prospectus was printed in the *Oddfellows' Chronicle*, April, 1848.

dictation. In female classes, history and domestic economy are taught in connection with reading. A distinct entrance into the Institution, and distinct rooms, are appropriated to females.

LIBRARY

The Library is open for the reception and delivery of books on Monday evenings, from fifteen minutes past seven till eight o'clock, and the same on Friday evenings; and from eight till nine o'clock on Wednesday evenings.

DAY SCHOOL

In this department arrangements have been made by which children above three years of age may be admitted. Fees—reading 3d.; reading and writing 5d.; reading, writing, arithmetic, algebra, grammar, book-keeping, etc. 7d. Hours of attendance: Morning, from nine till twelve; Afternoon, from half-past one to half-past four. All fees are pre-paid. Sewing, knitting, etc., are taught to girls.

READING-ROOM

The Reading-room is open every Saturday evening, from 4 p.m. till 10 p.m., and is supplied with London and Provincial newspapers and periodicals.

Here, then, is an Institution offering every advantage for mental and moral elevation that could possibly be expected from the smallness of its means. We continually hear it said that ignorance generates crime! Shall we continue to suffer the consequences of crime, while education, its antidote, can be obtained at so cheap a rate? Men of wealth, fathers and mothers, young men and women, remember the extent to which you encourage and avail yourselves of institutions like this, will show to what extent you are prepared to carry out the voluntary principle.

By order of the Directors,

J. WILD, Secretary

February, 1848.

Unemployment and the Affiliated Orders

IN the *Oddfellows' Magazine* in 1859 'J.H.' wrote: 'The chief officers have repeatedly stated—and it cannot be denied—that the order is affected by the position of the working classes; or, in other words, by the want of trade and the demand for labour.' [1] From about 1850 the two main affiliated orders were sufficiently well organised to be able to collect and to publish figures for their total membership which can be accepted as reliable. Moreover their membership was scattered over many occupations so that an isolated disturbance in one industry was unlikely to affect them greatly, while a general decline in trade was likely to concern many of their members or potential members, and to affect their rate of expansion.

Reliable figures for unemployment only become available from 1850. These figures seem to provide the best measure of the extent to which the 'want of trade' affected the working population from time to time. Accordingly the two graphs which follow attempt to show the degree to which the 'want of trade' (as reflected by the extent of unemployment among members of the main trade unions) affected the rate of growth of the Ancient Order of Foresters (as shown by the percentage increase in that Order's membership each year).

The rate of increase in the Ancient Order of Foresters follows broadly the percentage employed up to 1853 and again from 1860 to 1880. The greatest amount of unemployment occurred in the years 1852, 1858, 1862, 1868 and 1879; these troughs in the employment graph are reflected in the A.O.F. graph except for the later years of the 1850s—the trough in employment in 1858 appears to have had little effect on the growth of the Foresters. The period from 1854 to 1864 was the decade showing very rapid expansion of the Foresters, consequently, although adverse economic conditions bring the graph down in 1861 and 1862, yet the

[1] *Oddfellows' Magazine*, New Series, January, 1859, p. 45.

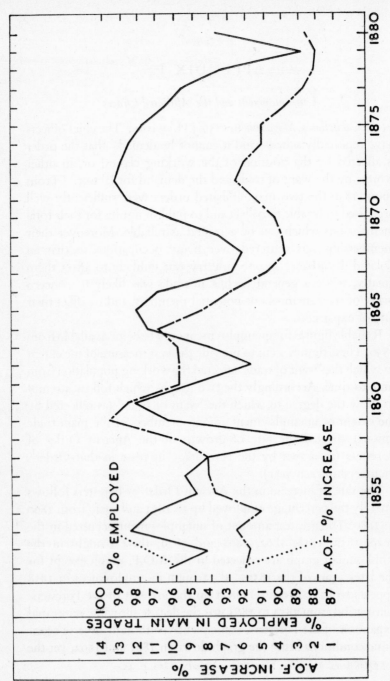

Percentage increase of A.O.F. and the percentage of employed in the principal trades, 1851–80.

TABLE 19

A comparison of the rate of growth of the Ancient Order of Foresters and the amount of employment in the principal trades, 1851–80

Year	A.O.F. per cent increase	per cent unemployed	Year	A.O.F. per cent increase	per cent unemployed
1851	5·9	3·9	1866	6·6	3·3
1852	5·6	6·0	1867	4·6	7·4
1853	6·4	1·7	1868	3·6	7·9
1854	5·0	2·9	1869	3·7	6·7
1855	7·6	5·4	1870	4·1	3·9
1856	7·9	4·7	1871	5·3	1·6
1857	8·0	6·0	1872	6·3	0·9
1858	9·6	11·9	1873	5·9	1·2
1859	13·5	3·8	1874	4·9	1·7
1860	12·5	1·9	1875	4·9	2·4
1861	9·5	5·2	1876	3·6	3·7
1862	9·5	8·4	1877	2·5	4·7
1863	9·6	6·0	1878	1·9	6·8
1864	10·8	2·7	1879	1·8	11·4
1865	8·3	2·1	1880	2·5	6·5

Note: In the graph opposite the percentage of unemployed has been subtracted from 100 and it is this figure which has been used to show the 'per cent employed' for purposes of comparison with the rate of increase of membership of the Foresters.

The figures for the A.O.F. are based upon the membership figures given in the annual Directories. The 'percentage unemployed' figures are from A. C. Pigou, *Industrial Fluctuations*, 1927, Appendix, Table I.

increase in those years can be seen to be at a much greater rate than in 1868 when the employment position was roughly similar. The apparent failure of the employment trough of 1858 to have its customary effect on the expansion of the Order may be due to the predominance of rural recruits among those who were joining the Foresters at that time, for they would not be included among the figures for the unemployed returned by the trade unions on which the employment graph is based. Agricultural wage rates, too, bore 'no very consistent relation' to general business cycle movements.[1] These were the years when old village clubs were becoming branches of the Ancient Order of Foresters which they could still do (until 1870) while maintaining their existing scales of charges and benefits.

[1] Gayer, Rostow and Schwartz, *Growth and Fluctuation of the British Economy*, vol. II, p. 953.

TABLE 20

A comparison between the rate of growth of the Manchester Unity of Oddfellows and the amount of employment in the principal trades, 1853–1880

Year	M.U.O.F. per cent increase	per cent unemployed	Year	M.U.O.F. per cent increase	per cent unemployed
1853	2·7	1·7	1867	2·9	7·4
1854	3·5	2·9	1868	1·9	7·9
1855	4·6	5·4	1869	2·1	6·7
1856	4·7	4·7	1870	2·1	3·9
1857	4·8	6·0	1871	2·9	1·6
1858	3·9	11·9	1872	2·6	0·9
1859	5·9	3·8	1873	2·5	1·2
1860	3·6	1·9	1874	3·1	1·7
1861	6·0	5·2	1875	2·5	2·4
1862	2·4	8·4	1876	1·9	3·7
1863	4·4	6·0	1877	1·5	4·7
1864	4·2	2·7	1878	0·9	6·8
1865	3·7	2·1	1879	0·4	11·4
1866	4·3	3·3	1880	1·8	6·5

Note: In the following graph the percentage of unemployed has been subtracted from 100 and it is this figure which has been used to show the 'per cent employed' for purposes of comparison with the increase of membership of the M.U.O.F.

The figures for the M.U.O.F. are based upon the membership figures given in the annual Lists of Lodges. Unemployment figures are from A. C. Pigou, op. cit.

The effect of unemployment on the growth of the affiliated orders which the experience of the Foresters suggested is confirmed by the graph showing the rate of increase in the size of the Manchester Unity for the years 1853 to 1880. This graph starts only in 1853 because the internal troubles from which the Unity suffered between 1845 and 1852 played a considerable part in governing the rate of expansion—or of contraction—of the Order in those years.[1] In this case all the troughs in the employment graph are reflected in the membership graph—those of 1858, 1862, 1868 and 1879. The rate of expansion of the Oddfellows was not nearly so great as that of the Foresters after 1850; consequently the graph for the increase in membership shows a less marked tendency to rise between the trough years than does that for the Foresters.

[1] The internal troubles included: (a) The dishonesty of the Corresponding Secretary, (b) The long conflict over the question of a graduated scale and actuarial soundness.

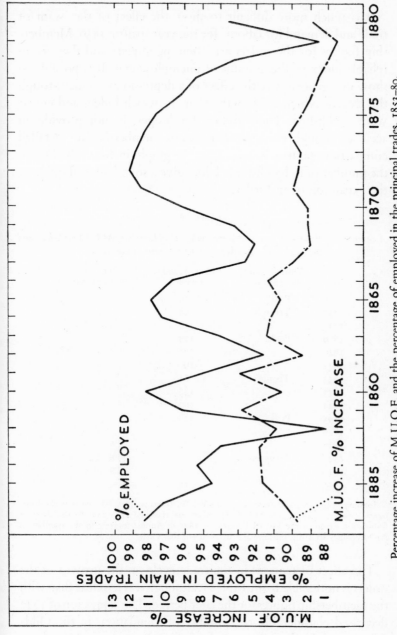

Percentage increase of M.U.O.F. and the percentage of employed in the principal trades, 1853–80.

It is much more difficult to show the effect of the 'want of trade and demand for labour' for the years before 1850. Membership figures for the orders are often incomplete and there is no reliable index of the amount of unemployment. It is possible to show in a general way the effect of a depression in trade through the records which exist of the years in which lodges and courts were established. These figures for lodges do not provide an accurate enough guide to increases in membership for detailed comparisons (as may be seen from the graphs in Appendix D) but the number of lodges founded does give a sound general guide to the expansion of an Order.

TABLE 21

A comparison of turning points of trade cycles, foundations of M.U.O.F. lodges and increases in the number of A.O.F. courts, 1836–1850

Year	Turning point of trade cycle	M.U.O.F. lodges founded	A.O.F. courts annual increase
1836	Peak	84	—
1837	Trough	91	—
1838		136	—
1839	Peak	174	—
1840		222	—
1841		190	—
1842	Trough	61	—
1843		143	—
1844		167	—
1845	Peak	128	158
1846		55	98
1847		24	Decrease
1848	Trough	18	Decrease
1849		9	Decrease
1850		11	21

Turning points in trade cycles are from W. W. Rostow, *British Economy of the Nineteenth Century*, 1948, p. 33. M.U.O.F. lodges are classified according to the dates of foundation given in the List of Lodges for 1875–6. Annual increase in the number of A.O.F. courts are from the annual Directories of that Order.

The effect of troughs in the trade cycle on the growth of the orders is noticeable from Table 21, although it is less clear than with the membership figures for the later period. The depression of 1842 decreased considerably the number of foundations in the Oddfellows, while the effect of that of 1848 seems to have been particularly severe in both orders, even allowing for the internal disputes in the Manchester Unity at that time. The trough of 1837 came during what was probably the most rapid decade of expansion in the Manchester Unity and its effect was certainly no more than to slow temporarily the rapid increase in new foundations. This becomes clearer when the number of new foundations is shown in the form of percentage increases:

> 1835—13 per cent increase
> 1836—13 per cent increase
> 1837—12 per cent increase
> 1838—16 per cent increase
> 1839—18 per cent increase.

BIBLIOGRAPHY

FRIENDLY SOCIETY SOURCES

THE most interesting and often the only records left by societies are their rules, small booklets of up to fifty pages setting out their aims, organisation, benefits and so forth. The large societies have also left a considerable amount of material in the form of annual reports or directories as well as monthly or quarterly magazines. Useful manuscript material relating to the years before 1875 seems to be practically non-existent. The Ancient Order of Foresters, for instance, have preserved at their head office a copy of virtually all directories and magazines that the Order has ever issued, but no manuscript material for these early years. The manuscript returns made to the Registrar from time to time by such societies as were registered have not been preserved since it was decided that they contained no 'historical matter of any importance but only the papers relating to the transactions of each society for the particular year. . . . No purpose can be served by retaining the returns after ten years' (Reprint of Statutes, Rules and Schedules governing the disposal of Public Records by destruction or otherwise, 1877–1913, Section 13, Friendly Societies Registry).

Parliamentary Papers are an important source, particularly towards the end of this period when the Royal Commission surveyed the position. During much of the nineteenth century strong opinions were held of the virtues or vices of various types of society and this helped to produce a considerable literature of books, pamphlets and articles containing useful material. Contemporary writers on such topics as the problem of the poor sometimes gave interesting information about the societies. The development of an actuarial science in this period led to the publication of material concerned especially with the finances of the societies but also throwing light on other aspects of their development. The most systematic and comprehensive private collection of information was that made by Walford and published in volumes IV and V of his Insurance Cyclopaedia.

The steadily increasing part played by the state in providing welfare services during the present century has led to a rapid decline in the relative importance of these societies and—perhaps as a consequence—in the last fifty years few writers have added much to our knowledge of their history.

(1) PRIMARY SOURCES

I. FRIENDLY SOCIETY RULES

The two principal collections of friendly society rules used here are those in the Goldsmiths' Library of the University of London and the Reading Room of the British Museum. There are rather more than four hundred sets of rules in these two collections. Nearly one hundred and fifty pamphlets containing the rules of different societies before 1847 are bound together in five volumes in the British Museum lettered Men's Permanent Societies; in the Goldsmiths' Library the sets of rules are bound and catalogued individually.

In this list no attempt is made to set out particulars of all of these, but only to give details of those rules from which quotations have been made or which have been referred to extensively in this book.

BLADON. Articles, Rules, Orders and Regulations of the Bladon Society. Newcastle, 1824.

BISHOP'S STORTFORD. Rules of the Bishop's Stortford Friendly Society. Bishop's Stortford, 1839.

BURFORD. Rules and Regulations of Burford Friendly Institution. Burford, 1826.

CAMPSALL. Rules and Orders of the Friendly Society held at Campsall in the West Riding of Yorkshire. Doncaster, 1796.

CARLTON. The Constitution and Rules of the Carlton Equitable Friendly Society with tables and calculations. London, 1834.

DARTON. Wilson's Darton Collieries' Club, Darton, Nr. Barnsley. Barnsley, 1833.

DINNINGTON. Rules and Orders to be observed and kept by the Friendly Society . . . held at the sign of the Falcon, Dinnington. Worksop, 1866.

DORSET. Rules, Regulations and Tables for a Friendly Society for the County of Dorset . . . upon legal and scientific principles, on the plan of the Reverend J. T. Becher. Blandford, 1825.

LEMINGTON. Articles, Rules, Orders and Regulations of Tyne Iron Friendly Society, Lemington. Newcastle, 1826.

LINDFIELD. Articles agreed upon by a Friendly Society meeting at the Sign of the Tiger in Lindfield. London, 1757.

NEWBURN. Articles, Rules and Orders of the Friendly Society of All Trades, Newburn. Newcastle, 1825.

NEWCASTLE. Rules and Regulations of the Friendly Society of Joiners instituted at Newcastle-upon-Tyne, 1 January, 1777. Newcastle, 1821.

NEWCASTLE. Articles, Rules and Regulations of the Miners' Society, Newcastle-upon-Tyne. Newcastle, 1829.

PATRINGTON. Articles of the Amicable Society of Patrington. Hedon, 1822.

WALLSEND. Rules and Regulations of Wallsend Colliery Relief Fund. Newcastle, 1832.

WESTMINSTER. Rules and Orders to be observed by the members of a Benefit Society called the Friendly Brothers held at the Duke's Head, Great Peter Street, Westminster. Southwark, 1810.

WHITWELL. Rules of the Independent Friendly Society held at the Jug and Glass Inn, Whitwell. Worksop, 1859.

FORESTERS. General Laws for the Government of the Ancient Order of Foresters (published frequently from 1834).

ODDFELLOWS. Laws for the Government of the Independent Order of Oddfellows, Manchester Unity Friendly Society (published frequently in
this period).

II. FRIENDLY SOCIETY PERIODICAL PUBLICATIONS

(1) *Foresters. Foresters' Miscellany*. Quarterly from 1836, originally published
Edinburgh.
Annual Directory, Published from *c.* 1840.
(2) *Oddfellows. Oddfellows' Magazine*, vols. 1–7, 1829–43, continued as
Oddfellows' Quarterly Magazine, vols. 7–9, 1843–47, continued as
Quarterly Magazine of the I.O.O.F.M.U., vols. 1–14, 1858–83, Manchester.
List of Lodges of the Manchester Unity of Oddfellows. Annually from
c. 1840, Manchester.
Oddfellows' Chronicle, vols. 1–4, 1845–48, Douglas, Isle of Man.
(3) *Other Societies. Rechabite Magazine and Temperance Recorder* (Independent
Order of Rechabites), Nos. 1–15, 1840–1, continued as
Rechabite Magazine, 1844–50, continued as
Rechabite Magazine and Journal of Progress, 1864–9, continued from 1870 as
Rechabite and Temperance Magazine, Manchester.
The Druids' Magazine, 1830–43, Manchester.

III. OFFICIAL SOURCES

A. Main Acts of Parliament

33 Geo. 3, c. 54 (1793). An Act for the Encouragement and Relief of Friendly
Societies. (Rose's Act.)

59 Geo. 3, c. 128 (1819). An Act for the further Protection and Encouragement
of Friendly Societies and for preventing Frauds and Abuses therein.

10 Geo. 4, c. 56 (1829). An Act to consolidate and amend the Laws relating to
Friendly Societies.

4 & 5 Wm. 4, c. 40 (1834). An Act to consolidate and amend the Laws relating
to Friendly Societies.

3 & 4 Vict., c. 73 (1840). An Act to explain and amend the Acts relating to
Friendly Societies.

9 & 10 Vict., c. 27 (1846). An Act to amend the Laws relating to Friendly
Societies.

13 & 14 Vict., c. 115 (1850). An Act to consolidate and amend the Laws
relating to Friendly Societies.

15 & 16 Vict., c. 65 (1852). An Act to continue and amend an Act passed in
the 14th year of the Reign of Her Present Majesty to consolidate and
amend the Laws relating to Friendly Societies.

18 & 19 Vict., c. 63 (1855). An Act to consolidate and amend the Law relating
to Friendly Societies.

R

38 & 39 Vict., c. 60 (1875). An Act to consolidate and amend the Law relating
to Friendly and other Societies.

B. *Other Official Sources* (*primarily concerned with Friendly Societies*)

Report from the Select Committee of the House of Commons on the Laws
respecting Friendly Societies. 1825, IV.

Report from the Select Committee of the House of Commons on the Laws
respecting Friendly Societies. 1826-7, III.

Report from the Select Committee of the House of Lords on the Provident
Associations Fraud Prevention Bill 1847-8, XXVI. (This is not available in the
State Paper Room but there is a copy in the Library of the House of Lords.)

Report from the Select Committee of the House of Commons on the
Friendly Societies Bill. 1849, XIV.

Report from the Select Committee of the House of Commons on Friendly
Society Laws. 1852, V.

Report from the Select Committee of the House of Commons on the
Friendly Societies Bill. 1854, VII.

Four Reports from the Royal Commission appointed to inquire into
Friendly and Benefit Building Societies, 1871-4.

> First Report, 1871, XXV.
>
> Second Report and Evidence, 1872, XXVI.
>
> Third Report, 1873, XXII.
>
> Fourth Report, 1874, with Appendices, 1874, XXIII.
>
> Reports of Assistant Commissioners, 1874, XXIII.

A List of the several Friendly Societies to which debentures have been
issued by the Commissioners for the National Debt. 1824, XVIII.

A List of Friendly Societies or other Institutions which have been registered
in virtue of the Act 59 Geo. 3, c. 128. 1824, XVIII.

Return of the number of Friendly Societies filed by Clerks of the Peace of
each County, etc., since 1 January, 1793. 1831-2, XXVI.

Return of the number of Friendly Societies filed by Clerks of the Peace of
each County, etc., since Michaelmas, 1831. 1834, XLI.

An account of the amount of fees received by the Barrister under the statute
10 Geo. 4, c. 56 for certifying the rules of Friendly Societies to 14 June, 1834.
1834, XLI.

A Return relating to Friendly Societies enrolled in the several counties of
England and Wales. 1837, LI.

A Return relating to Friendly Societies enrolled in the several counties of
England and Wales. 1842, XXVI.

List of Friendly Societies which have invested with the Commissioners for
the National Debt. 1849, XIV.

Return of all Friendly Societies registered, etc. 1852, XXVIII.

Abstract of returns respecting sickness and mortality of Friendly Societies in England and Wales during the five years ending 31 December, 1850. 1852–3, C.

Copy of a report and tables prepared by the Actuary of the National Debt Office on the subject of sickness and mortality among the members of Friendly Societies as shown by the quinquennial returns to 31 December, 1850. 1852–3, C.

Further report and tables by the Actuary of the National Debt Office on sickness and mortality among members of Friendly Societies, etc. 1854, LXIII.

Return of the number of societies which have deposited their rules with the Registrars of Friendly Societies, with the name and object of each, and when established, so far as relates to societies in England. 1867, XL.

Names of all societies whose rules have been deposited, etc. 1868–9, LVI.

Friendly Societies Act, 1875: Regulations approved by the Treasury. 1876, LXIX. Further Regulations. 1877, LXXVII.

Abstracts of the quinquennial returns of sickness and mortality experienced by Friendly Societies for periods between 1855 and 1875, etc. 1880, LXVIII.

Annual Reports of the Registrar of Friendly Societies in England: 1856 LVIII; 1857 XXXIX; 1858 L; 1859 XIX; 1860 XXXIX; 1861 XXXIV; 1862 XXIX; 1863 XXIX; 1864 XXXII; 1865 XXX; 1866 XXXIX; 1867 XXXIX; 1867–8 XL; 1868–9 LVI; 1870 LXI; 1871 LXII; 1872 LIV; 1873 LXI; 1874 LXII; 1875 LXXI.

Annual Reports of the Chief Registrar of Friendly Societies from 1876, especially: 1883 LXVII and LXVIII; 1886 LXI; 1890 LXIX; 1890–1 LXXIX; 1906 CXII.

C. Other Official Sources (not primarily concerned with Friendly Societies)

Abstract of answers and returns relative to the expense and maintenance of the poor in England. 1803–4, XIII.

Abstract of answers and returns relative to the expense and maintenance of the poor in England, 1813, 1814, 1815. Whole of England except London in 1818, XIX; figures for London, 1817, XVII.

Report from His Majesty's Commissioners for inquiry into the administration and practical operation of the Poor Laws with evidence and appendices. 1834, XXVII and XXVIII.

Annual Reports of the Poor Law Commissioners from 1834.

Official circulars of public documents and information issued by the Poor Law Commissioners, 1840–53.

Report from the Poor Law Commissioners on the employment of women and children in agriculture. 1843, XII.

Return of paupers in the workhouses of England having been members of a Benefit Society, etc. 1881, LXXIX.

Report from the Select Committee of the House of Commons on Labourers' Wages. 1824, VI.

Report from the Select Committee on Combination Laws with appendix. 1825, IV.

Supplementary Report of the Central Board of H.M. Commissioners appointed to collect information in the manufacturing districts as to the employment of children in factories (report from Dr. Mitchell), 1837, XIX.

Report from the Select Committee of the House of Commons on Accidents in Mines. 1835, V.

Salaries of Medical Officers and objections to the present system of Medical Relief. 1844, IX.

Report from the Select Committee of the House of Commons on Medical Relief. 1854, XII.

Report from the Select Committee of the House of Commons on Investments for the Savings of the Middle and Working Classes. 1850, XIX.

Parliamentary Debates. Relevant volumes.

IV. PRIVATE PAPERS—MANUSCRIPT AND PRINTED

LUDLOW, J. M. Collection of the papers which Ludlow accumulated as Secretary to the Royal Commission on Friendly Societies, 1870–4.—Goldsmiths' Library.

LUDLOW, J. M. Collection of pamphlets, articles, etc., concerning Friendly Societies and other social questions. 26 volumes.—Goldsmiths' Library.

PLACE, F. Place MSS.—British Museum.

PLACE, F. Place Collection. 180 volumes.—British Museum.

V. EARLY AND CONTEMPORARY WORKS

ACLAND, J. *A Plan for rendering the Poor independent of public contributions founded on the basis of Friendly Societies, etc.* London, 1786.

'ACTUARY'. *Considerations on the necessity of appointing a Board of Commissioners for the protection and encouragement of Friendly Societies.* London, 1824.

ALCOCK, T. *Observations on the Defects of the Poor Laws and on the Causes and Consequences of the Great Increase and Burden of the Poor.* London, 1752.

ANONYMOUS. *Essay upon the necessity and equity of a National Parish Bank and Annuity System adapted for the lower classes.* London, 1831.

—— *Some Suggestions for the improvement of Benefit Clubs and Assurances.* London, 1824.

—— *Strictures on Benefit or Friendly Societies ... in a dialogue between Mr. Goodwill and Mr. Frankley.* Stockport, 1798.

—— *The Old and the New Poor Law, who gains? and who loses?* London, 1835.

—— *Hints to Agriculturists in the neighbourhood of Colchester upon the advantages derived from Benefit Societies.* Colchester, 1827.

ANSELL, C. *A Treatise on Friendly Societies in which the Doctrine of Interest of Money and the Doctrine of Probability are practically applied.* London, 1835.

BAERNREITHER, J. *English Associations of Working Men.* (English edition revised and enlarged by the author from his German edition which was published at Tübingen in 1886, with a Preface by J. M. Ludlow.) London, 1889.

BARTLEY, G. C. T. *Provident Knowledge Papers.* London, 1878.

BAYLEY, P. *Observations on the Plan for an Institution for the promotion of Industry and Provident Economy among the manufacturing and labouring classes.* London, 1819.

BECHER, J. T. *The Constitution of Friendly Societies upon legal and scientific principles exemplified by the Rules for the Government of the Friendly Institution at Southwell.* London, 1824.

—— Observations upon the Report of the Select Committee of the House of Commons on Laws respecting Friendly Societies exemplifying and vindicating the Principles of Life Assurance adopted in calculating the Southwell Tables. Newark, 1826.

Beehive Newspaper. Article on Friendly and Industrial Societies, 13 June, 1874.

BENTHAM, J. *Pauper Management Improved.* London, 1812.

BONE, J. *The Friend of the People, etc.* London, 1807.

—— *The Principles and Regulations of Tranquillity,* an Institution for encouraging industrious individuals to provide for themselves. London, 1806.

BORTHWICK, J. and others. *The Jackson Prize Essays on Friendly Societies.* Leeds, 1885.

BRADBROOK, E. W. *The Friendly Societies' Bill.* (Reprint of a paper read by the Assistant Registrar to the National Association for the Promotion of Social Science.) London, 1875.

—— *Friendly Societies and Similar Institutions.* (Reprint of a paper read before the Royal Statistical Society.) London, 1875.

BROWNE, J. C. *Friendly Societies: A letter . . . on the evils of existing Friendly Societies to which are added Suggestions for the Formation of a Mutual Provident Association in the Parish.* London, 1849.

BUNYON. *Life Insurance.* London, 1854.

BURN, J. *An Historical Sketch of the Independent Order of Oddfellows, Manchester Unity.* Manchester, 1845.

BURNE, J. D. *A Glimpse at the Social Conditions of the Working Class during the early part of the present century.* London and Manchester, 1868.

CAMERON, C. What Legislation should follow on the Report of the Commission on Friendly Societies? *Transactions of the Social Science Assn.* 1874, pp. 794–805.

CHADWICK, E. *An Essay on the Means of Insurance against the Casualties of Sickness, Decrepitude and Mortality.* London, 1836.

CHEW, E. *Companion to the Harmonica of the Independent Order of Oddfellows.* Manchester, 1837.

CLAPHAM, S. *Friendly Society substitutes for Parochial Assessments:* a sermon preached at Christchurch, Hants, 1810. London, 1810.

CLAYDEN, A. *The Revolt of the Field.* London, 1874.

CLEGHORN, J. *Thoughts on the Expediency of a General Provident Institution for the benefit of the Working Classes.* London, 1824.

CLIFFORD, F. *The Agricultural Lockout of 1874.* With notes upon farming and farm labour in the Eastern Counties. Edinburgh and London, 1875.

COLQUHOUN, P. *A Treatise on Indigence.* London, 1806.

COWBRIDGE. Cowbridge Tracts: No. 5. *On Friendly Societies.* No. 6. *On Savings Banks.* (Published by the Society for the Improvement of the Working Population in the County of Glamorgan.) Cardiff, 1831.

COX, J. C. *The Rise of the Farm Labourer.* London, 1874.

CUNNINGHAM, J. W. *A Few Observations on Friendly Societies and their Influence on Public Morals.* London, 1817.

DAVIES, S. T. *Oddfellowship: Its History, Principles, Constitution and Finances.* Witham, Essex, 1858.

DAVIS, W. *Friendly Advice to Industrious and Frugal Persons recommending Provident Institutions or Savings Banks.* London, 1817.

DEFOE, D. *An Essay on Projects.* London, 1697.

DE SALIS, J. *A Proposal for Improving the System of Friendly Societies.* London, 1814.

DONSBERY, T. *A Warning Voice to the Members of Benefit Societies.* London, 1832.

DUNLOP, J. *Artificial Drinking Usages of North Britain.* Greenock, 1836.

EDEN, F. M. *The State of the Poor. 3 vols.* London, 1797.

—— *Observations on Friendly Societies for the Maintenance of the Industrious Classes during Sickness, Infirmity, Old Age and other exigencies.* London, 1801.

FARR, W. *Vital Statistics;* a memorial volume of selections from the reports and writings of W. Farr. London, 1885.

FAWCETT, H. *Economic Position of the British Labourer.* Cambridge, 1865.

FILKES, J. *A Sermon on behalf of those useful and benevolent Institutions called Friendly Societies,* preached at Navestock, Essex, 1802. London, 1804.

FINLAISON, J. Tables for Providing Relief in Sickness and Old Age, for Payments at Death and Endowments for Children. London, 1833.

FRASER, W. *On the History and Constitution of Benefit or Friendly Societies.* London, 1828.

FREEMAN of Exeter. *To the Farming Labourers of Great Britain and Ireland.* Exeter, 1837.

FYNES, R. *The Miners of Northumberland and Durham.* Sunderland, 1873.

GASKELL, P. *The Manufacturing Population of England . . . etc.* London, 1833.

GIFFEN, R. *The Progress of the Working Classes in the last half-century.* London, 1884.

GREGSON, H. *Suggestions for Improving the Condition of the Industrious Classes.* London, 1830.

GREIG, G. *Are Friendly Societies, Secret Orders, etc., safe? No!* London, 1850.

HARDWICK, C. *The Provident Institutions of the Working Classes; Friendly Societies, their History, Prospects, Progress and Utility.* Preston, 1851.

—— *A Manual for Patrons and Members of Friendly Societies.* Manchester, 1859.

—— *Insolvent Sick and Burial Clubs: The Causes and the Cure.* Manchester, 1863.

—— *A History of Friendly Societies.* Manchester, 1893.

H.M.S.O. *Instructions for Establishing Friendly Societies.* London, 1835.

—— *Statutory Rules for Friendly Societies.* London, 1846.

HOLLAND, G. C. *Vital Statistics of Sheffield.* Sheffield, 1843.

HUDSON, W. J. *The History of Adult Education,* in which is comprised a Full and Complete History of the Mechanics and Literary Institutions. London, 1851.

JAMES, J. H. *Guide to the Formation and Management of Friendly Societies for Assurance, Investment, etc.* London, 1851.

JARVIS, R. *A Plain Statement of the Facts relative to the Proceedings of the Hampshire Friendly Society.* London, 1837.

JOHNSTON, T. *The Records of an Ancient Friendly Society,* the Bo'ness United General Sea Box. Bo'ness, 1890.

KEBBEL, T. E. *The Agricultural Labourer, a Short Summary of his Position.* London, 1870.

LANGLEY, E. *A Statement of the Proceedings of the Dorking Provident Institution.* Dorking, 1817.

LEVI, L. *Wages and Earnings of the Working Class.* London, 1867.

LEWINS, W. *A History of Banks for Savings in Great Britain and Ireland.* London, 1866.

LUDLOW, J. M. On State Aid to Friendly Societies. *Transactions of the National Social Science Assn.* 1874, pp. 811–23.

—— Gilds and Friendly Societies. *Contemporary Review,* 1873, pp. 553–72 and pp. 737–62.

LUDLOW, J. M. and LLOYD JONES. *The Progress of the Working Classes, 1832–1867.* London, 1867.

McCULLOCH, J. R. *A Statistical Account of the British Empire.* 2 vols. London, 1839.

MILLAR, J. *The Friendly Society Guide;* or a Series of Letters, Conferences and Essays on the formation and improvement of Benefit or Friendly Societies. Dundee, 1825.

MITCHELL, J. *A Treatise on Benefit or Friendly Societies:* containing a Statement of the Laws of the Land respecting these Institutions; the Probabilities of Sickness, Mortality, Births and other Casualties; with Practical Instructions for the Formation of Rates, the Investment of Funds and General Management. London, 1828.

MORGAN, E. D. *Expedience and Method of Providing Assurances for the Poor and of Adopting the Improved Constitution of Friendly Societies.* London, 1830.

MULCASTER, S. *Tables for Friendly Societies agreeable to their old usage and customs.* London, 1833.

NEISON, F. G. P. *Contributions to Vital Statistics being a Development of the Rate of Mortality and the Laws of Sickness.* London, 1845.

—— *Observations on Oddfellow and Friendly Societies.* London, 1845.

NEISON, F. G. P. *The Manchester Unity of Oddfellows*. London, 1869.

—— *Legislation on Friendly Societies*. London, 1870.

—— Report on the Sickness Experience of the Ancient Order of Foresters Friendly Society for the year 1870. Newcastle, 1872.

—— Rates of Mortality and Sickness according to the Experience for the five years 1871–5 of the A.O.F. Friendly Society. London, 1882.

—— Rates of Mortality and Sickness in Friendly Societies. *Journal of the Statistical Society*, vol. VIII, pp. 290–343.

—— Rates of Mortality and Sickness in Particular Societies. *Journal of the Statistical Society*, vol. IX, pp. 50–76.

—— Some Statistics of the Affiliated Orders of Friendly Societies. *Journal of the Statistical Society*, vol. XL, pp. 42–81.

NICHOLLS, G. *History of the English Poor Law*. London, 1854.

NIHIL, (ps). *To the Inhabitants of Newtown, particularly the members of benefit societies*. Newtown, 1836.

ODDFELLOWS. *Oddfellows Song Book for 1811*. London, 1811.

—— *Harmonia of the Grand United Order of*. Sheffield, 1833.

—— Durham District, I.O.O.F.M.U., Annual Report for 1858 containing Reprint of 'Benefit Societies and the Times' from the *Durham County Advertiser*. Durham, 1859.

—— *The Complete Manual of Oddfellowship*. London, 1879.

PORTER, G. R. *Sketch of the Progress and Present Extent of Savings Banks in the United Kingdom*. London, 1846.

—— *Progress of the Nation*. 3 vols. London, 1836–43.

PRATT, J. TIDD. *The Laws Relating to Friendly Societies*. London, 1829. (This became a standard work, it was frequently revised and re-issued throughout the century.)

—— *Suggestions for the Establishment of Friendly Societies with Tables*. London, 1855.

—— Instructions prepared by J. Tidd Pratt, Esq., the Registrar of Friendly Societies in England, for the Establishment of Friendly Societies with Rules, Tables, etc. London, 1860.

Quarterly Review. Inquiry into the Poor Laws. 1812, vol. 8, pp. 319 ff.

—— The Poor Law Question. 1834, vol. 50, pp. 347–73.

—— Workmen's Benefit Societies. 1864, vol. 116, pp. 318–50.

RATCLIFFE, H. *Observations on the Rate of Mortality and Sickness existing among Friendly Societies calculated from the experience of members composing the Manchester Unity of the Independent Order of Oddfellows*. Manchester, 1850.

—— Revised edition of the above. Colchester, 1862.

RECHABITES. *Jubilee Record . . . a full report of the proceedings of the High Moveable Conference, August, 1885*. Exeter, 1885.

ROBERTS, G. *Social History of the People of the Southern Counties in Past Centuries*. London, 1856.

ROSE, G. *Observations on the Act for the Relief and Encouragement of Friendly Societies . . . by the gentleman who framed the Bill.* London, 1794.

ROSS, J. *A Few Loose Remarks on the Advantages of Friendly Societies;* a Scheme for supporting the Widows and Orphans of Teachers. London, 1804.

RUMSEY, H. W. *Medical Relief for the Labouring Classes on the Principle of Mutual Insurance.* London, 1837.

—— *Essays in State Medicine.* London, 1856.

RUSSOM, J. *An Essay on Oddfellowship; being an explanation and vindication of its principles, etc.* London, 1840.

SCRATCHLEY, A. *Observations on Life Assurance Societies and Savings Banks, etc.* London, 1851.

SCROPE, J. *Remarks and Suggestions on the Report of the Commissioners on Friendly Societies and the Bill of the Chancellor of the Exchequer.* London, 1874.

SMILES, S. *Self-Help.* London, 1859.

—— *Workmen's Earnings, Strikes and Savings.* London, 1861.

—— *Thrift.* London, 1875.

SMITH, H. L. *Alfred Societies; or a plan for very small sick clubs.* Southam, 1837.

SOLLY, H. *Trade and Friendly Societies in relation to Workmen's Trade Halls and Social Clubs.* London, 1870.

—— *Working Men's Social Clubs.* London, 1867.

SPACKMAN, W. F. *An Analysis of the Occupations of the People.* London, 1847.

SPRY, J. *The History of Oddfellowship: Its Origin, Tradition and Objects.* Manchester, 1867.

STANLEY, E. L. *What Legislation should follow on the Report of the Commission on Friendly Societies? Transactions of the Social Science Assn.* 1874, pp. 805–11.

STRATTON, J. Y. *Method of Improving the Labouring Classes by altering the Conditions of Poor Relief and providing them with a System of Insurance through the Post Office.* London, 1872.

—— On what principles should Friendly and other kindred societies be based? *Transactions of the Social Science Assn.* 1873, pp. 566–73.

TAMLYN, J. *A Digest of the Laws of Friendly Societies and of Savings Banks.* London, 1827.

TOMPKINS, H. *An Account of some Remarkable Friendly Societies.* Chester (1871?).

VIVIAN, R. *A Letter on Friendly Societies and Savings Banks, occasioned by Mr. Rose's letter.* London, 1816.

WALFORD, C. *The Insurance Cyclopaedia.* 5 volumes. London, 1870–8.

—— *Gilds.* London, 1888.

WARDLE, M. *Sketch of the Lives of John Lloyd, James Mansall, William Smith, William Armitt, Thomas Armitt and Thomas Wildey.* Manchester, 1832.

WHITE, N. *A Handy Book on the Law of Friendly Societies, etc.* London, 1865.

WILLIAMS, C. *Suggestions for the Improvement of Benefit Clubs and Assurances for the Lower Classes.* London, 1829.

WOOLLGAR, J. W. *Friendly Society Security:* an essay on testing the condition of a

Friendly Society by the valuation of all policies . . . without resorting to a professional actuary. Tables, etc. Lewes, 1844.

WRIGHT, J. *A Treatise on the Internal Regulation of Friendly Societies . . . also a code of rules with form for the use of magistrates in questions relative to such societies. . . . To which is added an appeal to the Rt. Hon. Lord John Russell on the present state of the law relating to such societies.* London, 1829.

—— *A Summary of Objections to Act 10 Geo. IV c. 56 and of the Grievances then resulting to Benefit Societies.* London, 1833.

YOUNG, A. Board of Agriculture Reports for Dorset, Sussex and Essex. London, 1807–15.

(2) SECONDARY WORKS

ASCHROTT, P. F. *The English Poor Law System, Past and Present.* London, 1888.

ASPINALL, A. *Early English Trade Unions.* London, 1949.

AXON, W. E. A. *The Rechabites and the Rechabim.* London, 1896.

BARKER, T. C., and HARRIS, J. R. *A Merseyside Town in the Industrial Revolution, St. Helens, 1750–1900.* Liverpool, 1954.

BEER, M. *History of British Socialism.* London, 1919.

BEVERIDGE, W. *Unemployment.* London, 1909.

—— *Voluntary Action.* London, 1948.

BEVERIDGE, W., and WELLS, A. *The Evidence for Voluntary Action.* London, 1949.

BOOTH, C. *The Aged Poor in England and Wales.* London, 1894.

BOWDEN, W. *Industrial Society in England towards the end of the Eighteenth Century.* New York, 1925.

BOWLEY, A. L. *Wages in the United Kingdom in the Nineteenth Century.* Cambridge, 1900.

BRADBROOK, E. W. *The Law of Friendly Societies.* London, 1897.

—— *Provident Societies and Industrial Welfare.* London, 1898.

BRIGGS, A. *Friends of the People.* London, 1956.

B.M.A. Report on Contract Practice. London, 1905.

BUER, M. C. *Health, Wealth and Population, 1760–1815.* London, 1926.

CAMPBELL, G. L. *Miners' Thrift and Employers' Liability.* Wigan, 1892.

CLAPHAM, J. H. *Economic History of Modern Britain.* 3 vols. London, 1930–8.

COLE, G. D. H. *Short History of the British Working Class.* London, 1925.

—— *A Century of Co-operation.* London, 1946.

COLE, G. D. H., and POSTGATE, R. *The Common People, 1746–1946.* (2nd edn.) London, 1946.

FINER, S. E. *The Life and Times of Sir Edwin Chadwick.* London, 1952.

FORESTERS. *Centenary of the Ancient Order of Foresters, 1834–1934.* London, 1934.

FOWLE, T. W. *The Poor Law, Friendly Societies and Old Age Destitution.* London, 1892.

FULLER, F. B. *The Law relating to Friendly Societies and Industrial and Provident Societies.* London, 1926

GAYER, ROSTOW and SCHWARTZ. *The Growth and Fluctuation of the British Economy, 1790–1850.* 2 vols. Oxford, 1953.

GEORGE, M. D. *London Life in the Eighteenth Century.* London, 1925.

GOULD, R. F. *History of Freemasonry.* 4 vols. London, 1884.

HAMMOND, J. L. and L. B. *The Skilled Labourer, 1760–1832.* London, 1919.

—— *The Village Labourer, 1760–1832.* London, 1911.

—— *The Age of the Chartists, 1832–1854.* London, 1930.

HARDY, R. P. *An Inquiry into the methods of representing and giving effect to the experience of a Friendly Society.* London, 1893.

HASBACH, W. *The History of the English Agricultural Labourer.* (Translated by R. Kenyon from the Leipzig edition of 1894.) London, 1908.

HOLYOAKE, G. J. *Sixty Years of an Agitator's Life.* London, 1906.

—— *History of Co-operation in England.* Revised edition, 2 vols. London, 1906.

HORNER, N. G. *The Growth of the General Practitioner of Medicine in England.* London, 1922.

HOWELL, G. *Trade Unionism—New and Old.* London, 1891.

HUTCHINS, B. L. *The Public Health Agitation, 1833–48.* London, 1909.

KNOOP, D., and JONES, G. P. *The Genesis of Freemasonry.* London, 1949.

LAYTON, W. T., and CROWTHER, G. *Introduction to the Study of Prices.* London, 1925.

LITTLE, E. M. *A History of the British Medical Association, 1832–1932.* London, 1932.

LOWNDES, W. L. *Thrift and the Poor Law.* London, 1892.

LYND, H. M. *England in the Eighteen-Eighties.* London, 1945.

MOFFREY, R. W., and others. *Forster Prize Essays on Friendly Societies.* London, 1879.

MOFFREY, R. W. *The Rise and Progress of the Manchester Unity of the Independent Order of Oddfellows, 1810–1904.* Manchester, 1904.

—— *A Century of Oddfellowship.* Manchester, 1910.

MORGAN, F. C. *Friendly Societies in Herefordshire.* Hereford, 1949.

MORRAH, D. *A History of Industrial Life Assurance.* London, 1955.

NEWMAN, T. S. *The Story of Friendly Societies and Social Security.* London, 1945.

OLIVER, T. (editor). *Dangerous Trades: the historical, social and legal aspects of industrial occupations as affecting health by a number of experts.* London, 1902.

PALGRAVE, R. H. I. (editor). *Dictionary of Political Economy.* 3 vols. London, 1894–9.

PERHAM, M. R. *Harting Old Club.* Haywards Heath, 1958.

PIGOU, A. C. *Industrial Fluctuations.* London, 1927.

RAYNES, H. E. *A History of British Insurance.* London, 1948.

ROGERS, J. E. T. *Six Centuries of Work and Wages.* London, 1909.

ROSTOW, W. W. *The British Economy of the Nineteenth Century.* Oxford, 1948.

ROUNDELL, C. S. *Progress of the Working Classes during the Reign of the Queen.* Skipton, 1890.

SAVILLE, T. (editor). *Democracy and the Labour Movement.* London, 1954.

SMART, W. *Economic Annals of the Nineteenth Century.* London, 1910–17.

TYLECOTE, M. *Mechanics Institutes of Lancashire and Yorkshire.* Manchester, 1957.

WALLER, W. C. *Early Huguenot Friendly Societies.* London, 1901.

WATSON, R. *Explanatory Treatise on the Valuation of Friendly Societies.* London, 1878.

—— *An Essay on Friendly Societies and Sick Clubs.* London, 1888.

WEARMOUTH, R. F. *Some Working Class Movements of the Nineteenth Century.* London, 1948.

WEBB, R. K. *The British Working Class Reader. Literary and Social Tension, 1790–1848.* London, 1955.

WEBB, S. and B. *Industrial Democracy.* London, 1898.

—— *History of Trade Unionism.* London, 1907.

—— *The State and the Doctor.* London, 1910.

—— *English Poor Law Policy.* London, 1910.

—— *English Local Government.* Vols. 8 and 9. London, 1929.

WILKINSON, J. F. *The Mutual and Provident Institutions of the Working Classes.* London, 1888.

—— *The Friendly Society Movement; Its Origin, Rise and Growth; Its Social, Moral and Educational Influences.* London, 1886.

—— *Mutual Thrift.* London, 1891.

WILLIAMS, ALFRED. *A Wiltshire Village.* London, 1912.

WOOD, G. H. *The History of Wages in the Cotton Trade during the past hundred years.* London, 1910.

WULCKO, L. M. *Some Early Friendly Societies in Buckinghamshire.* Chalfont St. Peter, 1951.

YOUNG, E. *Labour in Europe and America: a Report to the House of Representatives.* Washington, 1876.

YOUNG, G. M. *Early Victorian England, 1830–1865.* 2 vols. London, 1934.

YOUNG, T. E. *The German Law of Insurance of 1889—History, Analysis and Criticism.* London, 1891.

INDEX